Favorite American Regional Recipes
By Leading Food Editors

Selected and Introduced by
MARIAN TRACY

DOVER PUBLICATIONS, INC.
NEW YORK

Acknowledgment

The Publishers are indebted for his helpful cooperation to Mr. J. H. Sawyer, Jr., a member of the Chicago chapter of the American Association of Newspaper Representatives and formerly chairman of the Food Editors' Conference Committee. They are also grateful to the many food editors contributing their basic recipes, to the American Association of Newspaper Representatives and its President, Delwyn J. Worthington and to Ruth Ellen Church of the *Chicago Tribune,* who originally collected many of these recipes in booklet form for the American Association of Newspaper Representatives.

Published in Canada by General Publishing Company, Ltd., 30 Lesmill Road, Don Mills, Toronto, Ontario.

This Dover edition, first published in 1976, is an unabridged and corrected republication of the work originally published in 1952 under the title *Coast to Coast Cookery.* This edition is published by special arrangement with the original publisher, Indiana University Press, 10th and Morton Streets, Bloomington, Indiana 47401.

International Standard Book Number: 0-486-23415-0
Library of Congress Catalog Card Number: 76-24563

Manufactured in the United States of America
Dover Publications, Inc.
180 Varick Street
New York, N.Y. 10014

Contents

Introduction

1

States and Regions Represented

Notes on Regional Terms and Unusual Ingredients

General Index

Newspapers and Contributors

Introduction

In the beginning, American food was whatever the early settlers could find in their desperate struggle for existence—wild fowl, deer and other wild animals, corn, cranberries, all the wild plants they thought edible, and the fruitful plenty of our coastal waters—adapted to their traditional recipes, English, Dutch, French, and Spanish.

Now our food is as abundant and varied as the people in our land. Immigrants to America brought from many lands their seeds and slips of their favorite fruit trees and berry bushes, their seasonings and their ways of cooking. These ways, sometimes amplified, sometimes diluted, have been modified to fit our tastes, our skills, and the many foods that flourish here until they have become our own cuisine, as intermingled and intermarried as ourselves.

The recipes in this collection have been gathered from all sections of the country by those local and vocal experts, the newspaper food editors, who have put these traditional and often half-forgotten recipes into a workable idiom for present-day cooks, unfamiliar with the terse and sometimes cryptic instructions of our ancestors. Colorful but local nomenclature has been kept when the meaning seemed clear. Even so, some vivid but possibly confusing terms are listed in the Notes on Regional Terms with the regional variants. Instructions for procedures almost obsolete in homes, like preparing live snapper turtles, have been omitted as unsuitable to the skill and squeamishness of either sex these days and to the dimensions of most kitchens. Such processes these days are performed by specialists before the food gets to the home or even to a restaurant. Space has been given to the specialities of the different sections rather than to basic recipes that can be found in any good general cookbook, although this is a general cookbook of its own kind covering food for all parts of all meals. Dishes are indexed in as much detail as possible and can be found under categories, titles, and predominating ingredients.

The reader is warned that regional foods, both animal and vegetable, vary in size almost as much as individual capacities; hence the number of servings given for each recipe is only approximate. East and West Coast crabs and oysters, for instance, cannot be used interchangeably. The proportions of the other ingredients in recipes must be readjusted and allowance made for the variations in quantities.

In any selection such as this, made from many, many recipes for local specialities, arbitrary and personal idiosyncrasies are bound to creep in (for instance, "buttered" dishes and pans sound more appetizing than "greased" ones no matter what fat is used). The duplication and overlapping in the material makes one aware of the truly fluid population in this country. It is true that here and there isolated communities use unchanged the recipes that their parents and grandparents brought from the old country, but these are unusual.

These recipes, some simple and some complex, are exciting and persuasive lures from dull and routine food. Who can resist the tempting sound of Anadama bread and the story that goes with it, Maryland stuffed ham for Easter, Country Captain, a traditional Indian chicken curry, that name and all is now part of Southern cuisine, black walnut pie from the Ozark section, the subtle flavor of a West Coast eggplant and clam casserole, the nostalgic sound of salt-rising bread, wild blackberry pie, almond dice chicken, and so on into a rapturous infinity?

Marian Tracy
New York City, 1952

Alabama

Margaret Dillon (Sue Scattergood)

THE BIRMINGHAM NEWS

BIRMINGHAM, ALABAMA

Southern Alabama is a fertile region, up-and-coming in the matter of meat animals and general produce. Specialties here are pecans, peanuts, yams, and Kieffer or hard preserving pears. Figs grow abundantly throughout the state, but we have not included recipes using them because they grow in so few sections of the country. Fresh figs peeled and served with cream are delicious breakfast fruits. Because of the brief season, we preserve and pickle them.

Orange-Candied Pecans

3 cups sugar
1 cup orange juice
1 tablespoon butter

1 teaspoon grated orange rind
3 cups pecan halves

COMBINE sugar and orange juice and cook to the soft ball stage (236 degrees). Add butter and grated rind and remove from fire. Beat as you would fudge. Before the mixture is ready to set, add pecans and continue beating until mixture "sugars." Turn onto a greased surface and separate nuts with two forks. These are delicious Christmas confections.

Peanut Brittle

2 cups sugar
¾ cup light corn syrup
¼ cup water
Pinch of salt

2 cups raw peanuts, preferably the tiny Spanish variety
2 heaping teaspoons soda

COMBINE sugar, syrup, water, and salt in a large pot. Stir and bring mixture to boiling point. Add raw peanuts and cook to the brittle stage, stirring occasionally. When candy is brittle enough, it is just short of the scorched stage; if tried in cold water, the syrup will form brittle strings in the water.

At this point remove from the fire and quickly stir in the soda, which must be measured and ready beforehand. The mixture foams up when the soda is added.

Pour candy onto a buttered marble slab or porcelain table. Run a buttered knife under the sheet of candy. Use the same knife to spread the foamy portion and make as thin as possible.

When sufficiently cooked, this most brittle brittle will leave the table clean. If undercooked, it will stick to the table unmercifully.

Green Tomato Crisp

Makes about 6 pints

2 gallons water
3 cups ordinary garden lime
7 pounds green tomatoes, cut
into thick slices
4 pounds sugar

2 quarts vinegar
1 teaspoon each: cloves, ginger, cinnamon, allspice, celery seed, mace, and salt

MIX lime and water. Add the tomato slices and soak 24 hours. Drain well, rinsing off any particles of lime. Soak 4 hours in fresh cold water, changing water once each hour. Drain well.

Make a hot syrup of the sugar, vinegar, and spices. While boiling hot, pour over the tomatoes. Let stand overnight. In the morning, boil 1 hour and seal in sterile jars.

Pear Relish

This is a delicious meat relish.

Makes about 10 quarts

15 pounds preserving pears
6 large white onions
4 red, sweet bell peppers
1 tablespoon salt
1 tablespoon mixed whole
  spices
2 pounds sugar
5 cups vinegar

THE Kieffer or hard preserving pear is used in this recipe. Cut peeled pears very small—grinding causes them to turn dark. Grind onions and peppers; combine with pears. Add remaining ingredients. Bring to a boil and simmer 30 minutes. Seal in sterilized jars while hot.

Ben Cooper

THE MOBILE PRESS REGISTER
MOBILE, ALABAMA

Mobile, on the Gulf Coast, has her own style of cookery. It has Spanish, French, Indian, and English influences, with contributions from Africa via the Negro cooks and from ports around the world via the visitors from the seven seas.

The dishes Mobile features in her homes and on her café menus are her own interpretations of gumbo (a word deriving from the African gombo or okra), her own versions of baked or stuffed crabs, interesting chicken dishes, soft-shelled crabs, oyster dishes, and baked stuffed fishes such as flounder.

Every Mobile cook has his or her own recipe for gumbo. Essentially it is a soup of vegetables with seafood or chicken, thickened with okra or with filé—a powder of sassafras leaves first used by the Choctaw Indians.

Here are two sample Mobile recipes: a gumbo, and a smothered chicken that is spicy and different.

Seafood Gumbo

Serves 6 as a main dish

1 pint chicken stock
1 cup chopped celery stalks and tops
1 cup chopped sweet peppers
2 cups chopped fresh tomatoes or drained canned tomatoes
2 cups chopped onions
1 cup sliced okra
1 clove garlic, chopped
1 bay leaf
Salt and pepper to taste

1 dried red pepper or hot pepper sauce to taste (optional)
1 tablespoon flour mixed to a thin paste with cold water
1 cup green (raw) shrimp, fresh or frozen, cleaned, deveined, and chopped
1 cup oysters, fresh or frozen
½ cup crabmeat, fresh or frozen
1 tablespoon filé

IF you don't have stock on hand, make it by cooking chicken bones (with necks, gizzards, etc.) in a heavy pot in 6 cups of water with salt and pepper for about 2 hours, skimming carefully several times. The liquid should be reduced to about 1 pint. Strain carefully and discard the bones.

Add vegetables and seasonings to your stock. Simmer gently about 30 minutes. Stir in the flour mixed with cold water. Simmer 15 minutes. Add the shrimps, oysters, and crabmeat; taste the mixture, and add salt and pepper as needed. Simmer gently 15 minutes. Take 2 tablespoons of stock from the pot and dissolve the filé in it. Remove soup from the fire, stir in the filé, and serve immediately. Do not reheat after the filé has been added.

Note: Canned (undiluted) bouillon or stock made with chicken cubes can be used if necessary, but the gumbo will not be as rich.

Smothered Breast of Chicken

Serves 4

4 breasts of chicken (breasts of two chickens, split)
2 tablespoons olive oil
1 tablespoon butter
2 cloves garlic, chopped coarsely
1 onion, sliced
Salt and pepper
½ cup sherry and water, half and half
Generous pinch of dry mustard
1 sprig lemon basil or sweet basil (or ½ teaspoon dried sweet basil)
2 leaves sage (or ½ teaspoon dried sage)
1 whole clove
1 bay leaf
1 tablespoon flour, made into a thin paste with cold water
Milk

HEAT olive oil and butter in a medium-sized skillet (about 9 inches). In it sauté the garlic until it begins to brown, then discard the garlic.

Cook onion in the fat, over low heat, until translucent. Push it to one side of the skillet and sauté the chicken breasts until lightly browned. Add salt and pepper to taste. Add sherry and water and seasonings. Cover and simmer. When chicken is tender (about 1 hour), remove the chicken but keep it warm. Stir the flour paste into the mixture in the skillet. Add enough milk to make a thin gravy. Cover and let dish simmer about 5 minutes, or until gravy thickens. Add more milk, again thinning the gravy. Cover and cook slowly until gravy is of the desired consistency and the raw flour taste has disappeared. Correct seasoning with salt and pepper, and return chicken breasts. Green corn fritters are a traditional accompaniment for this dish.

Guyton Parks

THE ALABAMA ADVERTISER-JOURNAL
MONTGOMERY, ALABAMA

Pear Chutney De Luxe

A fine Southern recipe.

Makes about 6 or 7 pints

6 large firm pears	1 pound brown sugar
6 large ripe tomatoes	1 quart vinegar
4 medium-sized onions	3 tablespoons salt
4 red sweet peppers	1 teaspoon ground cinnamon
1 pound seeded raisins	

CHOP fine, cook slowly for 3 hours, put in sterilized jars, and seal.

Arkansas

Mildred Woods

ARKANSAS GAZETTE
LITTLE ROCK, ARKANSAS

Lemon Tarts

This is my great-great-grandmother's recipe, and my favorite of all the lemon pie family, for though satisfyingly rich, it is not the least cloying, as lemon meringues are likely to be. Especially nice for a buffet, as they can be eaten with the fingers if made the day before the party.

Makes 12 medium-sized tarts

2 cups sugar
½ cup butter
4 eggs

1 rounded tablespoon flour
Juice of 2 large, fat lemons
1 recipe for pastry

CREAM sugar and butter. Beat in the eggs, not separated. Add flour, then the lemon juice. Roll pastry thin (use your very best recipe) and line small tart shells or shallow muffin rings, filling them only half full. Bake in a moderate oven (350 degrees) until pastry browns and filling is set.

Albert Pike's Famous Champagne Punch

I found this Arkansas hero's drink pridefully listed in an old holograph cookbook, with the notation that the recipe had been given the writer by Dr. Charles Minor Taylor. Both those gentlemen had come to maturity in another portentous time, one of great evil from which came great good—somehow a hopeful thought.

TO make this punch, take 2 fresh pineapples, very ripe, finely cut up. Juice and pulp of 12 oranges. 2 large bottles of champagne (this means "magnums" which hold 2 quarts each, but you might try one on for size and proceed to the other at discretion), 1 wineglass each of curaçao and maraschino liqueurs. (Serve very cold, of course, but I wouldn't put ice in the punch bowl.)

Baked Catfish

1 large catfish or other lean fish around 4 pounds	1 teaspoon chopped pickle
	¼ cup melted butter
1 cup cracker crumbs	1 egg, well beaten
½ teaspoon salt	Strips of salt pork
½ teaspoon black pepper	Melted butter
1 teaspoon chopped onion	Flour
1 teaspoon chopped parsley	Court bouillon (*see* glossary)

CLEAN and dry fish. Make stuffing of cracker crumbs, seasonings, onion, parsley, pickle, and melted butter, all mixed together and bound with the well-beaten egg. Sew up the fish, or skewer it securely with toothpicks. Cut S-shaped gashes in the sides and fit strips of salt pork into them—the amount depends on the size of the fish, but at least two per side. Rub with melted butter, dredge with flour, put into a pan without any water, and bake in a moderate oven (350 degrees) for 40 to 60 minutes, depending on the size, basting frequently with court bouillon. Serve with its own sauce.

"Osgood" Pie

*This is a family recipe given me by some old and dear friends—
marvelous cooks.*

Makes 8- or 9-inch pie

1 recipe for pastry shell	6 teaspoons melted butter
4 eggs, separated	1 cup pecans, chopped
2 cups sugar	1 cup raisins
1 teaspoon cinnamon	3 teaspoons vinegar
1 teaspoon cloves	Liquor (optional)

LINE an 8- or 9-inch piepan with your best brand of crust. Beat egg
yolks light. Sift in a mixture of sugar, cinnamon, and cloves. Add
butter, nuts, raisins, and vinegar. Fold in the stiffly beaten egg
whites last. And the old rule ends engagingly: "Three tablespoons
of liquor make this perfect." Bake in a moderate oven (350 degrees) until the filling is set.

Rice Pudding

Serves 3 or 4

*This is another little rule-of-thumb job that won me high praise
both in Yankeeland and in Europe.*

ABOUT a cupful of cooked rice goes into a well-buttered baking dish,
with lots of raisins and a good dusting of cinnamon. The yolks of
two eggs are severely beaten, sweetened to taste, about half a cup
of milk and a few drops of vanilla added, and the resulting light
custard mixture stirred into the rice. Add a little more milk if in-
dicated. Again the dash of cinnamon and dots of butter, and bake

in a slow oven. When the pudding is fluffy and brown, slide on top a meringue made with the whipped egg whites and 2 tablespoons of sugar; finish cooking on top rack in the oven. Serve hot.

ARKANSAS DEMOCRAT
LITTLE ROCK, ARKANSAS

For recipes by *Bessie R. Murphy*, see pp. 221-223.

California

Katherine Kitchen

THE FRESNO BEE
FRESNO, CALIFORNIA

Oranges, apples, raisins, and figs, all found in California's fruit basket, suggest many wonderful pickles, preserves, salads, and desserts. These recipes come from kitchens of San Joaquin Valley homemakers, who have a wide reputation for their excellent food.

Favorite Raisin Pie

2 cups raisins
1½ cups boiling water
1 cup sugar
3 tablespoons cornstarch
Few grains salt
Juice of 2 lemons

Juice of 1 orange
1½ tablespoons grated lemon rind
1½ tablespoons grated orange rind
Pastry for 9-inch, 2-crust pie

COOK raisins in the boiling water for 5 minutes. Blend sugar, cornstarch, and salt. Add to raisin-water mixture and cook until thick. Remove from heat. Add lemon and orange juice and the grated rinds. Cool. Pour raisin mixture into 9-inch pastry-lined piepan. Adjust top crust and bake in hot oven, 425 degrees, for 35 to 45 minutes, or until done.

Apple-Orange Pie

Oranges and apples have been combined in this unique pie, which rates high with those who enjoy a richly flavored apple pie. It is especially pleasing when made with summer all-purpose Gravenstein apples from Northern California, or with winter Newtons, which are firm, all-purpose pippins.

½ cup orange juice
½ cup water
1 cup sugar
6 or 7 apples, thickly sliced
2 tablespoons flour blended with ¼ cup orange juice

2 teaspoons grated orange rind
1½ tablespoons lemon juice
1½ tablespoons butter or margarine
Pastry for 9-inch, double-crust pie

LINE pie dish or pan with pastry and chill in refrigerator while making filling. Add ½ cup orange juice and water to sugar and bring to boiling point in saucepan. Add sliced apples and cook them until barely tender. Drain and cool. Place apples in pastry-lined piepan. To 1 cup of syrup in which apples were cooked, add flour blended with ¼ cup orange juice and cook until thickened. Add grated orange rind, lemon juice, and butter or margarine. Cook 2 or 3 minutes longer. Cool to lukewarm. Pour over apples in unbaked pie shell. Cover with a plain or crisscross top crust and bake at 425 degrees for 30 to 35 minutes or until nicely browned.

If preferred, this mixture may be used in a graham cracker crust and sprinkled with a few of the crust crumbs.

Fig Pickles

Makes about 12 pints

7 pounds figs, white or black
5 pounds sugar
1½ pints vinegar

3 sticks cinnamon
2½ tablespoons cloves

WASH figs and boil in water (salted as for potatoes) until tender enough to pierce with a straw. Drain in colander.

Boil sugar and vinegar (with spices tied in cheesecloth bag) until clear. Add drained figs and let stand overnight.

The next day, drain figs and let syrup come to a boil. Put figs back into syrup. Repeat this process the third day. The fourth day, put all on stove together and boil until figs are clear. Put into clean sterilized jars and seal.

Zula I. Ferguson (Martha Grayson)
DAILY NEWS
LOS ANGELES, CALIFORNIA

California cookery in general, I suspect, is very much like my own particular cooking in California. It is suited to special occasions, to special known taste preferences.

For friends who are especially keen on foreign dishes, I may plan a Mexican, a Chinese, or an Italian meal. Of course, we have formal dinners in California, too, just as we have family dinners of beef pot roast, corned beef, boiled tongue, stew, and such.

Perhaps it is the very versatility of our California cooks, and their catholic tastes in cookery, that distinguish our cooking here. At any rate, I haven't known just what recipes to choose as typical of California cookery. Consequently, I have selected recipes of dishes that I didn't think of when I lived in my native Kentucky, but which I myself serve often in California.

Patio Sandwich

Serves 4

2 hard-cooked eggs, chopped fine	Canned green chili peppers
Mayonnaise	Sour cream
Salt, pepper	8 slices white bread

BLEND eggs with mayonnaise to spreading consistency. Add salt and pepper to taste. Spread four slices of bread with this egg mixture. Lay strips of chili peppers over mixture; dot with sour cream. Complete sandwiches with the other four slices of bread. Toast on both sides in 450-degree oven until mixture is heated and bread slightly browned.

Lamb with Western Barbecue Sauce

Serves 6

3 pounds breast of lamb   Salt, pepper
Wright's Liquid Smoke

BRUSH breast of lamb lightly with "liquid smoke." Wrap tightly in heavy waxed paper and allow to stand in refrigerator several hours. Remove from refrigerator and place, fat side down, in a shallow baking pan. Sprinkle with salt and pepper; brush with barbecue sauce. Bake until browned and tender in a 400-degree oven, basting frequently with barbecue sauce. Serve with remaining barbecue sauce, heated separately.

Sauce:

¼ cup salad oil
1 clove garlic, minced
1 large onion, minced or grated
1 teaspoon dry mustard
2 teaspoons chili powder
½ teaspoon freshly ground black pepper
1 teaspoon brown sugar
1 teaspoon salt
1 teaspoon paprika
Dash of cayenne
2 teaspoons Worcestershire sauce
1 tablespoon tomato catsup
3 tablespoons vinegar
2 to 2½ cups water

COOK onion and garlic in oil for 2 minutes; mix dry ingredients, then stir into the oil; add liquids and simmer about 25 minutes.

Eggplant and Clam Casserole

Serves 5 or 6

1 large eggplant
1 medium onion, chopped fine
3 tablespoons butter or margarine
2 7-ounce cans minced clams

2 cups dry bread crumbs
Salt
Freshly ground black pepper
Butter or margarine
¼ cup milk

WASH eggplant. Cut, unpeeled, into cubes; add enough boiling salted water to cover, and cook until tender (about 10 minutes); drain. Fry chopped onion in butter or margarine until amber-colored and soft. Drain clams, reserving liquid; mix onion and clams. In a greased casserole place a thin layer of bread crumbs, then a layer of eggplant, then a layer of clams; season each layer with salt and pepper. Repeat, making final layer one of crumbs. Dot with butter or margarine. Over all, pour liquid from clams, mixed with milk. Bake at 350 degrees for 45 minutes.

Guacamole

(Pronounced wahk-a-mo-leh)

This mixture is wonderful for cocktail "dunking."

Makes appetizers for 10 or 12

2 ripe avocados
1 small onion, minced
1 tablespoon canned green chili peppers, chopped (optional)
Salt, pepper to taste

1 medium-ripe tomato, chopped fine
1 tablespoon lemon juice
2 teaspoons sherry
Dash of cayenne (optional)

PEEL and mash avocados; add minced onion, canned green chili, and chopped tomato; then add lemon juice, sherry, and seasonings, blending well.

Barbecue Salad

Serves 10 to 12

Garlic
¾ cup olive oil or other salad oil
¼ cup wine vinegar
1 egg, coddled 1 minute and chilled

Salt
4 bunches chilled, crisp romaine lettuce
Freshly ground black pepper
1 cup grated Parmesan cheese

RUB wooden bowl with crushed clove of garlic; remove garlic. Add oil and vinegar alternately to "flavored" bowl, blending well after each addition. Add egg, salt, and pepper, blending thoroughly with oil and vinegar. Toss separated whole leaves of the romaine lettuce in this dressing, coating every leaf. Add grated cheese; toss again, but lightly. Pass the bowl around in the patio just before steaks are placed on the barbecue grill; let guests help themselves with their fingers to really enjoy this wonderful appetizer salad. (But have available plenty of paper napkins.)
Note: For table service, head lettuce, torn into bite-sized pieces, may be substituted; or a mixture of head lettuce and romaine may be used. A cup or two of crisp croutons may be added, too.

Fleeta Hoke (Marian Manners)

LOS ANGELES TIMES
LOS ANGELES, CALIFORNIA

Tamale Pie en Casserole

Italian spaghetti and tamale pie vie for first place as the favorite food to serve with our customary green salad and toasted garlic French bread at both indoor and outdoor parties, when friends gather informally to eat and drink. Tamale pie perhaps has a slight advantage because it can be completely prepared ahead of time, ready to pop into the oven for last minute reheating.

Serves 8

1 cup yellow cornmeal	2 cups ground beef
6 cups boiling water	2 cups canned or coarsely
1 teaspoon salt	chopped fresh tomatoes
1 medium-sized onion,	2 pimientos
chopped	¼ cup sliced ripe olives
2 tablespoons olive oil	1 teaspoon chili powder

COOK the cornmeal, water, and salt as for mush, for about 20 minutes. Fry onion in olive oil until brown. Add meat and fry until its red color disappears. Add tomatoes, pimientos, sliced olives, and chili powder. Line an oiled casserole with the mush, put meat mixture in center, cover with mush, and bake at 350 degrees for 2 hours.

Esther Hall

SAN FRANCISCO CHRONICLE
SAN FRANCISCO, CALIFORNIA

Native San Franciscans cook in many languages and take the unusual as a matter of course. Tempting dishes such as enchiladas and tortillas have drifted here from Mexico, while Italy, France, Germany, Japan, and China have also contributed to our cuisine.

Visitors from the East will be particularly aware of the unique flavors of Pacific Coast seafood. Since San Francisco is in the heart of the country's wine-growing area, wine is used frequently in cooking.

Avocados and artichokes are eaten as freely as oranges and other native fruits. Artichokes, cooked in water to which lemon juice, salt, and olive oil have been added, and served with a dressing of mayonnaise and mustard, are quite typically San Franciscan.

Crab Louis

ALLOW half a good-sized cooked crab for each serving. Flake the meat in as big pieces as possible, removing all bits of shell.

On each luncheon plate arrange a bed of shredded lettuce, on it a mound of crab, topped with big pieces from the legs. Around the crab arrange a ring of chopped hard-cooked eggs. Top with a few slices of egg and a sprinkling of chopped chives or green onions. Garnish with tomato wedges. Pass dressing separately.

Louis Dressing:

Makes about 2½ cups

1 cup mayonnaise	1 teaspoon grated horseradish
¼ cup French dressing	1 teaspoon Worcestershire
¼ cup catsup	Salt and pepper to taste
2 tablespoons chopped chives	¼ cup chopped ripe olives

MIX all ingredients together and chill well.

Chinese Sweet-Sour Spareribs

Serves 4 liberally

2 pounds spareribs	1 cup pineapple juice
1 tablespoon oil	1 tablespoon soy sauce
2 tablespoons brown sugar	1 bouillon cube
2 tablespoons cornstarch	¼ cup boiling water
½ teaspoon salt	½ cup diced onions
¼ cup vinegar	½ cup diced green peppers
¼ cup cold water	1 cup diced pineapple

HAVE spareribs separated and cut into 2-inch pieces. Cover with boiling, salted water; cook until tender (about 1 hour); drain. Heat oil in skillet and brown ribs. Meanwhile mix sugar, cornstarch, and salt, stir in vinegar, cold water, pineapple juice, and soy sauce. Dissolve bouillon cube in boiling water and add to sauce ingredients. Add this mixture to the ribs and cook, stirring, until sauce is thickened and transparent. Add onions, peppers, and pineapple, and cook until vegetables are tender but still crisp. Serve at once.

Shish Kebabs

(Served at Omar Khayyam's in San Francisco)

2 pounds lean lamb (leg or shoulder), cut in 1½-inch cubes	½ teaspoon pepper
	½ teaspoon dried orégano or rosemary (fresh or dried)
2 onions, sliced	½ cup sherry
2 teaspoons salt	2 tablespoons salad oil

MIX the meat cubes and onions. Sprinkle with salt, pepper, and crumbled or chopped herbs. Pour sherry and oil over all and let stand in refrigerator overnight or for several hours, stirring once.

Remove meat, string on metal skewers, and broil over hot coals or in oven broiler until well done. If desired, tomato quarters, onion quarters, and pieces of green pepper can be strung on the skewers between the cubes of lamb. Baste with oil mixture while broiling.

Eve Jolly (Prudence Penny)

THE SAN FRANCISCO EXAMINER
SAN FRANCISCO, CALIFORNIA

Chicken Sauté Madras

Serves 4

2 cantaloupes	2 tablespoons drippings
2 broiling chickens	2 tablespoons flour
Salt and pepper	1½ cups milk
Flour	1 (or more) teaspoon curry powder
½ cup washed raw rice	
1¼ cups boiling water	

CUT melons in halves and scoop out seeds. With a teaspoon, scoop meat from the melon halves. Put it in four individual dishes and chill in refrigerator. Cut the broilers in quarters, wash, dry, season with salt and pepper, and dredge generously with flour. Cook rice in boiling water for 25 minutes. Fry quartered chickens in hot shortening until well done (about 35 minutes). Make a gravy of pan drippings, flour, milk, and curry powder. Put each melon half on an ovenproof plate. Fill with cooked dry rice, arrange two quarters of chicken on each melon, cover with curry gravy, and place the plates in a hot, 400-degree oven for 15 minutes. Serve with the individual dishes of chilled cantaloupe meat on the side.

Chow Mein

Serves 6

1 pound lean pork, thinly sliced
3 tablespoons shortening
1 cup finely chopped onions
1 cup bean sprouts
1 cup finely chopped celery
1 cup finely chopped mushrooms
1 tablespoon molasses
1½ tablespoons soy sauce
⅔ cup meat stock or chicken broth
2 8-ounce packages thin egg noodles
Deep fat for frying
1 egg
1 bunch green onions

SAUTÉ pork in shortening for 15 minutes over a moderate fire. Add onions, cook 3 minutes longer, then add bean sprouts, celery, and mushrooms. Cook 10 minutes; add molasses, soy sauce, and stock. (The vegetables should retain their crispness.)

In the meantime cook the noodles in plenty of boiling salted water. When tender, pour into a colander, drain thoroughly, and spread out for a few minutes to dry. Then fry, a few at a time, in deep hot fat.

Beat the egg slightly and pour into about 1 tablespoon hot short-

ening in a frying pan, and cook slowly until set and dry, then remove to a board and shred. Cut green onions in lengthwise strips.

To serve, place fried noodles on a big platter, pour the vegetables
over them, then garnish with onion strips and shredded eggs.

Green Goddess Salad

Serves 10

1 clove garlic
4 or 5 anchovy fillets
1 small white onion, sliced
1 teaspoon chopped parsley
A few tarragon leaves, chopped
1 head chicory, broken in small pieces

1 head romaine and an equal amount of escarole, both broken in small pieces
1½ cups mayonnaise
1 tablespoon tarragon vinegar
1 tablespoon chopped chives

RUB salad bowl with cut clove of garlic. Mix together the anchovies,
onion, parsley, and greens. Add mayonnaise, vinegar, and chives.
Mix all together lightly.

Fillets of Chicken

Serves 6

3 broiling chickens, breasts and wings
Salt, white pepper
Heavy cream
Flour
2 tablespoons shortening

2 tablespoons butter
6 slices of raw ham, broiled or sautéed briefly
Hollandaise or Mornay sauce
Grilled pineapple slices (optional)

REMOVE skin from breasts of uncooked chickens and with a sharp
knife remove the breastbones, leaving the wing bones intact. Sprinkle with salt and pepper and dip into heavy cream, then dredge

with flour and fry lightly in shortening. Dot with bits of butter, cover, and bake in a 400-degree oven for 20 minutes. When tender, place each fillet on a slice of grilled ham and cover with a Hollandaise or Mornay sauce. Serve with grilled slices of pineapple if desired.

Chocolate Cake Unique

Yield: 3-layer, 9-inch cake; half the recipe makes 2-layer, 8-inch cake

1 cup shortening	¼ cup lukewarm water
2 cups sugar	1 cup chopped nutmeats
¾ cup grated, unsweetened chocolate	1 cup milk
	2¾ cups sifted flour
3 eggs, well beaten	1 teaspoon soda
1 cake compressed yeast	3 teaspoons hot water

CREAM shortening thoroughly, add sugar gradually, and cream together well. Melt chocolate over hot water. Add chocolate, then the eggs; blend thoroughly. Dissolve yeast in lukewarm water and add to chocolate mixture. Add nuts, then milk. Gradually fold in the flour. Mix well and let stand until morning.

The following morning, mix soda and water and add to the batter. Pour into three greased, 9-inch cake pans and bake in a moderate oven (350 degrees) for 25 to 30 minutes. Cover with custard frosting.

Custard Frosting:

1 tablespoon cornstarch	1 egg, beaten
2 tablespoons sugar	3 tablespoons butter
¾ cup milk	Powdered sugar

BLEND together cornstarch and sugar, and cook with milk over hot water until thick. Add beaten egg and cook 2 minutes longer. Cool. Cream butter until very soft. Add to it, alternately, the custard and enough powdered sugar to make a mixture stiff enough to spread.

Ruth Thompson

THE SAN FRANCISCO NEWS
SAN FRANCISCO, CALIFORNIA

Fritto Misto

Serves 4

½ pound raw zucchini

6 artichoke hearts, parboiled 25 minutes

1 bunch celery, parboiled 20 minutes

1 small head cauliflower, cooked 10 minutes

2 sets raw calves' brains

3 tablespoons olive oil for frying

1 teaspoon salt

⅛ teaspoon pepper

1 egg

1 lemon, sliced

SLICE fine zucchini across. Slice artichoke hearts, celery, and cauliflower. Soak brains in cold water 30 minutes. Bring to a boil in salted water. Cool, remove skin, and cut into cubes.

Sauté calves' brains in olive oil for 5 to 7 minutes. Season with salt and pepper. Dip each piece of meat and vegetable into beaten raw egg. Transfer to skillet, stir around, and cook just until egg coating is done. Serve on a warm platter garnished with lemon.
Note: This recipe can be made with sweetbreads, liver, or small fish instead of brains. Almost any other vegetable can be used, too.

Pickled Italian Bell Peppers

TO 5 gallons of red wine vinegar add 1 cup salt. Wash and dry as many peppers as the liquid will take—probably about 5 pecks. Be sure they are perfect—no bruises or bad spots. Bruised peppers will spoil. Drop the peppers in the brine and allow them to stand at least 2 weeks before serving. They will keep for months and of course are better when they have stood some time.

Serve these peppers as an appetizer, by cutting them into strips.

Swiss Chard, San Francisco Style

1 tablespoon olive oil	2 tablespoons water
1 tablespoon butter	Salt and pepper to taste
1 clove garlic, minced	3 cups cooked, chopped
2 eggs, beaten	Swiss chard

HEAT oil and butter in a skillet. In this cook minced garlic gently for a moment. Mix beaten eggs with water, salt, and pepper. Add cooked chard to beaten egg mixture. Pour into skillet; stir and mix well until the egg is set. Serve hot at once.

Fresh Asparagus with Gorgonzola Sauce

BOIL fresh asparagus and serve hot with individual servings of sauce.

Gorgonzola Cheese Sauce:

(*One serving—multiply by the number of people*)

1 tablespoon red wine vinegar	1 tablespoon Gorgonzola
	Salt and pepper to taste

ADD cheese to vinegar and mash fine with a fork until it is a paste. Season lightly with salt and pepper to taste. Serve in individual dishes. Dip each hot spear of asparagus in the sauce.

Marinated Fava Beans

2 cups boiled fava beans (horse beans!)	4 tablespoons olive oil
1 clove garlic, minced	3 tablespoons red wine vinegar
1 tablespoon chopped parsley	Salt and pepper to taste

SHELL and boil favas in salted water until tender. Drain and cool. Place in a deep bowl. Pour over the mixture of all other ingredients and let stand overnight. Serve as relish or salad.

Colorado

Helen Messenger

THE DENVER POST
DENVER, COLORADO

Denver, often referred to as the "Mile-High City," is just a 30-minute drive from trout-filled streams and big game. Sportsmen from all over the country are lured to the crystal-clear streams and rivers during the summer months. Colorado trout not only enjoy popularity here but are shipped to restaurants throughout the country.

A few herds of buffalo are still to be found in the state, and buffalo meat is featured at a few Western community affairs.

Denver is also considered a livestock center of the Rocky Mountain area, so it is not surprising that barbecued meats are especially popular.

We have our share of good vegetables, too, grown in the fertile mountain and country soil, and the western slope of the state boasts famous peaches and pears, which begin coming to markets during late August or early September.

Secret Sauce (Barbecue)

One of Denver's leading restaurateurs, Everette Peterson, who specializes in barbecued foods at his restaurant, "The Apple Tree Shanty," serves a barbecue sauce that is typical and very popular.

Makes about 2½ cups

1 small onion
1 clove garlic
½ cup raisins
½ cup thick catsup or tomato paste
2 tablespoons vinegar
1 teaspoon dry mustard
⅔ cup butter
½ teaspoon basil
½ teaspoon monosodium glutamate

1 tablespoon mixed tarragon, rosemary, thyme, and marjoram
2 tablespoons brown sugar
1 teaspoon salt
Juice of ½ lemon
¼ teaspoon freshly ground black pepper
2 tablespoons A-1 or Worcestershire sauce
½ cup red wine (optional)

GRIND onion, garlic, and raisins very fine. Combine all ingredients and cook in the top of a double boiler for 45 to 60 minutes, stirring often. Red wine may be added just before removing from the fire.

The sauce is delicious served separately and warm with spareribs, beef, or chicken. It may also be used as a basting sauce.

Trout Amandine

We like to dress up our native trout for company by serving them with a sauce of almonds, butter, and wine.

Serves 4

6 ounces almonds
3 tablespoons butter
4 trout

5 tablespoons brown sugar
6 ounces sherry
Chopped parsley

WASH and blanch almonds, dry, and cut into slivers. Sauté in butter until golden brown, being careful not to scorch butter.

Slowly fry trout in a little extra butter until well done and golden brown (about 10 minutes). Meanwhile finish the sauce, as follows. Add brown sugar to almonds and butter and let simmer for 4 to 5 minutes, stirring occasionally. Add sherry and simmer for an additional 2 to 3 minutes.

Place cooked trout on a warm platter or serving plate, cover with sauce, and sprinkle with chopped parsley. Serve immediately.

Carol Untiedt

ROCKY MOUNTAIN NEWS
DENVER, COLORADO

One is hard put to find a true native in Denver. Most people are residents of five and ten years' standing and, of course, have brought their favorite regional recipes with them. Mexicans and Spaniards, too, have added to Colorado's collection of recipes. Ranchers have contributed the knack of using every piece of a slaughtered lamb or steer in delicious stews and hashes.

Rocky Mountain Squaw Corn

Serves 4 to 6

½ pound bacon
1 large onion, chopped
1 No. 2 can whole-kernel corn

1 No. 2½ can tomatoes
1 teaspoon salt
¼ teaspoon pepper

CUT bacon into small pieces. Put into a skillet and partially brown. Then add onion and brown. Pour off about half the bacon grease. Add tomatoes, corn, salt, and pepper. Cook until fairly thick in consistency.

Cream of Pascelery Soup

Colorado Pascal celery is nationally famous.

Serves 4

1 cup diced Pascal celery
1 cup boiling water
3 tablespoons butter or
    margarine
1 tablespoon minced onion

3 tablespoons flour
2½ cups milk, scalded
2 teaspoons salt
¼ teaspoon pepper

COMBINE celery and water and simmer in a covered pan until celery is tender. Melt butter and in it brown onion. Add flour and stir until smooth. Add milk slowly, stirring constantly. Cook in the top of a double boiler until smooth and thick. Add celery and the water in which it was cooked. Season with salt and pepper. Serve hot with crackers or toast.

Western Swiss Steak

Serves 4

2 pounds round steak, 1
    inch thick
1 cup flour
3 tablespoons fat

1 onion, sliced
1 No. 2 can tomatoes
2 teaspoons salt
½ teaspoon pepper

POUND flour into steak, ½ cup on each side. Melt fat in a skillet; when hot, drop steak into the pan. Brown nicely on both sides. Add onion and tomatoes. Add enough water to cover the meat. Cover with a tight lid and cook in a slow oven (325 degrees) for about 2½ hours. Just before the steak is done, add salt and pepper. Serve very hot.

Red Flannel Stew

A lusty and filling dish to satisfy outdoor appetites—can be made on location out of the usual camp supplies. This version has been adapted from Round-Up Recipes by Bonnie and Ed Perlow.

Serves 6

2 tablespoons butter, margarine or bacon fat

1 large onion, chopped fine

1 can corned beef or corned beef hash, or 1 to 2 cups cooked, chopped meat

1 No. 2½ can kidney or pinto beans

1½ cups tomatoes, or 1 cup tomato sauce

1 small can red chili sauce

Salt

MELT shortening. Fry onion; add meat, beans, tomatoes, and chili sauce. Salt to taste. Simmer 10 minutes, and serve very hot.

Connecticut

Edrie Van Dore

THE HARTFORD TIMES
HARTFORD, CONNECTICUT

There are probably no typical, exclusively Connecticut foods. With the rest of New England we share blueberries, squash, onions, maple syrup. We raise poultry, chickens, and turkeys. Like all coastal states, we have an abundance of seafoods.

Blueberry Slump

While blueberry muffins and pie are not limited to New England, blueberry slump is distinctive of the region. This recipe comes from Secrets of New England Cooking, *by Ella Shannon Bowles and Dorothy S. Towle (Barrows).*

Serves 6

SPRINKLE 1 quart of blueberries with ½ cup sugar. Cook over a slow fire until the berries are slightly soft and covered with a thin syrup. Strain off the berries and put syrup back on the stove. When it begins to boil, drop squares of thinly rolled biscuit dough into the syrup. Cover closely and cook 20 minutes. Pour blueberries over these dumplings and serve with heavy pan cream. Serve hot.

Squash Pie with Maple Cream Topping

Maple syrup and butter make a particularly good seasoning for squash. This recipe is offered by the Extension Service nutritionist at the University of Connecticut.

Pastry for 9-inch pie shell	½ teaspoon nutmeg
3 eggs, well beaten	½ teaspoon ginger
¾ cup brown sugar	2 cups top milk, scalded
1 teaspoon salt	2 cups cooked, strained
½ teaspoon cinnamon	squash

LINE a 9-inch piepan with pastry. Make a fluted standing rim. Combine eggs, sugar, salt, and spices. Gradually stir in hot milk, and then add the strained squash. Pour squash mixture into pastry-lined pan and bake in a hot oven (450 degrees) for 10 minutes. Then reduce the heat to 325 degrees and continue baking for about 30 minutes more, or until firm. Cool the pie. Just before serving, cover with

Maple Cream Topping:

½ pint heavy cream	¼ cup maple syrup

WHIP cream until stiff. Pour maple syrup in a fine stream over the cream, folding it in carefully. Cover the surface of the pie with the topping, swirling it to make an attractive appearance.

Raw Cranberry Relish

Raw cranberry relish is both easy and good. Put through food chopper 4 cups cranberries, 3 apples, cored, 1 whole seedless orange, and 2 cups of sugar. Mix well. Let stand 24 hours before using. Keeps well in covered container in refrigerator.

Cranberry Pie

1½ cups cranberries	⅔ cup water
1 cup sugar	1 tablespoon butter
2 tablespoons flour or fine cracker crumbs	1 recipe for pastry

COOK cranberries, sugar, water, flour, and butter for 10 minutes. Cool. Place in pan lined with rich piecrust, add a top crust (usually a lattice crust), and bake.

Baked Boneless Shad

Connecticut River shad, a large, soft-fleshed, meaty white fish, is much in favor in the spring when it "runs" up the river from the ocean for spawning. No one seems to know where the shad spends the rest of the year. One reader sent us this recipe for cooking shad.

Serves 6 generously

ORDER a 5-pound shad cleaned, trimmed, and split for stuffing, with head removed. Fill cavity with the stuffing given below. Sew up cavity, pour a little vinegar down the backbone, let it stand a few minutes, then drain and place the fish in a large baking pan. Cover with 2 quarts of milk and bake in a slow oven, 300 degrees, for about 5½ hours. The bones will be completely soft.

Stuffing:

1 cup diced celery	2 teaspoons powdered sage
1 cup boiling water	1 quart lightly packed day-old bread cubes
3 tablespoons minced onion	
6 tablespoons butter or margarine	¾ teaspoon salt
	¾ teaspoon pepper

COOK celery in boiling water for 15 to 20 minutes, or until tender. Drain and reserve 4 tablespoons of liquid. Cook onion in butter until brown. Mix together the sage, bread cubes, salt, and pepper. Add the celery, liquid, onions, and butter, and mix thoroughly with a fork. Cover and let stand for 5 to 10 minutes. This is enough for a 4- or 5-pound fish.

Maine

Because there is no food editor in the group from Maine, and because Maine is partly responsible for two of our leading food products—potatoes and corn—I am including a recipe for Corn Chowder with Potatoes. Another Maine favorite is the inevitable, popular, and hearty succotash. According to Secrets of New England Cooking *(see p. 32 above), there are two kinds of succotash: in winter it's made of dried corn and dried beans, in summer of fresh corn and string beans.*

Corn Chowder with Potatoes

Serves 6

¼ pound salt pork
1 large onion, sliced
4 potatoes, sliced
2 cups water
6 soda crackers

3 cups milk
1 No. 2 can cream-style corn
1 teaspoon salt
½ teaspoon paprika

CUT salt pork into cubes and brown in a large saucepan. Remove salt pork and drain off all but about 2 tablespoons fat. Add onion and cook until yellow; add potatoes and water and cook until potatoes are soft. Stir in crackers soaked in the milk; add corn, salt, and paprika. Heat to simmering. Before serving sprinkle with crisp salt pork.

Florida

Sarah Ellen Merritt

MIAMI DAILY NEWS
MIAMI, FLORIDA

Lime-Flavored Meringues

Serves 6

3 egg whites	⅛ teaspoon salt
¼ teaspoon cream of tartar	¾ cup sugar

BEAT egg whites until foamy; add cream of tartar and salt; beat until stiff but not dry. Add sugar gradually, beating until very stiff. Cover baking sheet with buttered brown paper. Pile meringue into six rounds each about 3 inches in diameter. Make 2-inch depressions in the centers. Bake in a very slow oven (225 degrees) for 1 hour.

Filling:

3 egg yolks	1½ teaspoons grated lime rind
¼ cup sugar	1 cup heavy cream, whipped
4 tablespoons lime juice	

BEAT the egg yolks; add sugar and lime juice. Cook over boiling water, stirring constantly until thickened. Add lime rind. Remove from heat; chill. Fold into whipped cream. Fill the cooled meringue shells. Chill 6 to 12 hours in the refrigerator.

Green Mango Pie

3 or 4 large green mangoes 4 tablespoons butter
2 cups sugar   1 recipe for pastry
1 teaspoon nutmeg

LINE a pie plate with pastry. Peel and slice thin, enough green mangoes to fill the plate. Mix sugar and nutmeg; spread over mango slices. Dot with butter. Top the mango slices with a solid or lattice-type crust. Bake for 15 minutes at 425 degrees. Reduce temperature to 350 degrees and bake 45 minutes longer. This makes a very tart pie; for one less acid, use partially ripe mangoes. Half-and-half apple and green mangoes makes an interesting flavor combination.

Jeanne Voltz

THE MIAMI HERALD
MIAMI, FLORIDA

Cooking in subtropical Florida is a fascinating adventure in exotic raw materials, deliciously different tropical fruits and vegetables, and fresh-from-ocean seafood.

The specialty most often asked for by visitors to Miami's tropical wonderland is lime pie. Most of the limes produced in this country are grown within a few miles of Miami.

Lime Chiffon Pie

1 envelope unflavored gelatin   ¼ teaspoon salt
¼ cup cold water   1 teaspoon grated lime rind
4 eggs, separated   ½ cup heavy cream, whipped
½ cup lime juice   1 9-inch baked pie shell or
1 cup sugar   graham-cracker crust

SOFTEN gelatin in cold water. Put beaten egg yolks in top of double boiler. Add lime juice, ½ cup sugar, and salt. Cook over hot water, stirring constantly, until mixture thickens slightly. Remove from heat. Add softened gelatin and stir until dissolved. Add lime rind. Cool slightly. Beat egg whites until stiff peaks form; then gradually beat in remaining ½ cup sugar. Fold egg whites into gelatin mixture, then whipped cream.

Turn into baked pie shell and chill until firm.

Diana Rowell

ST. PETERSBURG TIMES
ST. PETERSBURG, FLORIDA

Florida gives us many delightful fruits: avocados, calamondins, guavas, loquats, lychee fruit and "nuts" (dried fruit), mangoes, and papayas, among others.

One of the less known avocado recipes that is especially delightful is the following: Cut the avocado in half, remove stone, and serve one half to each person. In the cavity of each portion put one heaping teaspoonful of powdered sugar and the juice of one lime. Everyone who hears of this thinks it is a terrible concoction, but everyone who has tried it considers it superior to all other methods of serving.

Now that lychee trees are planted in Florida, the delicious fresh fruits, which resemble large strawberries, are being shipped north. They are covered with a tough, red, warty skin that peels off readily, revealing the glistening white pulp, which is sweet, juicy, and a trifle acid. For centuries it has been the favorite fruit of the Chinese.

The mango fully merits the title "king of fruits." Now that the fibrous, turpentine-tasting fruit of earlier days has given place to the sweet-flavored, fiberless mangoes of today, more and more persons are learning to enjoy them.

The mango has a high nutritive value and should be included in every home planting in subtropical areas. It may be considered the tropical equivalent of the apple in the diet. Mangoes are usually eaten sliced, without sugar or cream, for dessert or breakfast, or combined with fruit salads.

Calamondin Marmalade

Calamondins make marmalade of distinctive flavor. The juice also is ideal for "ades" and can be used instead of lemon or lime for fish.

WASH the fruits thoroughly. Cut in halves and remove all seeds. Put through the food chopper, using a fine blade. Measure resulting pulp and to each measure of fruit add three measures of water. Let stand several hours or, if more convenient, overnight. Boil, uncovered, until pulp is tender, about 30 or more minutes. For each measure of the fruit mixture, add an equal measure of sugar. Cook rapidly in a heavy aluminum saucepan, stirring occasionally from the bottom of the pan until the mixture no longer runs off the side of the spoon but hangs on in a thick sheet. Allow mixture to cool slightly, with gentle stirring, before being poured into containers. This permits the even distribution of the peel throughout the jelly.

Loquat Pie

In late winter and early spring, loquat trees with their yellow fruits make handsome ornaments in our gardens. The fruits should not be eaten until they are fully ripe on the tree, as they fail to develop sugar after they are gathered. As the ripe fruit bruises easily, it does not ship well.

3 pints seeded, skinned loquats
1 rounded tablespoon flour or cornstarch

2 cups sugar
2 tablespoons butter
Cinnamon
1 recipe for pastry shell

SCALD large, ripe fruits and remove skins, seeds, and membranes around seed cavities. Put fruit in baking dish, add a mixture of the sugar, flour, and butter; sprinkle with cinnamon. Put piecrust over the top (there is no bottom crust), and bake in a 350-degree oven until crust is golden brown. Too long cooking ruins the flavor. Serve hot or cold. Do not add any water to the fruit, since loquats are approximately 80 per cent water.

Mango Chutney

Many experts consider it is simply not possible to make mango chutney without tamarinds, which add a tart piquancy.

¼ pound ripe tamarinds
1½ pounds brown sugar
3 pounds green mangoes, just beginning to turn yellow
1 pint vinegar (or ½ pint grapefruit juice and ½ pint vinegar)

1 pound dry currants
1 pound raisins
¼ ounce whole cloves
¼ ounce cardamon seed
6 ounces fresh or dry ginger root (or 4 ounces candied or preserved ginger)

REMOVE the tamarind shells, boil pulp 3 hours, let cool overnight. Boil again, and with a grater remove all pulp from seeds. Add half the sugar and boil down until syrupy. Slice green mangoes, including the skins. Add the remaining ingredients, and boil 2 hours, adding water if the mixture thickens too quickly. Add remaining sugar last, and cook to desired consistency. Pack in sterilized jars.
Note: If the dried ginger root is used, it is advisable to boil it and the whole cloves separately for a few hours in advance.

Roast Opossum

This recipe came from one of the old pioneer families of Florida. I've treasured it purely because of its age.

THE opossum is a very fat animal with a peculiarly flavored meat. To dress, immerse in very hot water (not boiling) for 1 minute. Remove and use a dull knife to scrape off hair so that skin is not cut. Slit from bottom of throat to hind legs and remove entrails. Remove head and tail if desired.

Wash thoroughly inside and out with hot water. Cover with cold water to which has been added 1 cup salt, and let stand overnight. Drain off the salted water and rinse with clean boiling water.

Stuff opossum and place in roaster; add 2 tablespoons water and roast in moderate oven (350 degrees) until tender. Baste every 15 minutes with drippings. Skim fat from pan gravy; serve gravy separately with baked yams or sweet potatoes.

Stuffing:

1 large onion, minced
1 tablespoon fat
Opossum liver, uncooked
1 cup bread crumbs

1 sweet red pepper, chopped
1 hard-cooked egg, chopped
Salt

BROWN onion in the fat. Add chopped liver and cook until liver is tender. Add bread crumbs, pepper, egg, salt, and enough water to moisten.

Greek Salad

Greek cookery is popular in some parts of Florida. This recipe is from Can the Greeks Cook! *by Fannie Venos and Lillian Prichard, of Tarpon Springs, Florida.*

4 Greek anchovies
½ head lettuce
3 stalks celery, chopped fine, leaves included
1 medium cucumber
2 medium tomatoes
1 small onion, sliced thin
½ green pepper

½ avocado
4 slices feta cheese
⅓ cup olive oil
Juice of 1 lemon or 1 teaspoon vinegar
Salt, pepper, and orégano
8 Greek olives

WASH anchovies thoroughly. Wash and clean vegetables. Arrange them on a large platter as follows: lettuce, celery, cucumber, tomatoes, onion, green pepper, avocado, and olives. Decorate with anchovies and feta cheese. Sprinkle olive oil, lemon juice or vinegar, salt and pepper, and orégano over entire salad.

Barbara Clendinen

THE TAMPA TRIBUNE
TAMPA, FLORIDA

Because almost a third of the people in this bay city are Spanish, Italian, or Cuban, the cuisine of Tampa is a fascinating blend of Deep South and continental fare. In many, perhaps most, Tampa homes, the fare is typically Deep South, but in our restaurants and in many homes, Spanish, Italian, or Cuban cooking has an important or even a controlling influence.

Stop by a kitchen door in any block and you'll smell the rich, pungent aroma of salt-water mullet frying in deep fat, with corn-meal hush puppies tumbling and turning gold in the same kettle. Take a few steps to the next house. You'll catch a breath and wish they'd ask you to share the arroz con pollo (chicken with yellow rice) that sends its inviting fragrance through the window. In our res-taurants you will find thick, saffron-tinted garbanzo bean soup; crisp Cuban bread baked in banana leaves; pompano al papillo, baked in parchment with a velvety sauce rich with shrimp and crabmeat; and fillets Cacerola or Catalana. And because we live on a small penin-sula near the Gulf of Mexico, not too far from Key West and within banana-boat distance of Cuba, our menus boast a profusion of sea-foods.

Young Tampa hostesses serve thin, salty chips of plantain at cock-tail parties. Plantain is the giant red banana that is shipped into few ports other than Tampa and New Orleans. Green plantain sliced thin and fried in deep fat turns into a crunchy tidbit similar to a potato chip. Ripe plantain sliced lengthwise and sautéed in fat, then sprinkled with sugar, is a favorite vegetable to serve with broiled ham steak.

Huge Key West shrimp are available most of the year in Tampa seafood markets, most of which have their own boats and unload directly into their own back doors. Fresh scallops, crayfish which take the place of their lobster kin, red snapper, Spanish mackerel, yellowtail, mullet, pompano, turtle steaks, soft- and hard-shelled crabs, grouper, and trout are plentiful most of the year.

We like our crayfish split, stuffed with seasoned whipped potatoes or with a thick seafood sauce, and baked. Turtle steaks are a fast-growing favorite, too, particularly since they sell consistently below beef prices and resemble the less tender cuts of beef. They're best braised with red wine and onions.

Shrimp we eat often and in so many ways that no one has ever selected the prime favorite. Shelled and cleaned, dipped into egg and cornmeal and fried in deep fat, they're tender and flaky-crisp. Simmered in water with a fat pod of garlic and a few slices of lime, they turn rosy red and are perfect teamed with pungent yellow rice. (Saffron turns the rice yellow; garlic, onions, and green pepper make it savory.)

We eat shrimp Creole style with peppery seasonings, and cut them into pieces to fry in delicate little puffballs. We sauté them with green pepper and onion, add a little tomato and bay leaf, and spoon the mixture into pastry-lined tart shells. Topped with a rich crust, they bake into wonderful little pies.

Arroz Con Pollo (Yellow Rice with Chicken)

Serves 8 generously

2 garlic pods
6 tablespoons olive oil
1 4-pound chicken, cut into serving pieces
4 medium onions, chopped
1 large bell pepper, chopped
3 large, ripe tomatoes, peeled and chopped
5 cups water

2 teaspoons salt (about)
1 envelope dried saffron or 1 small packet powdered saffron
2½ cups uncooked rice, washed
¾ cup sauterne or dry sherry
Tiny green peas
Pimiento strips

COOK one garlic pod in oil until it turns brown. Remove it from oil. Wash chicken pieces, dry, salt, and pepper. Brown them lightly on both sides in hot oil. Remove chicken. In the oil, sauté onions, bell pepper, and one garlic pod, cut fine. Add tomatoes, browned chicken, water, and salt to taste. Cover and let simmer 1 hour. Add saffron and simmer until chicken is tender. (If dried saffron is used, heat it on pan top, mix with a little cold water, and add. Powdered saffron can be used straight from the package.) Add rice, stir well, add wine, cover, and cook 40 minutes or until liquid is absorbed and rice is fairly dry. The rice will be a glossy yellow, the chicken golden brown. Garnish with tiny green peas and strips of pimiento. Serve with green salad and crisp Cuban (or French) bread. Hot coffee and a fruit dessert finish the meal.

Black Beans with Rice

Violently sable in hue, black beans startle the amateur. They're not for nervous digestions, but eaten by sturdy folk, they make the best of all bean soups. The Spanish restaurants serve them as a meat substitute, particularly on Fridays. Tampa partygoers usually end up at midnight at a Spanish restaurant to sup on black beans and rice before going home.

Serves 8

1 pound black beans	2 bay leaves
1 small ham hock	1 cup olive oil
3 onions	1 tablespoon vinegar
3 buttons garlic (more if desired)	Salt and pepper to taste
	Steamed rice
½ bell pepper	Onions, finely chopped

SOAK well-washed beans overnight. Drain, reserving water. The water will be very dark, but that's the nature of the dish. If necessary, add enough fresh water to make 2 quarts. Start beans cooking slowly in their water, with ham hock. Cut up onions, garlic, bell pepper, and bay leaves, and sauté in olive oil. Add, with vinegar, to the beans. Cook very slowly 3 or 4 hours, until done. Season to taste. Serve atop fluffy, steamed rice and top with finely chopped onions and a lacing of vinegar and olive oil.

Garbanzo Bean Soup

This sturdy, thick, and rich soup, served with a salad and crisp bread, makes a meal.

Serves 8

1 pound Spanish beans
  (*garbanzos*)
2-pound ham hock
4 large onions
2 buttons garlic
1 bell pepper

3 tablespoons olive oil
2 bay leaves
½ teaspoon powdered saffron
2 Spanish sausages (*chorizos*)
4 large potatoes
Salt and pepper to taste

WASH beans; soak overnight. Wash well next morning. Cover ham hock well with cold water, add beans, and start cooking slowly. Cut up onions, garlic, and bell pepper, and sauté quickly in olive oil. Add to soup, together with bay leaves and saffron. Cut sausages into quarters and add. When beans are beginning to be tender (and this takes long, slow cooking), add potatoes, cut into eighths. Season to taste with salt and pepper. Always cook slowly. More water may be needed but soup should be thick. The longer it cooks, the better it is. And it's even better reheated the following day.

Coquina Soup

Coquinas are tiny, clamlike sea life that color the Gulf beaches with rainbow hues. Children gather them enthusiastically in sand buckets because, opened, their shells form tiny butterflies. Gourmets gather them just as fervently, for they make a delicate, light broth.

WASH 6 quarts coquinas very well in several waters to rid them of sand. Just cover with cold water, cover the utensil, and bring them slowly to a boil. The wee shells will open and the juice and infinitesimal meat will flavor the water. Simmer 10 minutes after the coquinas reach the boiling point, stirring occasionally. Pour through a fine sieve and serve hot or chilled with salty crackers. Marjorie

Kinnan Rawlings mentions this soup in her *Cross Creek Cookery*. She suggests that 2 tablespoons of thin cream and a small lump of butter be added to each serving. That is richer treatment than coquinas usually get.

Crab Enchilada

Crab cooked this way is not a dish to serve with your fine linens. Better newspapers and a lawn supper, for the crabs are plucked out of their pungent sauce and eaten out of the hand.

Serves 12

1 head of garlic, cut fine
1 pound onions, cut fine
3 large green peppers, cut fine
2 cups olive oil
3 No. 2 cans tomato paste
3 No. 2½ cans whole tomatoes, strained

1 pint white wine
2 small hot peppers
1 pint hot water
Salt to taste
5 dozen crabs, hard-shelled cooked and cleaned

COOK garlic, onions, and green peppers slowly in olive oil until soft but not brown. Add tomato paste and tomatoes, then wine, hot peppers, water, and salt to taste. Simmer slowly 2 hours.

Clean crabs under running water, leaving the meat in the shells. Place in sauce, cook 45 minutes. Serve with lots of paper napkins, crisp bread, and a salad.

Georgia

Agnes Reasor Olmstead

THE ATLANTA CONSTITUTION
ATLANTA, GEORGIA

Georgia's favorite foods like those of many Southern states, stem from the English settlers, but reflect the skills of many generations of cooks, both white and Negro, in dealing with native foods. We share with other Southern states such staples as corn bread, hominy, brandied peaches, and greens cooked with fat back. But if we think of specifically Georgian foods we are likely to include these: Brunswick stew, egg bread (no flour is used; the real Southern cornmeal is sufficiently fine to hold the bread together), fried corn (fresh sweet corn fried in bacon drippings in a black iron skillet), grits (served hot with butter for breakfast or supper), cracklin's and cracklin' bread (no egg), hush puppies, fat back (salt pork, not smoked, no lean streak in it), and buttermilk biscuits as staple foods to be found almost anywhere, any time.

Also very characteristic are: Hoppin' John, pecan pie, boiled peanuts (green peanuts in the shell, boiled in salted water about 15 minutes), syllabub (made with a syllabub churn, served in tall parfait glasses), sweet-potato pudding (always using grated raw sweet potato and cooked in an iron skillet so the pudding will turn dark), Lane cake, eggnog (a Christmas drink), hog jowl and black-eyed peas (always served on New Year's Day at noon), fried chicken and cream gravy (a traditional Sunday breakfast), smothered chicken *(use raw chicken, roll in flour, brown in fat, then add ¼ cup water, dot with butter, put in 350-degree oven uncovered), ambrosia (a typical Christmas or holiday dessert), and "Tipsy Squire" (a layer of sponge cake soaked in wine or sherry, a layer of boiled custard, a layer of whipped cream; repeat; stud the top with blanched, quartered almonds).*

Syllabub

Some cookbooks call syllabub a drink, some say it is a dessert. It's first cousin to eggnog but not so well known. It came to this country from England in early colonial days and is best known along the Southern coast: Virginia, South Carolina—especially in Charleston —and parts of Georgia. It is a traditional Southern dessert for holidays and other gala occasions.

A good way to start an argument is to claim your recipe is the best. No two families seem to agree, but most Southerners would admit that this recipe is a good one.

Serves 8 to 10

1 pint thick cream	1 pint sweet milk
½ cup sugar	½ cup bourbon (or a bit more)

MIX all the ingredients together in a bowl deep enough for the froth to rise. Place churn in the center of the bowl; hold churn firmly as you pump the dasher up and down with an easy and steady motion. Or beat with a rotary beater. When the top of the bowl is well covered with froth, skim off with a spoon and put into tall glasses or goblets. Continue to beat, skimming off the froth periodically until the mixture is used up. Syllabub will keep in the refrigerator for a week—provided the refrigerator is locked.

Syllabub may be beaten ahead of time, placed in glasses, and kept cold until served. Or you may bring out your prettiest bowl to the party and make it right at the table. It may be served with fruit cake, old-fashioned tea cakes, pound cake, or angel-food cake. Salted pecans, stuffed dates, and crystallized fruit are also good with it.

Hush Puppies

The hush puppy is a truly Southern dish, and derived its name from a true Southern incident.

When General Sherman was making his flight through Georgia to the sea, back in the days of the War Between the States, the pursuing gallant boys in gray had trouble carrying enough supplies, and the dogs that invariably follow armies were going somewhat hungry. Each time mess would be prepared they would surround the cooking places and howl dismally. Cooks usually would hurl them scraps of corn pone and admonish, "Hush, puppy."

To the dyed-in-the-wool hush puppy fundamentalist a hush puppy is an accoutrement of a fish dish, just as an egg is essential to a nog.

If you asked a good Georgia cook how to make a hush puppy, she might tell you something like this:

TAKE cornmeal, preferably water-ground. Break into it sufficient eggs to give it something of a sticky texture, then add beer, milk, or just plain water to make a malleable mess. Mix in finely chopped onions. Form into small pones, using the hands. Drop into hot deep fat and cook until golden brown. Remove, place on brown paper to drain, and serve hot.

Here, however, is a tested recipe, used in one of Atlanta's famous tearooms.

Makes 20 to 25 hush puppies

2 cups cornmeal	1 egg, beaten
1 tablespoon flour	3 tablespoons finely cut onion
½ teaspoon soda	1 cup buttermilk
1 teaspoon salt	

MIX dry ingredients, add beaten egg, onion, and buttermilk. Mix well and drop by teaspoonfuls into hot (about 350 to 375 degrees) deep fat. When they float they're done.

Lane Cake

1 cup butter	1 cup milk
2 cups sugar	1 teaspoon vanilla
3¼ cups sifted flour	8 egg whites
2 teaspoons baking powder	

CREAM butter and sugar. Sift together flour and baking powder and add to creamed mixture alternately with milk and vanilla. Fold in stiffly beaten egg whites. Pour into three shallow cake pans. Bake in a moderate oven (350 degrees) until golden brown.

Filling:

½ cup butter	1 cup chopped pecans
1 cup sugar	1 teaspoon vanilla
8 egg yolks, beaten	1 wineglass brandy
1 cup seeded raisins	

CREAM butter and sugar. Add beaten egg yolks and cook in a double boiler until thick. Add remaining ingredients and spread between layers of cake.
Note: It helps to first soak the raisins in the brandy for an hour or more.

Icing:

2½ cups sugar	2 egg whites, beaten until
⅛ teaspoon salt	foamy
⅓ cup dark corn syrup	1 teaspoon vanilla
⅔ cup water	

DISSOLVE sugar, salt, and syrup in the water. Cook syrup mixture; when it reaches the boiling point, pour 3 tablespoons into the beaten egg whites. Continue beating eggs until stiff but not dry. Boil syrup mixture to 240 degrees, or until it spins a thread at least 10 inches long, then pour slowly over egg whites, beating until the frosting begins to lose its gloss and hold its shape. Spread over cake. If the frosting becomes hard, add a drop or two of hot water to the mixture. This frosting does not form a crust that cracks when the cake is cut.

Fried Cream

The cream of all accompaniments for broiled chicken.

Serves 4

1 stick of cinnamon
1 pint milk
9 tablespoons sugar
2 tablespoons cornstarch
(mixed with 3 additional
tablespoons milk)
3 egg yolks, beaten

1 tablespoon flour (add to
cornstarch mixture)
1 tablespoon butter or margarine
½ teaspoon vanilla
Sifted cracker crumbs

COOK cinnamon in milk. When just about to boil, add sugar and cornstarch-flour mixture. Stir for 2 minutes, remove from fire, stir in well-beaten egg yolks, and return to fire only until thickened. Take out cinnamon; stir in butter or margarine and vanilla extract.

Grease a deep platter with butter or margarine. Pour in mixture to a depth of about ⅓ inch. When cold and stiff, cut into pieces about 1 inch wide and 3 inches long. Roll carefully in sifted cracker crumbs, sauté in a little more butter until colored brown, and place in hot oven for 4 or 5 minutes to soften. Serve immediately.

Grace Hartley

THE ATLANTA JOURNAL
ATLANTA, GEORGIA

Peach-Berry Sponge Roll

Serves 8 to 10

4 eggs, separated
¾ cup granulated sugar
2 tablespoons cold water
1 teaspoon vanilla extract

¾ cup sifted cake flour
1 teaspoon baking powder
¼ teaspoon salt
Confectioners' sugar

1 cup whipping cream
3 tablespoons granulated
sugar

4 to 6 peach halves
1 cup sliced strawberries

BEAT egg whites until stiff. Gradually beat in ⅜ cup sugar. Beat yolks until thick. Gradually beat another ⅜ cup sugar, then cold water and vanilla. Fold in egg whites. Sift together flour, baking powder, and salt; fold into egg-sugar mixture. Pour into a waxed-paper-lined pan (about 10 by 15 inches). Bake in a moderately hot oven (375 degrees) for 15 to 20 minutes. Turn out at once onto a clean cloth thickly dusted with confectioners' sugar. Trim off crusts and roll as for jelly roll. Cool. Unroll and spread with sweetened whipped cream. Dice thoroughly drained peaches to make 1 cup. Spread peaches and strawberries over cream; roll up again. Decorate with whipped cream and fruit. Cut in slices to serve.

Chicken Pie

Serves 8 generously

2 fowl
1 onion
Salt and pepper
¼ pound butter
4 tablespoons flour

1 4-ounce can mushrooms
6 hard-boiled eggs, chopped
fine
Salt and pepper
1 recipe for pastry

BOIL fowl until tender. Separate meat from bones and replace bones in liquor in which fowl were boiled, together with onion, salt, and pepper. Cook for 1 hour and strain. Cut up the white meat in bite-sized pieces. Run dark meat and skin through chopper, and add to white meat. Melt butter, and flour, chicken stock, chicken meat, mushrooms, eggs, additional salt and pepper to taste, and reheat. Line a baking dish with piecrust and bake it in a medium oven (350 degrees). When a light brown, pour in chicken mixture; make a top crust and finish baking.

Pepper Relish

Makes about 4 pints

12 sweet red peppers, chopped
12 sweet green peppers, chopped
1 pod hot pepper
9 onions

1 cup sugar
1 tablespoon mixed pickling spices
1 tablespoon salt
2 cups vinegar

COVER peppers and onions with boiling water, let stand 5 minutes, and drain. Cover again with boiling water, let stand 10 minutes, and drain. Add sugar, seasonings, and vinegar. Cook 15 minutes. Pack into sterile jars; seal at once.

Watermelon Rind Pickle

Makes 4 or 5 pints

2 quarts prepared rind
2 quarts limewater or salt water
4 to 6 cups sugar
1 quart vinegar

1 tablespoon whole allspice
1 tablespoon whole cloves
1 stick cinnamon
1 tablespoon crushed ginger root

TRIM the flesh from large pieces of thick, firm watermelon rind. Soak rind in limewater (1 tablespoon slaked lime to 1 quart water) 4 hours, or soak overnight in salt water (4 tablespoons salt to 1 quart water). Limewater makes a crisper pickle. Drain, rinse, cover with fresh water, and boil 1½ hours. Cool, then cut into small pieces. Trim off the green skins and measure rind. (This may be done at the time the pink meat is removed but is easier to do after the rind has been partly cooked.) Boil 2 cups sugar, 1 quart fresh water, 1 cup vinegar, and the spices for 5 minutes. Add rind. Simmer 30 minutes. Let stand overnight. Add remaining sugar and vinegar, and boil gently until the syrup is almost as thick as honey and the rind clear. Add boiling water if the syrup becomes too thick before the rind is tender and translucent. Pack into sterile jars; seal at once.

Pecan Pie

3 eggs
1 cup sugar
1 cup molasses
½ cup melted butter or margarine

1 cup pecans (halves)
¼ teaspoon salt
1 teaspoon vanilla
1 recipe for pastry shell

BEAT eggs until light, add sugar, and beat again. Then add molasses, melted butter or margarine, pecans, salt, and vanilla. Mix and pour into 9-inch piepan lined with plain pastry. Bake for 10 minutes in a hot oven (400 degrees), then lower heat to 350 degrees and bake until custard is set.

Cordelia Rhodes

AUGUSTA HERALD-AUGUSTA CHRONICLE
AUGUSTA, GEORGIA

President Eliot of Harvard once inquired of an old gentlewoman what it was, in all her long life, that had given her the most pleasure. She answered, promptly and enthusiastically, "My vittles." Georgia folk have for generations taken pleasure in their "vittles" and have been proud of the bounteous tables which they set. Good Southern cooking is a heritage claimed by many Georgia women.

Blackberries grow wild in Richmond County. The highways are lined with the bushes, and in the spring the white blooms are pretty to ride along and see, but come hot weather the luscious blackberry becomes the hunting goal of many.

Barbecue Sauce

When Augustans entertain a large gathering, they are likely to have a barbecue. With the barbecued pork and chicken will come corn on the cob, cabbage slaw, rice, Brunswick stew, thick red slices of tomatoes, and a quantity of iced tea. The meat is cooked over pits of smoldering hickory and oak logs—roasted, basted, and turned for a period of about 12 hours. The barbecue fires usually burn the entire night before the barbecue.

Makes about 2 cups

1½ cups tomato juice
¼ teaspoon red pepper
2 teaspoons salt
¼ teaspoon pepper
¼ teaspoon powdered mustard
1 teaspoon sugar

4½ teaspoons Worcestershire sauce
1 bay leaf
¾ cup cider vinegar
3 peeled garlic buds cut in pieces
3 tablespoons butter

SIMMER all ingredients together for 10 minutes. Baste the roasting chicken or pork every 10 minutes with this sauce.

Sweet Pickled Peaches

Georgia women have learned many ways of using up surplus peaches, pickles being one of the most popular.

Makes about 4 pints

7 pounds peaches
3¾ pounds sugar
1 quart vinegar

2 ounces whole cloves
2 ounces stick cinnamon

PEEL the peaches; stick a clove into each peach. Boil sugar and vinegar with cinnamon sticks for 5 minutes, then drop in the peaches. Cook peaches until tender; remove from syrup. Boil the syrup, reducing its volume nearly one half. Pour over the peaches, which have been packed into sterilized jars. Seal.

Southern Fried Chicken

Serves 2

1 2-pound fryer, cut up   Shortening (bacon drippings
Salt, flour   are especially good)

POUR into a frying pan (black iron is best) enough drippings to come up 1 inch in the pan. Heat to smoking. Dredge chicken, which has been salted, in flour. Drop into hot fat; cover tightly. Chicken should not be turned more than two times. When chicken is brown on one side, turn and replace cover. When brown on both sides remove cover and let cook until tender. When removing chicken from the pan, hold each piece over the hot fat a few minutes to draw all the fat from the chicken. Drain on brown paper. Serve hot or cold.

Georgia Hoecake

ONE quart of meal, 1 teaspoon salt; mix with cold water, or buttermilk and soda if preferred. Make a very stiff batter; spread half an inch thick on a hot greased griddle. Cook over a quick fire.

Blackberry Wine

MASH berries thoroughly; to 1 gallon of fruit, add 2 quarts water. Let this mixture stand for 36 hours in a stone crock until it ferments. Then strain through a coarse piece of muslin. To 1 gallon of the liquid add, for a sweet wine, 3 pounds of sugar, or for one not so sweet, 2¼ pounds sugar. Put in a demijohn. Tie a piece of cloth over the top until the second fermentation is finished, probably 2 to 3 weeks. Pour off into bottles and cork tightly. The wine will be ready for use in 5 to 6 months.

Latimer Watson

LEDGER AND ENQUIRER
COLUMBUS, GEORGIA

I believe that any Georgian would tell you that chicken is the favorite meat in this part of the country. If you narrow it down to Columbus, Georgia, the answer would come, quick as a flash, "Country Captain." This very special way of preparing chicken was originated by a famous Columbus hostess and belle, Mrs. W. L. Bullard, to be served to Franklin Delano Roosevelt and some of his distinguished guests at a dinner at her Warm Springs cottage. This was long before Mr. Roosevelt became President.

This recipe has been given to a star-studded list including General Pershing, General Patton, General Eisenhower, General Bradley, and General Marshall. General Patton once wired, when he was to spend only a few hours in Columbus, "If you can't give me a party and have Country Captain, put some in a tin bucket and bring it to the train."

Country Captain

Serves 4

3½- to 4-pound young, tender fryer
Flour, salt, and pepper
Lard
2 onions, finely chopped
2 green peppers, chopped
1 small garlic bean, minced
1½-teaspoons salt
½ teaspoon white pepper
3 teaspoons curry powder

2 No. 2 cans tomatoes
½ teaspoon chopped parsley
½ teaspoon powdered thyme
¼ pound almonds, scalded, skinned, and roasted to golden brown
3 heaping tablespoons dried currants
2 cups cooked rice
Parsley for garnish

CUT up the chicken in pieces for frying. Remove skin and roll pieces in flour, salt, and pepper. Brown in lard. Remove chicken from the pan but keep it hot. (This is a secret of the dish's success.)

Into the lard in which the chicken has been browned put the onions, peppers, and garlic. Cook very slowly, stirring constantly. Season with salt, pepper, and curry powder. (Test curry to suit taste of your family. Some like more.) Add tomatoes, parsley, and thyme.

Put chicken in roaster and pour mixture over it. If it does not cover the chicken, rinse out skillet in which mixture has been cooked and pour over chicken also. Cover roaster tightly. Bake in moderate oven about 45 minutes, until the chicken is tender.

Place chicken in center of a large platter and pile around it the rice, cooked very dry and with each grain standing alone. Now drop currants into the sauce mixture and pour over the rice. Scatter almonds over the top. Garnish with parsley, and you have food for the gods.

Idaho

Sylvia Johnson

THE IDAHO STATESMAN

BOISE, IDAHO

Idaho is most famous in the culinary world for her baking potatoes and wild game, so we have included a simple recipe for the preparation of each of these. We add, also, a cake recipe for the housewife who may be baffled by the effect of high altitudes on her baking, a problem many Idaho housewives have had to master.

Idaho Baked Potatoes

WASH and dry potatoes of the same size. Put into medium-hot oven and cook until tender (from 40 to 60 minutes). If a soft skin is desired, rub the potato with a little fat before baking. To economize on fuel, bake the potatoes with other foods requiring a medium heat. When the potatoes are soft, take them from the oven and gash each one on the side in the form of a cross. Pinch the potato slightly so that it fluffs up through the break in the skin. Into the break pour meat drippings, pieces of crisp salt pork, butter, etc.

Baked potatoes may also be stuffed. Cut the baked potato lengthwise, scoop out, mash, season with melted fat, hot milk, and salt, restuff potato skins, brush with fat, and brown in the oven. Cheese may be sprinkled over the top of the stuffed potato for added flavor.

Venison, Elk, or Beef Steak

TO oven-broil, take a medium to thick steak and wipe with a damp cloth. Preheat broiler to 350 degrees, and place steak on broiler rack. Leave oven door slightly ajar while broiling meat. When the meat is brown on top, salt and turn. A 1-inch venison sirloin should be medium well done in 15 to 20 minutes. Elk takes slightly longer to cook than the corresponding cut of beef. Many people prefer game rare to medium, as long cooking kills some of the wild flavor. To pan-broil the steak, preheat the skillet and grease slightly. Cook over a medium flame. Salt and turn when half done.

Mile-High Cake

(For altitudes around 3000 feet)

2 cups sifted cake flour
1¾ teaspoons baking powder
¾ teaspoon salt
1¼ cups sugar
½ cup vegetable shortening

¾ cup, plus 1 tablespoon milk
1 teaspoon vanilla
2 eggs

PLACE in a sifter the sifted cake flour, baking powder, salt, and sugar. Have shortening at room temperature. Stir it just enough to soften, and sift in the dry ingredients. Add vanilla to the milk. (If butter, margarine, or lard is used as shortening, decrease amount of milk to ¾ cup.) Add three-quarters of the milk and mix until all the flour is damp. Beat 2 minutes. Add remaining milk and un-beaten eggs. Beat 1 minute. If an electric mixer is used, beat using low speed. Count only actual beating time or number of strokes, counting 150 full strokes to a minute. Scrape spoon and sides of bowl often during beating. Pour batter into two 8-inch layer-cake pans lined with greased paper. Bake in 375-degree oven until done (about 25 minutes). The cake may also be baked in a pan 9 by 9 by 2 inches or one 10 by 10 by 2 inches in a 350-degree oven for 25 to 35 minutes. Frost as desired.

Illinois

Ruth Ellen Church

CHICAGO TRIBUNE

CHICAGO, ILLINOIS

Probably a typical Midwestern menu would include a breakfast of bacon and eggs or oatmeal with cream, toast and coffee, plus orange juice or some fruit in season; lunch of macaroni and cheese, lettuce and tomato salad, gingerbread and milk; dinner of fried chicken or pork chops with milk gravy, mashed or baked potatoes, baking-powder biscuits, buttered peas or scalloped corn (corn on the cob, in season), apple pie, and coffee.

Those foods are typically Midwestern, but Midwestern families, particularly Chicagoans and others who have access to city markets, also enjoy more cosmopolitan foods. They prepare dishes brought by people from many lands and many other regions of this country. We thus find among Midwest favorite foods Mexican chili, English roast beef with Yorkshire pudding, Hungarian goulash, Bohemian Kolacky, the many Swedish smörgasbord delicacies, Italian spaghetti and pizza, and Chinese egg rolls. Maine lobster is eaten in restaurants, but Chicagoans dote on lobster tails, shrimp, and other seafoods from the Eastern and Southern coastal regions, which they prepare at home. New England baked beans, the West's Caesar salad, "Southern" fried chicken, corn bread—these have become Midwestern, too.

Chicago is the world's livestock market, and Chicagoans are meat eaters. They love thick T-bone steaks served almost charred on the outside, rare within. With steak they want French-fried potatoes and probably a slice of onion or tomato. Not much else. A good, aged steak is a meal in itself, and the dinner plate must not be cluttered with distracting vegetables.

Midwestern cooks are beginning to cook with spices, herbs, and wines, but their basic cooking accessories are and always have been milk and cream and cheese, eggs and butter, of which the Midwest has an abundance.

Readers of the Tribune ask for recipes for French pastry, Italian cannoli, East Indian curry; they want to know how to cook pheasant in wine and to make rich, extravagant desserts. But they also want to know how to fix the more everyday foods such as potato salad, coleslaw, bread pudding, and corned beef hash. The recipes here represent popular requests and, I believe, typical Chicago and Midwestern food choices.

Turkey Casserole

Serves 6

½ pound sliced mushrooms
4 tablespoons butter
¼ cup flour
½ teaspoon salt
⅛ teaspoon pepper
1 teaspoon minced onion
1 cup cream

1 cup clear turkey or chicken broth or bouillon
2 cups diced, cooked turkey
¼ cup chopped green peppers
¼ cup sliced ripe olives

SAUTÉ mushrooms in butter for 5 minutes. Sprinkle flour over mushrooms and add salt, pepper, and onion. Stir until blended. Gradually add turkey or chicken broth and cream, stirring constantly until thickened and smooth. (As much as ½ cup dry white wine may replace some of the broth.) Add turkey, green peppers, and olives. Cook only until the turkey is heated through. The mixture may then be turned into a hot casserole or transferred to a chafing dish for serving.

Oven Barbecued Spareribs

Serves 6

4 pounds spareribs
1 teaspoon salt
⅛ teaspoon pepper

4 thin slices of lemon
1 large onion, chopped fine

PLACE spareribs, meaty side up, in a dripping pan. Sprinkle with salt and pepper. Top with lemon slices and onion. Bake in a hot oven (450 degrees), uncovered, for 30 minutes.

Sauce:

1 teaspoon chili powder
1 tablespoon celery seed
¼ cup brown sugar
¼ cup vinegar

¼ cup Worcestershire sauce
1 cup tomato catsup
2 cups water
Few drops of Tabasco sauce

COMBINE ingredients and bring to the boiling point. Pour over ribs and continue baking in a moderate oven (350 degrees) for 1 hour longer. Baste ribs two or three times during baking.

Shrimps de Jonghe

Here is famous fare in Chicago, where the dish originated.

Serves 8

¾ cup butter
1 teaspoon salt
1 clove garlic, minced
1 cup fine, dry bread crumbs
¼ cup minced parsley

½ cup sherry
Dash of cayenne pepper
Dash of paprika
3 pounds shrimp

CREAM butter and mix in salt and garlic. Add crumbs, parsley, sherry, and seasonings. Mix thoroughly. Shell and clean the cooked shrimps. Arrange in eight individual greased casseroles. Cover with a layer of the crumb mixture. Bake 20 to 25 minutes in a moderately hot oven (375 degrees).

Chicken-Baked Pork Chops

Serves 6

6 thick pork chops
1 teaspoon salt
¼ teaspoon pepper
2 tablespoons drippings

1 cup quick-cooking rice
1 can condensed cream of chicken soup
1 cup milk

SEASON chops with salt and pepper; brown in drippings in a frying pan. Place in a baking dish or casserole. Cover with rice. Mix soup with milk and pour over the chops and rice, being careful to cover rice with the liquid. Cover tightly. Bake in a moderate oven (350 degrees) for 1¼ hours. The chicken soup will be absorbed by the chops and rice.

Pepper Steak

Serves 4

1½ pounds round steak
Flour
4 tablespoons fat
3 medium green peppers, chopped

2 medium onions
2 teaspoons Worcestershire sauce
2½ cups water
Salt and pepper to taste

CUT steak in pieces about 2 by 3 inches. Roll in flour and brown in fat. Add peppers, onions, Worcestershire sauce, and half the water. Season well, cover, and simmer over a low flame until tender, about 1½ hours. Add the remaining water from time to time during the cooking.

Dorothy Cooley Thompson

CHICAGO HERALD-AMERICAN
CHICAGO, ILLINOIS

Roast Sweet Corn

In the heart of the great concentrated corn-growing area of the Middle West we think we know some of the best ways to cook sweet corn. There is steamed fresh sweet corn, sweet corn cooked in milk, fried corn, and best of all, the freshly picked ears roasted slowly over glowing coals in the damp, clean husks of the corn itself.

ROAST corn not more than 4 or 5 hours after picking. Remove outer husks, leaving a layer three or four husks deep. Remove the silk and damaged ends, and place in a kettle or pail of cold water. Allow the ears to soak for 30 to 60 minutes.

Meantime build up your outdoor fire and allow it to reduce to glowing coals. Arrange corn on a rack over the coals and allow the ears to roast slowly, turning occasionally, for 40 to 45 minutes. Strip off the husks and serve with butter, salt, and freshly ground pepper.

Cannibal Appetizers

1 pound lean beef, ground
1 egg yolk
Capers
Sweet onion, thinly sliced

Thinly sliced icebox (salty) rye bread, buttered
Salt and pepper

HAVE all fat and thick membranes removed from high-quality beef (but not necessarily round steak), and have it ground twice. Pile the raw beef in the center of a chop plate and make a nest in the center. Break the egg yolk into this, being careful to keep out any white, and garnish with capers. Surround with overlapping slices of onion. Around the outside arrange overlapping slices of the rye bread. Serve with salt and coarsely ground black pepper.

Quick Kolacky

This is a Bohemian recipe popular with readers of the Herald-American.

Makes 12 or more Kolacky

2 cups sifted flour
2 teaspoons baking powder
2 tablespoons sugar
¼ teaspoon salt
1 cup butter or margarine

3 packages (3-ounce size) cream cheese
2 eggs, beaten
Filling

SIFT flour with baking powder, sugar, and salt. Cream butter and cheese together. Blend in the sifted dry ingredients, then add beaten eggs and stir to form a stiff dough. Chill.

Roll out ¼ inch thick on a lightly floured board. Cut with a floured biscuit cutter. In the center of each round of dough place a spoonful of prune, apricot, cottage-cheese, or poppy-seed filling, or a thick jam. Bake on an ungreased cooky sheet in a 375-degree oven for 15 minutes, or until delicately browned.

Great Lakes Fish Boil

On the shores of the Great Lakes a favorite outdoor or shore dinner is the fish boil—a meal in one kettle that couldn't be easier to prepare or more delicious to eat. Pack up a bowlful of salad greens and garden-ripe tomatoes to make a giant tossed salad to go with this, and pass cold bottles of beer or steaming cups of coffee.

Medium potatoes
Salt
Lake trout or white fish

Cooking onions
Parsley
Celery tops

ALLOW one or more potatoes for each person, and one or more thick fish steaks, cut 1½ to 2 inches thick. Bring a large kettle of water to a boil and add salt, allowing 1 teaspoon for each 2 quarts. Add potatoes, which have been thoroughly scrubbed and rinsed. Bring to a boil again. Cook gently for 20 minutes, then add a "bouquet" of parsley and celery tops, onions cut in quarters, and the fish steaks. Simmer gently about 10 minutes, or until the fish is tender. Lift fish from the liquid onto a large platter, surround with unpeeled potatoes, and serve with plenty of butter.

Houska Twist

And here is another Bohemian sweet bread.

Serves 10 to 12

2 cups milk, scalded	½ pound seeded white raisins
2 cakes compressed yeast	(1½ cups)
1 cup sugar	¼ pound blanched almonds,
½ cup butter or margarine	slivered (1 cup)
1 egg	6 cups sifted flour (about)
2 egg yolks	1 egg white
1 teaspoon nutmeg	Almonds
1 tablespoon salt	Confectioners' sugar

SCALD the milk and cool to lukewarm. Crumble yeast into a small bowl, add 1 teaspoon sugar and ¼ cup milk, and allow to stand for about 5 minutes. Cream butter, add remaining sugar, and cream together thoroughly. Add egg and egg yolks and beat well. Add nutmeg, salt, raisins, almonds, and enough flour to make a dough that can be kneaded. Knead on a floured board until smooth and elastic. Place in a lightly greased bowl and allow it to rise until doubled in bulk. Divide the dough into nine pieces—four large, three medium, and two small. Roll them into ropelike strands, braid the four large pieces, and place on a greased cooky sheet. Braid the three medium pieces and place on top, then twist the two small strands and place on top. Allow to rise until doubled in bulk. Brush with slightly beaten egg white and sprinkle with more almonds. Bake in a 350-degree oven for 45 to 60 minutes, or until done. Cool; sprinkle with confectioners' sugar.

Lillian Martin

CHICAGO SUN-TIMES
CHICAGO, ILLINOIS

*The recent influx of D.P.'s and immigrants from central Europe
has brought to Chicago many of the so-called Continental foods:
hearty, well-seasoned soups of the main-course variety, veal in new
guises, excellent yeast baking,* torten *of the Viennese type, minia-
ture butter and nut cookies, and fine chocolates. These augment
our average-American everyday good cooking—with strong empha-
sis on fine beef, for which the Middle West has long been famous.*

*During the Passover, the following prize-winning Jewish dish
was submitted in the* Sun-Times *recipe contest. It's good the year
around, and may be served as an accompaniment to the main course
or for desert.*

Egg Mold with Caviar Dressing

*Egg appetizers are popular here for luncheon and dinner. This one
is served in individual slices atop a foundation of bright, shredded
greens.*

Serves 8 as a lunch dish; more as an appetizer

12 to 14 hard-cooked eggs
1 green pepper
1 small can pimientos
1 teaspoon Worcestershire
   sauce
1 teaspoon salt

½ teaspoon pepper
2 teaspoons onion juice
Mayonnaise as needed
Thousand Island dressing
Black caviar

GRIND eggs, pepper, and pimientos through a food chopper and mix.
Add seasonings and enough mayonnaise to hold the mixture together. Mold and refrigerate about 12 hours. Unmold. Serve with
Thousand Island dressing to which a small jar of caviar has been
added. Crabmeat can be used instead of caviar.

Noodle and Cheese Kugel

Serves 6

½ pound medium-broad
  noodles
Salt
4 eggs, beaten
1 pint cottage cheese

¾ cup sugar
3 teaspoons cinnamon
1 cup chopped pecans
¼ pound butter, melted

COOK noodles in salted water. Drain; rinse under cold water. Add the remaining ingredients. Place in a greased casserole or loaf pan and bake at 350 degrees until nicely browned, 20 to 30 minutes.

Vanilla Cream Torte

The contributor of this recipe had been in America less than three months.

6 egg whites, whipped until
  stiff
6 egg yolks
7 tablespoons sugar

¾ cup plus 2 tablespoons
  flour
Butter

ADD egg yolks, sugar, and flour in rotation to egg whites. Butter and flour the bottom, only, of a torte pan, and pour in the batter. Bake in a moderate oven (350 degrees) about 1 hour. When the torte layer is cool, cut it in half through the middle to make two layers.

Filling:

3 egg yolks
½ teaspoon potato meal or all-
  purpose flour
6 tablespoons sugar
1 teaspoon vanilla

¼ cup milk (scant)
7 tablespoons sweet (un-
  salted) butter
1 tablespoon rum
¾ cup raisins, plumped

COMBINE egg yolks, meal, sugar, vanilla, and milk in the top of a double boiler. Cook over boiling water, beating constantly, until thickened. Cool. Cream butter, and add to it the cream mixture. Add rum and raisins. Spread this cream on the lower half of the torte.

Meringue:

3 egg whites
⅞ cup sugar   Apricot jam

BEAT egg whites until frothy. Add half the sugar; beat until stiff. Add the remaining sugar. Beat until glossy. Use a pastry tube to apply meringue in the form of a spiral on the top half of the torte, beginning at the center. Bake in a slow oven (275 degrees) until the meringue is done. When cool, make a second spiral of apricot jam in between the ridges of the meringue. Put the two layers of the torte together.

Almond-Rum Cream Pie

Immigrants from Central Europe have adopted the American love for pie, but combined it with the European taste for cream and rum.

⅔ cup fine granulated sugar   1½ cups milk, scalded
⅓ cup sifted all-purpose   9-inch crumb piecrust, well
   flour   chilled
Dash of salt   5 tablespoons currant jelly
2 large eggs, slightly beaten   ½ cup shredded, toasted
3 tablespoons rum or 1 table-   almonds
   spoon rum flavoring extract 1 pint fresh strawberries

MIX sugar, flour, and salt and sift into the top of a double boiler. Stir in eggs and rum or extract. When well blended, add scalded milk almost drop by drop. Cook over hot water, stirring constantly, until the mixture thickens. Cool.

Remove the pie shell from the refrigerator and brush the bottom and sides with barely melted currant jelly. Sprinkle with almonds, and pour into it the cooled filling. Cover with ripe berries brushed with melted currant jelly. Top with whipped cream if desired. Serve very cold.

Note: This pie has a definite rum flavoring. Be sure you like it before adding too much. If you prefer, use orange juice.

Nevah Simmons

PEORIA STAR
PEORIA, ILLINOIS

Sausage and Scalloped Potatoes

This standby is popular in the Midwest, where pork is usually in plentiful supply, and is adaptable to either summer or winter menus.

Canadian-style bacon, sliced ham, or pork chops may be used instead of sausage.

Serves 4 to 6

6 medium potatoes	Salt and pepper to taste
1 pound sausage	Milk
2 tablespoons flour	

PARE potatoes and cut into thin slices. If bulk sausage is used, form it into small patties. Sauté the sausage briefly to remove excess fat. Place alternate layers of potatoes and sausage in a greased casserole, sprinkling each layer of potatoes with flour, salt, and pepper. Add milk until it can be seen between the slices of potato. Make the top layer sausage. Cover and bake in a moderate oven (375 degrees) for 60 minutes. About 20 minutes before the end of the cooking time, remove the cover and continue baking until the potatoes are tender and the sausage browned.

Pineapple Cake

This cake is light and moist, with a delicious fruit flavor. It is easy to prepare and has almost universal appeal.

½ cup butter or vegetable shortening
1½ cups sugar
1 teaspoon vanilla
⅛ teaspoon salt
3 teaspoons baking powder

3 egg whites
1 cup crushed pineapple, just as it comes from the can
¼ cup water
2½ cups sifted cake flour

CREAM butter with sugar, vanilla, salt, and baking powder. Add unbeaten egg whites one at a time. Then alternately add pineapple, to which the water has been added, and flour, making the last addition flour. Place in two buttered layer-cake pans and bake 25 to 30 minutes in a moderate (350-degree) oven. Use any desired frosting.

Phoebe Thompson

ROCKFORD STAR-REGISTER-REPUBLIC
ROCKFORD, ILLINOIS

Swedish Cabbage Rolls (Káldomar)

Makes 12 rolls

1 pound beef, ground
½ pound pork, ground
1½ teaspoons salt
½ teaspoon pepper

½ cup grated onion
½ cup raw rice
1 head cabbage

COMBINE meat, seasonings, onion, and raw rice. Shape into twelve loosely formed rolls. Remove the core from the head of cabbage and steam until the leaves begin to wilt. Or peel the leaves off, lay them in a small amount of hot water, and steam 2 or 3 minutes. Wrap one leaf around each meat roll, fastening it with a toothpick or skewer. Place in a baking dish and cover with water. Cook, covered, in a moderate oven (350 degrees) for 1½ hours.

Chili Con Carne
(Basic Stock)

Serves 8 to 10, depending on amount of beans

1 pound beef kidney suet, chopped	Garlic
	Chili powder
2 pounds round steak, ground	Salt

PURCHASE only suet from beef kidneys for the best results. Use a coarse grinder for the round steak. Chop the suet fine and render it slowly in a large, heavy skillet. This takes about 15 minutes. Add coarsely ground beef, chili powder (quite a bit of it), finely chopped garlic, and salt to taste. Stir; simmer together for 45 minutes, uncovered. This basic stock keeps very well and may be stored in a covered dish in the refrigerator, where it becomes very hard. When you want to serve chili, break off pieces of this brittle stock and heat it with kidney beans and tomatoes. For this quantity, two cans each of kidney beans and tomatoes is about the right amount.

Swedish Rye Bread

Makes 4 loaves

2 yeast cakes	1 tablespoon salt
1 tablespoon sugar	½ cup sugar
1 cup lukewarm water	4 tablespoons shortening
4 cups milk, scalded	6 cups white rye flour
1 cup molasses	6 cups white flour

DISSOLVE yeast and 1 tablespoon sugar in water. Mix together milk, molasses, salt, sugar, and shortening. Cool to lukewarm. Add the dissolved yeast and white rye flour; beat well. Add 5 cups white flour (leaving 1 cup for kneading the dough). Mix well and turn onto a floured board. Knead for 10 minutes. Place in a greased bowl. Cover and let rise in a warm place until doubled in bulk. Shape into four loaves. Let rise again, until doubled in bulk. Bake at 350 degrees for 1 hour.

Molded Cheese Appetizer

1 5-ounce jar Old English cheese

2 3-ounce packages cream cheese

1 5-ounce jar Roquefort-type cheese

¼ pound bleu cheese

⅓ cup finely chopped parsley
Salt
¼ small onion, grated
1 bud garlic, cut fine
1 tablespoon Worcestershire sauce

SOFTEN the cheeses. Mix together with a fork and add seasonings. Take a sheet of waxed paper, sprinkle with parsley. Drop the cheese hard on top of the parsley, thus forcing the parsley bits into the cheese so there is no danger of its dropping off later. Mold cheese into one large ball, using the hands. Fold the edges of the waxed paper over the top of the cheese balls; place it in a small bowl. Pack firmly, and put in the refrigerator for at least 24 hours. To serve, turn the bowl upside down on a platter, with the parsley side on top. Peel off the waxed paper. Serve at room temperature for the best flavor. Garnish the serving platter with potato chips, whole-wheat wafers, or soda crackers.

Indiana

Joan Schoemaker

THE INDIANAPOLIS TIMES
INDIANAPOLIS, INDIANA

Hoosier cookery represents a cross section of the cooking tastes of the remainder of the country. German and Swiss, Amish and Mennonite—all have established their settlements and left their marks, but none has left a dish typically Hoosier. A Pennsylvania Dutch influence can be found in some locales, but not in others.

Indiana's plentiful products include corn, tomatoes, and other fresh vegetables, as well as apples and peaches and livestock. If there is anything typically Hoosier, it's the fried chicken, corn on the cob, and apple cobbler which Indiana farm wives whip up for "company."

Corn on the Cob

FOR best results, drop husked ears of corn in boiling water (unsalted, to prevent the corn from getting tough). Boil 5 to 6 minutes and set the kettle aside. Let the corn remain in the water 5 to 10 minutes longer before serving time.

Some farm families return leftover ears of corn to the water it was cooked in. It remains there until the next meal and is eaten cold. Returning it to its original cooking water keeps the kernels plump and tender.

Apple Brown Betty

Serves 6

¼ cup melted butter	¼ teaspoon salt
1½ cups soft bread crumbs	1 teaspoon cinnamon
3 cups tart apples, diced	2 tablespoons lemon juice
⅔ cup brown sugar	⅓ cup water

ADD melted butter to bread crumbs. Combine apples, sugar, salt, and cinnamon. Place a layer of buttered bread crumbs in the bottom of a buttered casserole. Add a layer of apples and another of crumbs. Continue alternating the layers; the bread crumbs should be on top. Combine lemon juice and water and pour over the mixture. Bake at 350 degrees for 1 hour.

Thelma Michael

THE INDIANAPOLIS NEWS
INDIANAPOLIS, INDIANA

Summer weather in Indiana finds many families turning to the outdoor grill, and barbecued pork or beef is a favorite. The meat has already been baked, with a little water added. It is shredded and simmered for 1 hour in barbecue sauce made of tomatoes, chili sauce, mustard, and other seasonings.

Winter dishes include spareribs and sauerkraut, pork loin roast, pot roast, turkey, meat stew with dumplings, custard, hickory-nut cake, pumpkin and mince pie, persimmon pudding, and cranberry sauce.

Popular dishes in spring and summer include fried chicken or stewed chicken and noodles, baked beans, potato salad, pickled beets, deviled eggs, sliced tomatoes, meat loaf, and pot roast cooked in a Dutch oven.

Pumpkin Pie

Makes 2 pies

2 cups sieved, cooked or
canned pumpkin
½ teaspoon salt
3 tablespoons flour
2 teaspoons cinnamon
⅛ teaspoon nutmeg
⅛ teaspoon mace
Dash of cloves
3 egg yolks

2 cups sugar (you may substitute honey or sorghum
molasses for half the sugar,
or use all light brown
sugar)
1 cup light cream
3 egg whites, beaten stiff but
not dry
2 unbaked pie shells

COMBINE all ingredients but the egg whites. Then add the beaten whites to the pumpkin mixture and pour into the pie shells. Bake in a hot oven (425 degrees) for 1 hour, or until a silver knife inserted into the pies comes out clean.

Steamed Persimmon Pudding

Serves 6 generously

1 pint sieved, ripe persimmons
1 No. 2 can evaporated milk
2 cups sifted flour
1 cup graham cracker crumbs
1 cup sugar
2 eggs

1 teaspoon cinnamon
Dash of cloves, ginger, and
mace
¼ teaspoon soda
Pinch of salt
Raisins and nuts, ½ cup each
(if desired)

MIX together all ingredients. Place in a buttered mixing bowl and cover with waxed paper. Place in a steamer and steam 1 hour. If cooked in a pressure cooker, steam in a tightly covered mold for 15 minutes without pressure, and 30 minutes at pressure. Serve with cream or hard sauce.

Uncooked Persimmon Pudding

1 cup persimmon pulp   1 cup sugar
½ cup nut meats   12 marshmallows, cut up
24 graham crackers, rolled

MIX and let stand in the refrigerator overnight before serving.

Fried Green Beans

WASH 2 pounds of green beans, drain, and break into pieces. Cook
in boiling salted water until tender. Drain.

Cube six slices of bacon; fry brown. Drop green beans in the
pan with bacon; add onion if desired. Cook 15 minutes, uncovered. Add 1 teaspoon sugar, cover, and steam for 1 hour.
(Ed. note: These are typical Southern cooking instructions. Cooks
in other regions might prefer to steam briefly.)

Tomatoes and Corn

BROWN 2 tablespoons butter in the bottom of a kettle. Add six fresh,
medium-sized tomatoes, quartered, and salt, pepper, and ½ teaspoon sugar. After the tomatoes have boiled 30 minutes, add uncooked whole kernels cut from two ears of corn, and cook 20 minutes. Serve in individual saucedishes.

Iowa

Naomi Doebel

THE GAZETTE
CEDAR RAPIDS, IOWA

Two groups of early settlers, one Czechoslovakian and the other predominantly of Germanic origin, have given to this area some of its most distinctive dishes. Since Iowa produces more hogs than any other state in the Union, we have many favorite ways of preparing pork products.

Cedar Rapids, one of the nation's largest Czechoslovakian centers, with approximately 20 per cent of its population of Czech descent, enjoys many delicacies having their origin in old Bohemia. Among these are kolacky (sweet rolls filled with poppy seed, fruit mixtures, or with Dutch cheese mixed with eggs, milk, and sugar). A typical meal is roast goose with dumplings, sauerkraut with caraway seed, kolacky, and coffee.

Residents of the Amana colonies, established near Cedar Rapids almost a century ago, have popularized another type of cookery. This settlement of seven towns, which existed as a communal society until 1932, when it was reorganized as a corporation, originally had communal kitchens. In them women prepared dishes that had been handed down for generations by their ancestors in Europe. Given here is their recipe for air-light fritters that melt in your mouth.

Kolacky

These may be eaten for breakfast or as a dessert.

Makes about 75. Divide the recipe for family use

½ cup sugar	1 quart lukewarm milk
½ cup shortening	2 tablespoons salt
4 egg yolks, beaten	⅛ teaspoon mace
1 ounce fresh yeast	8 or 9 cups sifted flour

MIX sugar and shortening. Add egg yolks and beat. Dissolve yeast in ½ cup warm milk and add to the mixture. Add salt and mace; mix. Add milk and flour alternately, until the dough seems stiff enough to work with. Let rise in a warm place until doubled.

Put dough on a work board, cut into small pieces, and shape into balls. Brush well with shortening and let rise. Then press the dough from the center of the ball outward, and fill the depression with a fruit filling. Let stand 5 minutes, then bake in a well-greased pan in a moderate oven (350 degrees) for about 15 minutes, or until golden brown.

When baking watch the kolacky. Fifteen minutes is about maximum time; they may be ready to come out of the oven sooner.

Fillings:

(All these should be cooled before they are put in the dough.)
Prune. Stew prunes, put through a strainer, and mix with a little cream and sugar. Or, stew prunes, then chop them up with stale cooky crumbs, nuts, and coconut.
Cherry. Heat canned cherries, sweeten; thicken with cornstarch.

Poppy seed:

1 cup ground poppy seed	⅓ cup each of raisins and
⅔ cup milk	walnuts
½ teaspoon cinnamon	A little mace, about ¼ tea-
½ cup sugar	spoon

COMBINE ingredients. Bring to a boil over a slow fire and cook 3 minutes. If too thin, add a crumbled cooky; if too thick, add milk.

Fritters

Serves 6

½ cup sifted flour	2 eggs, separated
⅛ teaspoon salt	½ teaspoon sugar
⅜ cup milk (¼ cup plus 2 tablespoons)	Deep fat for frying
	Powdered sugar

SIFT together flour and salt. Add milk and egg yolks. Beat well. Beat egg whites stiff, and add sugar slowly. Beat again until almost dry, and then fold into the batter. Drop by teaspoonfuls into deep hot fat and fry until a golden brown. Sprinkle with powdered sugar and serve piping hot.

These fritters are now usually eaten with syrup, but in the olden days they were often served with a dish of mixed blackberries and currants, sugared.

Wilma Phillips Stewart

THE DES MOINES REGISTER AND TRIBUNE
DES MOINES, IOWA

Foods most typical of Iowa include fried chicken, roast pork with sage dressing, baked ham, pickled salt pork, fried rabbit, broiled steak, broiled ham and eggs (with accent on juicy ham), corn on the cob, vegetables served in cream without thickening (especially corn and string beans), boiled potatoes served in the skin—to be dunked in butter (right at the table), and two-crust apple pie.

Roastin' Ears

USE garden-fresh corn. Cut corn close to the cob and remove all but four or five leaves. Cut back leaves at the tip end to the point of the ear. Pull out the silk or leave it on, since in this method of cooking it disappears.

Have ready a good bed of coals. Arrange the ears on grids about 6 inches above the coals. After about 5 minutes over the coals, start turning the ears. Cooking time is about 15 to 20 minutes, depending upon the type of corn used. When the ears are cooked, pull back what husks are left, then stir up the flames and let the husks burn off. This gives the corn a slightly brown color and a smoky flavor that is indescribable, slightly reminiscent of parched corn.

Sage Dressing

Makes stuffing for a large turkey or two roasting chickens

½ cup fresh sage, or 1 tablespoon dried sage
1 pound loaf bread
½ cup melted butter
1 teaspoon salt

1 good-sized onion, chopped quite fine
¼ teaspoon freshly ground pepper
Milk or water

CRUMBLE sage, not too fine. Break up bread, stir in melted butter and the rest of the ingredients. Add just enough milk or water to bind the ingredients together. Add more salt if necessary. Use for roast pork, chicken, or turkey.

Kentucky

Cissy Gregg

THE COURIER JOURNAL
LOUISVILLE, KENTUCKY

In Kentucky, we have our sugar-cured, hickory-smoked old Kentucky hams, our beaten biscuit, Sally Lunn, fried chicken, hot biscuit, corn breads, green beans cooked with meat, burgoo, and turtle soup, as well as cakes, pies, and sauces galore. We won't go so far as to say we can choose a "best"—these are just examples of some of our fine foods.

Miss Jennie's Rum Cake

A number of years ago there was a restaurant and catering shop in Louisville, named "Jennie Benedict's." "Miss Jennie" catered the fine parties in these parts, and her place was famous both as a restaurant and as a bakery.

1 cup butter
2 cups granulated sugar
1 cup milk, not too cold
8 egg whites, beaten stiff but not dry

3½ cups sifted cake flour
3½ teaspoons baking powder
1 teaspoon vanilla
Pinch of salt

CREAM butter and gradually add sugar, a little at a time. Add one-third each of milk, flour, and stiffly beaten egg whites, beating well after each addition. Keep out 2 tablespoons flour, and mix baking powder with it. Add this mixture after the preliminary beating is over. Then beat well. At the very last add vanilla and salt. The beating should be given special attention—in fact, use vim and vigor.

Bake in two 9-inch buttered and paper-lined cake pans, rather deep ones, for 20 to 30 minutes, at 350 degrees. Turn out on racks and allow to cool before adding the filling.

Filling:

2½ cups powdered sugar   ½ cup rum
⅔ cup butter

CREAM sugar and softened butter together; beat and blend until soft and smooth. Sifting the sugar beforehand makes the blending light work. Add rum and mix well again. Put in the refrigerator until firm enough to spread. The filling should be ½ to ¾ inch thick. After the filling is spread on the cake, put cake and filling into the refrigerator until the filling is firm.

Frosting:

2 cups sugar   12 marshmallows
2 egg whites   1 to 2 teaspoons rum

MOISTEN sugar well with water. Boil together until the syrup will spin a thread. Pour slowly in a fine stream over the stiffly beaten egg whites. While the mixture is still hot add marshmallows, a few at a time, and the rum. Spread over the sides of the cake and pile high on top.

Miss Jennie's Eggnog with Ice Cream

Miss Jennie also willed us, and you, her eggnog, which is a little out of the ordinary.

Makes about 40 servings

12 eggs, separated
12 tablespoons sugar
12 tablespoons whisky (¾ cup)
12 tablespoons rum
1½ pints cream, whipped
Vanilla ice cream (1½ to 2 quarts)

BEAT the egg yolks until light, which takes good beating muscles unless you have an electric beater. Add sugar gradually and beat again until light. Then add whisky and rum very slowly, beating all the time. This is in order to "cook" the yolks. Fold in the stiffly beaten egg whites, and last, fold in the whipped cream. Set aside in a cold place to age.

When ready to serve, pour into your best punch bowl and add small dollops of vanilla ice cream. Each person gets a little ice cream plus the eggnog, and is given a spoon—at any rate, spoons should be available in case one wants to dig right in and not hang around until the ice cream melts.

Beaumont Inn Corn Pudding

Now, to show you that we appreciate all ways of using corn, here is a corn pudding that originated in Kentucky and wound up recently winning a national prize.

Serves 6 to 8

8 tablespoons flour
2 cups corn, cut and scraped from the ears
3 teaspoons sugar or honey
1 teaspoon salt
2 tablespoons melted butter
2 pints milk
4 eggs

MIX flour and corn. Add sugar, salt, and melted butter. Beat milk and eggs together, stir into the corn, and pour into a buttered pan or baking dish. Bake at 350 degrees for about 1 hour, stirring two or three times during the first 30 minutes to keep the corn from settling.

Marguerite T. Finnegan

**THE LOUISVILLE TIMES
LOUISVILLE, KENTUCKY**

Kentucky is south of the Mason and Dixon line, and Louisville is the "Gateway to the South," so we consider ourselves Southerners. We follow many Southern traditions in the preparation of food. For example, no true Kentuckian would ever put sugar in corn bread.

Individual Strawberry Shortcakes

Serves 4

1½ cups sifted flour
2¼ teaspoons baking powder
2 tablespoons sugar
Few grains of salt
¼ cup shortening

⅓ to ½ cup milk
Melted butter or margarine
1 pint strawberries
Sugar

SIFT together flour, baking powder, sugar, and salt. Cut in shortening with two knives or a pastry blender. Add enough milk to make a soft dough. Roll out ½ inch thick on a lightly floured board. Cut with a round cutter 3½ inches in diameter. Place on a baking sheet; brush with butter or margarine. Bake in a very hot oven (450 degrees) for 15 minutes. While hot, split; spread with butter or margarine. Wash and hull strawberries. Crush; add enough sugar to sweeten. Place strawberries between and on top of the biscuits. Serve with plain cream, whipped cream, or ice cream.

Louisiana

NEW ORLEANS ITEM
NEW ORLEANS, LOUISIANA

Gourmets as well as their less demanding brothers find in New Orleans a cookery that ranks with the best in the world. Whether the meal is intended for a dock laborer who likes his rice with red beans, or an epicure who demands superb gumbos and distinctive fish dishes, New Orleans chefs and housewives can provide it.

They have a rich background in the art of preparing food. The French who settled here brought their roux, their delicate touch with spices, their exquisite sense of just enough and not too much. The Spanish arrived with their crushed garlic and love of fiery foods. The Indians, already here, contributed their knowledge of the native bay leaf and the filé that makes such wonderful gumbos. And the Negroes added their genius for blending herbs and condiments, for making the lowliest fare into dishes that kings would not scorn. Then the American know-how combined them all into the fabulous Creole cooking.

Most visitors have sampled at least some of the city's most famous dishes: the seafood and okra gumbos, rich with spices and topped with a mound of rice; turtle soup, made with Madeira or sherry, best in the world; fresh fish, fried French style in deep fat; all the wonderful oyster dishes, from Rockefeller to en brochette;

shrimp Creole with rice, a concoction exclusively Orleanian; luscious trout meunière, *pompano* en papillotte, *and dozens of others.*

Never ignore red beans cooked with a piece of ham and served with fluffy rice. Or chicken Clemenceau, financière, *or other chicken dishes.* Or crayfish bisque!

Orleans chefs take full advantage of the plentiful supplies of fish at their doorstep. Salt-water fish arrive at the kitchen with the Gulf still clinging to them. The oysters, shrimp, crayfish, and the fat, delicious crabs all are challenges that the Creole cook takes in his stride.

But fish is not the limit of Creole good cooking. The things a chef does to chicken, ham, veal, and beef delight the most particular dinner guest. Creole garlic bread is world famed. And to finish off, Cherries Jubilee *and* café brûlot.

Oysters Rockefeller

Serves 4

5 tablespoons butter
5 tablespoons finely minced spinach
2 tablespoons finely minced onion
1½ tablespoons minced, cooked lettuce
2 teaspoons minced celery

3 tablespoons fine, dry crumbs
¼ teaspoon herb blend (for fish)
¼ teaspoon anchovy paste
Few grains of pepper
¼ teaspoon salt
24 oysters on half shells

HEAT butter, add spinach, onion, lettuce, celery, dry crumbs, herb blend, anchovy paste, pepper, and salt. Mix well. Remove oysters from the shells. Scrub the shells; boil to be sure every particle of sand has been washed away. Set six shells on each of four pie plates holding hot rock salt. Place an oyster in each shell. Broil slowly for 5 minutes. Place a spoonful of the spinach mixture on each oyster. Broil until thoroughly heated. Serve immediately.

Garlic Bread

TAKE a loaf of French bread and rub the entire outside crust with garlic. Slice the loaf lengthwise and brush the cut surfaces thickly with melted butter. Sprinkle with grated Parmesan cheese, finely chopped parsley, and (very lightly) bland paprika. Put in the oven until it becomes crisp and hot.

Pompano en Papillotte

Serves 6

3 medium-sized pompano
3 cups water
1 chopped shallot or 2 tablespoons chopped onion
6 tablespoons butter
2¼ cups dry white wine
1 cup crabmeat
½ clove garlic, minced

1 cup chopped, cooked
   shrimp
8 onions, chopped (1½ cups)
Pinch of thyme
1 bay leaf
Salt and pepper
2 tablespoons flour
2 egg yolks

CLEAN pompano; remove heads and backbones; cut into 6 fillets. Combine heads, bones, and water; simmer until there are 2 cups of stock. Sauté shallot and fillets in 2 tablespoons butter; add 2 cups wine. Cover; simmer gently until the fillets are tender, about 5 to 8 minutes. Sauté crabmeat, shrimp, and half the garlic in 1 tablespoon butter. Add onions and the remaining garlic; cook 10 minutes. Add thyme, bay leaf, salt, pepper, and 1¾ cups fish stock; simmer 10 minutes. Blend together 2 tablespoons butter and flour; gradually add the remaining ¼ cup fish stock. Add to the crabmeat mixture with the wine stock drained from the fillets. Cook, stirring constantly, until thickened. Beat egg yolks; add the hot sauce and the remaining ¼ cup wine. Mix thoroughly. Place in the refrigerator to chill until firm. Cut six parchment-paper hearts 8 inches long and 12 inches wide. Oil well, place spoonfuls of sauce on one half of the hearts; lay poached fillets on the sauce; fold over. Crimp the edges to seal. Lay the sealed hearts on an oiled baking sheet. Bake in a hot oven (450 degrees) 15 minutes, or until the paper hearts are browned. Serve immediately in the paper hearts. Note: Fresh salmon, sea trout, or striped bass may be used instead.

Café Brûlot

Serves 4

1-inch stick of cinnamon
8 whole cloves
Peel of 1 lemon, cut thin

3 lumps sugar
3 jiggers brandy
3 cups strong coffee

PUT into brûlot bowl or chafing dish cinnamon, cloves, lemon peel, and sugar. Place brandy in a large ladle; ignite it and pour it over the ingredients in the bowl. Continue ladling until the sugar is dissolved. Gradually add coffee, ladling the mixture until the flames fade. Serve immediately.

Marie Louise Ferguson and Julia D. Bowes

NEW ORLEANS TIMES-PICAYUNE
NEW ORLEANS, LOUISIANA

Sweet Potato Salad

Serves 8 a hearty lunch or supper salad

1 cup grated raw sweet potatoes
2 cups diced apples
½ cup pecans, broken into pieces

¾ cup raisins
½ cup chopped celery
Mayonnaise or French dressing to moisten

MIX ingredients lightly; serve on lettuce.

Shrimp Supreme

Serves 6 generously

3 pounds raw shrimp
½ cup butter or margarine
4 tablespoons sherry
½ cup finely chopped onions
¼ cup chopped parsley
1 small clove garlic, chopped
1 cup chopped mushrooms

1 pound fresh tomatoes,
  peeled and diced
1 cup consommé
1 teaspoon chili powder
Salt and pepper
½ cup pimiento, chopped

WASH and peel shrimp; remove the black veins. Heat butter in a skillet, then reduce the heat. Add shrimp and fry until lightly browned. Add sherry, onions, parsley, garlic, mushrooms, tomatoes, and consommé. Add chili powder, salt, and pepper to taste; add pimiento. Cover and simmer for 20 to 30 minutes.

Shrimp and Okra Gumbo

Serves 6 generously

3 pounds raw shrimp
1 pound okra
2 tablespoons shortening
⅓ cup shortening
½ cup flour

1 large onion, chopped
6 cups water
1 tablespoon vinegar
Salt, red and black pepper
Filé powder

WASH and peel shrimp; remove the black veins. Wash and cut okra into ¼-inch pieces. Heat 2 tablespoons shortening in a skillet, add okra, and cook at medium heat, stirring occasionally, until it smoothes.

Heat ⅓ cup shortening in a pan. Add flour, cook at medium heat until a rich, dark brown, stirring constantly. Add chopped onion, okra, water, and vinegar. Season to taste. Cook slowly for 30 minutes. Add shrimp and cook 15 to 20 minutes longer. Serve piping hot over steamed rice, with a dash of filé.

Crab Gumbo

Serves 4 to 6

12 hard-shelled crabs
2 tablespoons flour
2 tablespoons fat
1 cup finely minced onions
4 quarts water
Salt
Pepper

1 to 3 tablespoons minced parsley
2 tablespoons finely minced green onion tops
2 tablespoons finely minced garlic
Filé powder

WASH crabs, scald, cool, and clean. Pull off claws and crack them. Cut the crab bodies in half. Make a *roux* by browning the flour in fat. Be careful not to burn it, but do allow it to brown. Add onions, stirring constantly until they begin to turn yellow. Add water, salt, and crab claws and bodies. Simmer slowly for about 45 minutes. Add minced parsley, green onion tops, garlic, and pepper, and simmer for another 15 minutes. At serving time, sprinkle 1 teaspoon filé in each bowl and add the gumbo.

Note: Filé must not be cooked. It is always added at serving time.

Sweet Potato-Pecan Pie

2 pounds sweet potatoes
1½ cups hot milk
1 cup brown sugar
1 tablespoon butter or margarine
1 teaspoon ginger

1 teaspoon cinnamon
1 teaspoon nutmeg
1 teaspoon salt
3 eggs
Unbaked 9-inch pie shell
½ cup finely chopped pecans

PUT peeled, cooked sweet potatoes through a sieve to make 2 cups. Stir in hot milk, sugar, butter, and seasonings. Add gradually to beaten eggs. Pour into the unbaked pie shell with a standing rim. Sprinkle with pecans. Bake in a hot oven (425 degrees) about 35 minutes, or until the filling is set.

Shrimp Remoulade

Serves 3 or 4

1 pound shrimp
Court bouillon
4 tablespoons olive oil
2 tablespoons tarragon
vinegar
1 teaspoon salt
2 tablespoons Creole mustard

½ teaspoon paprika
4 stalks celery, finely minced
4 small onions, finely minced
4 sprigs parsley, finely minced
1 tablespoon horseradish
2 tablespoons anchovy paste

MAKE a court bouillon by simmering water, onions, garlic, sliced lemon, bay leaf, salt, and red pepper. Peel, clean, and de-vein the shrimp, and add the shells to the court bouillon. Boil the shrimp in it until pink—not more than 20 minutes. When cooked, drain; discard the liquid and shells.

Make a dressing of the oil, vinegar, and salt. Add the other ingredients and mix well. Pour over the shrimp and let stand 24 hours in the refrigerator. Serve on shredded lettuce.

SHREVEPORT TIMES
SHREVEPORT, LOUISIANA

For recipes by *Bessie R. Murphy*, see pp. 221-223.

Maryland

Maria B. Wooden

THE BALTIMORE NEWS-POST
BALTIMORE, MARYLAND

Any native of Maryland, a state noted especially for its out-of-this-world seafood dishes, can convince the inquiring gourmet, either at his favorite eating spot or his own dining-room table, that Maryland food is superb.

Oyster Bisque

Serves 4 to 6

1 pint oysters	1¾ teaspoons salt
1 quart milk	¼ teaspoon pepper
1 slice of onion	2 stalks celery
Sprig of parsley	⅓ cup butter
1 bay leaf	⅓ cup flour

DRAIN and chop oysters. Add the oyster liquor and heat slowly to the boiling point. Scald milk with onion, parsley, bay leaf, salt, pepper, and celery; strain. Melt butter and blend in flour. Add milk and cook until thick, stirring constantly. Add oysters and serve at once.

Crab Cakes

Serves 5 or 6

2 slices bread
½ cup melted butter
1½ pounds crab flakes or 1 pound crab claw meat
2 eggs, separated
1 tablespoon chopped parsley

1 teaspoon Worcestershire sauce
⅛ teaspoon dry mustard
½ teaspoon salt
Dash of paprika
Shortening

TRIM crusts from bread and pour melted butter over them. Allow to stand about 1 hour, then break into small pieces. To these add crabmeat, yolks of eggs, parsley, and seasonings. Mix lightly with a fork; then fold in stiffly beaten egg whites and shape the mixture into cakes. Brown in a hot skillet that has been brushed with fat.

Lobster Thermidor

Serves 4

2 1½-pound lobsters, boiled
¾ cup sliced mushrooms
¼ cup butter
¾ teaspoon mustard
1 tablespoon minced parsley

Dash of paprika
½ cup sherry
1½ cups cream sauce
2½ tablespoons grated Parmesan cheese

CUT lobsters lengthwise into halves. Remove meat and break it into small pieces. Cook mushrooms for 5 minutes in butter. Add mustard, parsley, paprika, sherry, and 1 cup of the cream sauce. Combine thoroughly and fill the lobster shells with the mixture. Cover with the rest of the cream sauce and sprinkle with cheese. Bake in a hot oven (450 degrees) for about 10 minutes.

Maryland Scrapple

Serves 6 generously

1 cup white cornmeal   1 pound pork sausage
1 quart boiling, salted water   ¾ teaspoon mixed herbs

COMBINE ingredients; stir thoroughly to prevent lumps. Cook in a double boiler for 1½ hours, stirring frequently. Pour into oblong pan. Cool, slice, and fry.

Massachusetts

Agnes Mahan

THE BOSTON GLOBE

BOSTON, MASSACHUSETTS

Visitors coming to Boston are often under the impression that Bostonians eat only baked beans and codfish, but that is not all they can boast of. Massachusetts waters abound in all kinds of fresh fish; in fact, more fish comes into the port of Boston than into any other port in the world. Lobsters and oysters, too, are plentiful here. Cotuit oysters are known far and near for their fine quality.

With quantities of apples, eggs, fish, oysters, and clams at their disposal, is it any wonder Massachusetts homemakers have established for themselves the reputation of being fine cooks?

Lobster Stew

Serves 8

3 cooked lobsters, 1½ pounds each	¼ cup butter
	3 cups milk
½ onion, sliced	Salt
1 stalk celery	Paprika

REMOVE meat and liver from lobsters. Put aside. Break shells in pieces; cover with 1 quart cold water; add onion and celery. Cover tightly and cook ½ hour. Cream butter; add lobster liver. Scald milk and add the butter mixture. When the lobster-shell mixture has boiled down to 1 pint, strain and add to milk. Season with salt and paprika. Put a few pieces of finely cut lobster into each portion.

Fish Chowder

Serves 8

2 slices salt pork, diced
1 medium onion, cubed
2 pounds fillet of haddock
1 quart milk

4 or 5 medium raw potatoes, cubed
1 tablespoon butter
Salt and pepper

TRY out the pork and brown onion in the same fat. Meanwhile cover fish well with water, about 1 quart, and boil for about 20 minutes; drain and flake fish. Save the liquor, and in it boil the potatoes. When they are tender, add the flaked fish, onion, milk, butter, salt, and pepper. Let come to a boil once. Serve hot with crackers.

Boston Cream Pie

Makes 2 pies

3 eggs
1 cup sugar
4 tablespoons cold water
1¼ cups flour

½ teaspoon flavoring, as desired
2 teaspoons baking powder
¼ teaspoon salt

BEAT eggs, add sugar, beat well, then slowly add cold water and flavoring. Now add the dry ingredients. Put into two 9-inch Washington-pie tins. Bake 15 minutes or longer in a 350-degree oven. When cool, split and fill with filling.

Filling:

3 tablespoons sugar   1 cup milk
2 tablespoons flour   1 egg, beaten

MIX sugar and flour in a double boiler. Add milk and cook over boiling water 10 minutes, stirring frequently. Slowly add about 1 tablespoon of hot sauce to the egg, beating well. Put this mixture back into the remaining sauce and cook about 2 minutes, stirring constantly. Cool before putting into the pies.

Muriel Caswall

THE BOSTON SUNDAY POST
BOSTON, MASSACHUSETTS

Maple Butternut Candy

A simple but delightful candy is made by mixing 2 cups maple sugar (broken up or shaved) with ½ cup cream, and letting it boil until it threads. Then stir in 1 cup nuts (butternuts are well liked and are easily available in New England). Cool on a buttered cookie sheet.

Broiled Scrod

This is a favorite New England dish, as these fish are plentiful. There have been many arguments as to whether a scrod is a young cod or a young haddock. As a matter of fact, it may be either.

TO broil, split the fish down the back, having removed the backbone except for a small portion near the tail. Sprinkle the fish with melted butter or dip it in olive oil, then in fine crumbs, with a dash of salt and pepper added, and then place, flesh side up, on a well-greased broiler or in a shallow pan. Broil 2 inches from the heat unit for about 15 minutes, or until the flesh flakes when tried with a fork. Then broil with the skin side up until skin is crisp and light brown.

New England Clam Chowder

This chowder is quite distinct from Rhode Island clam chowder, even though "Little Rhody" is as much a part of New England as Maine is. But for some reason or other the Rhode Islanders insist on having stewed tomatoes in their chowder (as New Yorkers also do, in Manhattan chowder). This is unheard of in Boston.

Serves 8

1 quart clams
½ cup of ½-inch cubes of fat salt pork
1 onion, sliced
4 cups raw potatoes cut in ¾-inch cubes
1 tablespoon salt
⅛ teaspoon pepper
Flour
4 cups milk, scalded
4 tablespoons butter
8 common or Boston crackers
Cold milk

PICK over the opened clams and clean in a cup of water. Reserve the liquor from the shells, heat to the boiling point, and strain. Now finely mince the hard parts of the clams, putting aside the soft portions. Try out the pork in a frying pan; add onion and cook about 5 minutes. Drain pork and onion on a paper towel and place in a large saucepan deep enough to hold the chowder.

Cook potatoes separately for 5 to 10 minutes in boiling water to cover. Drain and put half of them in the bottom of the saucepan, add the chopped (hard) clams, half the seasonings, and dredge well with flour. Add the rest of the potatoes, the rest of the salt and pepper, sprinkle again with flour, and add 2½ cups boiling water. Cook for about 10 minutes. Add scalded milk, the soft parts of the clams, and butter. Boil for 3 minutes, then add the crackers, which have been split and soaked in enough cold milk to moisten.

Reheat the clam water (which you reserved in the beginning) to the boiling point; thicken if necessary with 1 tablespoon butter and flour mixed with a little of the boiling mixture, and cook like any sauce, stirring until thick. Add to the chowder at serving time, since the clam water may curdle the milk if added during cooking.

Josephine H. Peirce

WORCESTER TELEGRAM AND EVENING GAZETTE
WORCESTER, MASSACHUSETTS

New England Foods

ANADAMA BREAD

This was invented by a fisherman who had a lazy wife and often had to do his own cooking. The results of his experiments with bread he named "Anna, damn her," but this was modified by polite society to "Anadama."

APPLE PANDOWDY

Also known as Apple Jonathan, Apple Potpie, Yankee Apple John, and Apple Betty.

BAPTIST BREAD

Bread fried in deep fat (immersed). In Connecticut it is known as Holy Pokes, in Maine as Huffjuffs.

BIRD'S-NEST PUDDING

Yankees disagree on both the name and exact ingredients of this dish, but agree that it must be made of apples. Sometimes known as Crow's Nest, Apple Cobbler, and Apple Shortcake. In Connecticut it is made without a biscuit topping; instead, a custard mixture is poured over the apples before baking. In Massachusetts shaved maple sugar is usually served on it, but in Vermont a sour sauce is preferred.

BLUEBERRY SLUMP

Dumplings served with cream. Known on Cape Cod as Blueberry Grunt, although in other places a "grunt" is a steamed pudding. Can be made with blueberries or apples.

BOAT STEERERS

Clam fritters.

BOSTON BAKED BEANS

Always baked in earthen pots, just as the Indians baked them. After pea beans were introduced from California, only beans of that size were popular. Puritan housewives baked the beans all day Saturday, served them fresh for Saturday night, warmed them over for Sunday breakfast (in later years they were served with codfish cakes Sunday morning), and served them again for Sunday noontime lunch.

BOSTON BROWN BREAD

Always accompanied the beans. The hard crusts of brown bread were cut off and simmered in milk or cream, then served as a pudding known as Brown Bread Brewis or New England Hard-Scrabble.

BOSTON CREAM PIE

A two-egg butter cake baked in two layers in round cake pans, with a cream filling between layers and powdered sugar sifted over the top. Not to be confused with Washington Pie, which has raspberry jam spread between the layers.

Boston's Parker House put on chocolate frosting and listed the famous dessert as Chocolate Cream Pie, thus confusing outlanders who expected an open piecrust filled with chocolate pudding and covered with whipped cream.

BOSTON STYLE FISH CHOWDER

Made with milk and/or light cream and plenty of haddock.

BROTHER JONATHAN'S HAT

A steamed pudding named after Governor Jonathan Trumbull of Connecticut; also called Deacon Porter's Hat, after Deacon Porter, an early trustee of Mt. Holyoke College.

CHERRY BOUNCE

Black cherries in New England rum.

COB-APPLE PIE

A deep-dish apple pie served upside down. An old Newport recipe.

EEL STIFLE

A scalloped dish made with eels, onions, potatoes, and salt pork. A favorite on Martha's Vineyard.

ELECTION CAKE

A cake served during Town Meeting Day; said to have originated in Hartford, Connecticut.

FOOL

A dish of fruit, crushed or stewed, served with whipped cream and sugar.

FLUMMERY

Cornstarch pudding made with water and cooked fruit, served with cream and sugar.

GAP'N SWALLOW

An emergency dish much like Hasty Pudding, made of cornmeal. Also a plum pudding served with maple syrup.

GINGERBREAD

One of the first breads baked in New England, for recipes are in the earliest English cookbooks, and there are old recipes for Dutch, French, German, and Flemish gingerbreads. Muster Day Gingerbread goes back to early New England days when there were celebrations known as "Muster" and "Training" days. Muster Day Gingerbread was made in squares, glazed on top, and was sold by food peddlers for ten cents a slab.

A very special Sea-Voyage Gingerbread was supposed to be a preventative for seasickness. It was a hard variety, cut in small rounds, that would keep during a long voyage.

While most gingerbread is made with molasses and spices, it is also made with white or brown sugar or honey. Candied orange peel was a popular ingredient, as well as caraway seed. Sometimes coriander seed and candied citron were added. Very "Superior Gingerbread" called for eggs, a wineglass of wine, and one of brandy. This was baked in squares and would keep a month. Banana Gingerbread originated in Wellfleet on Cape Cod, when, seventy-five years or more ago, Captain Lorenzo Dow Baker brought some bananas back from a voyage.

HALLELUJAH

or Cape Cod Stifle, a stew made of salt pork, onions, and potatoes.

HASTY PUDDING

Today called cornmeal mush. Also known as Stir-About Pudding. It was served also with meat and gravy, or as a dessert, with maple syrup, and was the main dish for breakfast, dinner, or supper.

INDIAN PUDDING

One of New England's oldest desserts; always baked in a slow oven. Also known as Injun Pudding, Whitpot, and Whitspot.

MEAD

An old-time drink made of water, honey, and ginger fermented.

PANHAS

Broth, remaining after making headcheese, thickened with corn-meal and made into mush. It is sliced, browned in hot fat, and served for breakfast.

PORTABLE SOUP

The original bouillon cube, made for travelers to carry with them.

QUAKING CUSTARD

Made like Spanish Cream, but egg whites are not added to the custard. Instead they are beaten and served around it like a sauce.

SEA PIE

So called because a sea captain introduced it. A combination of stewed pork, veal, or game birds, plus sweet dried apples, molasses, and dumplings.

SIZZLERS

Blueberry turnovers, fried in deep fat.

SLAPPERS

or Fried Indian Cakes; also called Flatjacks and Flapjacks.

SWITCHEL

Cold water flavored with sugar, molasses, vinegar, and ginger—for haymakers.

TOADS

Cornmeal fried in deep fat.

Anadama Bread

Makes 2 loaves

2 cups water	2 cakes compressed yeast
½ cup yellow cornmeal	½ cup lukewarm water
2 tablespoons shortening	7½ cups flour (about)
½ cup molasses	Melted butter
2 teaspoons salt	

BRING the 2 cups water to a boil and add cornmeal gradually, stirring constantly. Add shortening, molasses, and salt, and let stand until lukewarm. Add crumbled yeast cakes to lukewarm water and combine with the cornmeal mixture. Stir in the flour to make a stiff dough. Knead well. Place in a greased bowl, cover, and let rise in a warm place until doubled in bulk. Cut through the dough several times with a knife, cover, and let rise again for about 45 minutes, or until light. Toss onto a floured board and knead well. Add more flour if necessary. Make into two loaves and place in greased loaf tins. Cover and let rise in a warm place until doubled in bulk. Bake in a hot oven (400 degrees) for 15 minutes, then reduce the heat to moderate (350 degrees) and bake about 45 minutes longer, or until done. Brush with melted butter and remove the bread from the pans to a cake rack.

Apple Pandowdy

Serves 6

6 apples	Butter
1 cup light brown sugar	Biscuit dough
½ teaspoon nutmeg	1 teaspoon cinnamon
1 cup warm water	

PEEL, quarter, and slice apples into a baking dish. Sprinkle with sugar, nutmeg, and cinnamon mixed together. Add water and dot generously with butter. Prepare a rich biscuit dough (or use a prepared mix), roll it out ¾ inch thick, and cover apples, first cutting a decorative design in the center. Crimp edges around the outside of the baking dish. Bake in a slow oven (300 degrees) for 2 to 3 hours. Serve hot in the baking dish with Maple Sugar Sauce, or cream sweetened with sugar and flavored with nutmeg.

Maple Sugar Sauce:

1 cup maple sugar	1 teaspoon vanilla
½ cup cream	2 tablespoons butter

MELT sugar in cream. When smooth, add vanilla and butter and serve at once. Good with Apple Pandowdy or other apple dessert.

Sizzlers

Makes about 20 sizzlers

1 cup sifted flour
1 tablespoon sugar
1 teaspoon baking powder
½ teaspoon salt
2 tablespoons butter

1 egg, beaten
½ cup milk
Canned blueberries, drained
Fat for deep-frying

SIFT together flour, sugar, baking powder, and salt. Cut in butter until the mixture is the consistency of coarse cornmeal. Combine egg and milk and stir into the dry ingredients. Roll thin on a floured board and cut about the size of a saucer. Place 1 tablespoon blueberries on each round of pastry and seal the edges with water. Fry in deep hot fat (370 degrees) until a golden brown. Serve hot.

Boston Baked Beans

Serves 8

1 quart pea beans
½ pound fat salt pork
2 teaspoons salt

¼ cup molasses
½ teaspoon dry mustard
1½ tablespoons brown sugar

WASH and pick over the beans. Soak overnight in cold water. In the morning, drain, cover with fresh water, and simmer until the skins break; turn into a bean pot. Score pork and press into the beans, leaving ¼ inch above the surface. Add salt, sugar, molasses, and mustard. Add boiling water to cover. Cover; bake in a slow oven (250 degrees) for about 8 hours without stirring. Add water occasionally if needed to keep the beans covered. Uncover during the last half hour to brown.

A large onion nestled in the center while baking is popular in some parts of New England, and in Vermont maple syrup is used in place of molasses. Yellow-eye beans are also liked in New England.

Boston Brown Bread

1 cup rye flour
1 cup yellow cornmeal
1 cup graham flour
¾ tablespoon soda
1 teaspoon salt

¾ cup molasses
2 cups sour milk or 1¾ cups
 sweet milk
1 cup raisins (optional)

MIX and sift dry ingredients; add molasses and milk. Stir until well mixed, turn into a well-buttered mold, and steam 3½ hours. The cover should be buttered before being placed on the mold, and then tied down with string; otherwise the bread, in rising, may force it off. Never fill the mold more than two-thirds full. A melon mold or 1-pound baking-powder can makes the most attractive loaves, but any mold available may be used. For steaming, place the mold on a trivet in a kettle containing boiling water, allowing the water to come halfway up around the mold; cover closely and steam, adding more boiling water as needed. Lightly floured raisins or even a cup of dates may be added just before placing in the molds. Mix well to keep the fruit from settling.

Michigan

Kay Savage

DETROIT FREE PRESS
DETROIT, MICHIGAN

The people of Michigan have come from all over the world; in Detroit alone, the oldest major city in the United States west of the Atlantic coastal region, more than one-fourth of the two million residents were born in another country.

Agriculturally, Michigan is a leading producer of beans, apples, cherries, celery, chicory, peaches, sugar beets, soft winter wheat, potatoes, rhubarb, mushrooms, onions, and grapes. On a smaller scale and to supply local needs, the countryside is dotted with farms and orchards growing a myriad products suitable to this moderate climate.

Its watery Great Lakes borders—Lake Erie, Lake St. Clair, Lake Huron, Lake Michigan, Lake Superior, and connecting rivers— spill into the state huge quantities of fresh fish, winter and summer.

With so many different nationalities and such variety of food products, it would be difficult to pin down typical dishes. These, however, are two favorites.

Celery Relish

Makes about 6 quarts

4 quarts chopped celery
1 quart chopped onions
8 sweet red peppers
8 sweet green peppers

7 cups vinegar
2½ cups sugar
4 tablespoons mustard seed

COOK celery and onions separately in boiling, salted water (2 teaspoons salt to 1 quart water). Drain when tender. Chop peppers. Mix all the ingredients and simmer 20 minutes. Pack into sterilized jars and seal at once.

Raised Buckwheat Cakes

1½ cups buckwheat flour
½ cup white flour
2 cups boiled water, cooled
   to lukewarm
½ cake compressed yeast dissolved in 2 tablespoons
   warm water

1 teaspoon salt
1 tablespoon brown sugar or
   molasses
¼ teaspoon soda
¼ cup lukewarm water

WHEN the batter is first started, it should be set in the evening. Mix together the flours, 2 cups water, dissolved yeast, and salt. Beat to a smooth batter, cover, and set in a warm place to rise overnight. The following morning dissolve sugar and soda in the ¼ cup warm water and stir into the first mixture. Let stand 10 minutes, then bake in cakes on a hot, well-greased griddle.

Save a cupful of this batter each morning, and use it the next day in a new batter, instead of fresh yeast. After two mornings add ½ teaspoon soda in 2 tablespoons boiling water, and beat thoroughly into the dough. You can continue to do this for 3 weeks before making a fresh sponge.

Ruth Gorrell

DETROIT TIMES
DETROIT, MICHIGAN

Fried Smelt

These tiny, scaleless, silvery fish run in many Michigan streams every spring. They are so numerous that fishermen stand on the banks or wade in the streams and scoop them up with anything that comes to hand—a bushel basket, a fine net, or what have you!

Joe Muer's, out on Gratiot, is noted for delicious fish. Ernst Zeltwanger, the chef, gave us his elaborate directions for preparing smelt, but they involve three kettles of boiling fat and are too complicated for the average household. Here we have adapted them to home-kitchen facilities. In general, the procedure involves frying the batter-covered fish very quickly in hot fat that is kept as nearly as possible at a uniform temperature. This is the reason for having several vessels of fat.

The first requisite is to have very fresh fish; nothing but the best will do. The heads of the smelt are snipped off with shears and the bodies slit, then thoroughly washed. No scaling is necessary.

Serves 4

16 to 20 cleaned smelt	1 pint milk
1 egg	Cracker meal
1 tablespoon flour	Vegetable shortening for
½ teaspoon salt	frying

BEAT egg, add flour, salt, and milk, and blend until smooth. The batter should be very thin (this is important).

Dip the smelt in the batter, then in cracker meal, coating them well. Have two pans of vegetable shortening heated to 375 degrees.

Place the smelt in a French-fry basket and lower into the hot fat. In about 15 seconds they should be lightly browned. Move to the other pan of fat and leave for 30 seconds. Return to the first pan of fat, now hot again, and finish frying, about 45 seconds more.

Cornish Pasties

Pasties (and pronounce the "a" as in mast, not as in mace) are typical of the Michigan Upper Peninsula. They were introduced to this country back in the seventies and eighties when experienced miners from Cornwall, England, first came here to mine our copper. The Cornish women used to rise in the wee, small hours of the morning, prepare and bake the pasties, and have them ready, wrapped in clean towels, for their husbands to take to the mines.

Pasties provide a whole meal that is filling, heart-warming, and nourishing. They are wonderful for picnics or for late buffet suppers, where seating and serving are problems. They can be kept hot for hours.

Serves 4

¼ cup lard
3 cups flour
1 teaspoon salt
1 cup suet
6 to 7 tablespoons cold water
2 small raw potatoes, sliced thin

2 small raw turnips, sliced thin
1 raw onion, chopped
1 pound beef, diced
½ pound pork, diced
Butter

BLEND lard into flour and salt with a pastry blender. Add suet, which has been put through a food chopper, using the finest blade. The suet is important, as it gives the pastry a very flaky texture. Work it in with the flour mixture. Add cold water to make a soft dough, moister than ordinary pastry but not as soft as biscuit dough.

Divide into four pieces and roll each piece to an 8- or 9-inch circle. On half of each circle place a ½-inch layer of potatoes, seasoned with salt and pepper. Over these place a thin layer of turnips, then a layer of onions. Top each with one quarter of the beef and pork, mixed together, and season again. Dot with butter. Fold the uncovered portion of the pastry circle over the filling and crimp the edges together. Make a 1-inch slit in the top and place on a greased cooky sheet. Bake at 400 degrees for 1 hour. Eat out of hand.

Michigan Baked Beans

The controversy as to whether to add tomatoes or catsup to baked beans waxes hot in many parts of the country. I believe I am safe in saying that in Michigan, tomatoes are out. I am giving you my recipe, which came down from my great-grandmother, so it should be pretty typical of the original settlers. You see, my grandfather was the first white boy born in Livingston County, Michigan.

Serves 6 to 8

1 pound Michigan navy beans	1 teaspoon salt
	2 tablespoons brown sugar
1 medium onion	2 tablespoons white sugar
¼ pound chunk salt pork	

SOAK beans overnight in water to cover. Drain. Cover with fresh water, add the whole onion, salt pork, salt, and brown sugar. Simmer over very low heat until the beans are tender. Add more water occasionally, if needed.

Pour the beans into a baking pan. Remove the onion. Score the rind side of the salt pork, cutting about ½ inch deep. Bury all but the rind into the beans. The liquid should come just to the top of the beans. Sprinkle lightly with granulated sugar. Bake at 350 degrees until golden brown and some of the liquid has been absorbed.

Mary Walker

THE GRAND RAPIDS HERALD
GRAND RAPIDS, MICHIGAN

In the early days of Grand Rapids, furniture manufacturers brought in many Dutch furniture craftsmen to work in the factories. They established their churches and homes on the same patterns as in their mother country, Holland. Although the population now includes descendants from many nationalities, the Dutch influence is still strong. Many of the true Dutch dishes are still favored by third- and fourth-generation descendants of the original workers.

Dutch foods are not highly seasoned, nor are they expensive. Rather, the more common foods such as cabbage, spinach, and the less costly cuts of meat are the mainstays of their menus.

Split-Pea Soup

Serves 8 to 10

1 pound dried, split green peas

3 to 4 quarts water

2 medium onions, sliced

1 pound mettwurst, skinned and cut in ½-inch slices

2 teaspoons salt

⅛ teaspoon pepper

SOAK peas for 1 hour in enough water to cover. Add water, mettwurst, onions, salt, and pepper. Simmer for 2 to 3 hours.

Note: If mettwurst cannot be obtained, garlic frankfurters or a spiced bologna may be substituted.

Wilted Dutch Spinach

Serves 4

4 slices bacon, diced

3 cups chopped raw spinach

3 tablespoons flour

1½ cups hot water

1 tablespoon sugar

2 tablespoons vinegar

½ teaspoon salt

⅛ teaspoon pepper

2 hard-cooked eggs

FRY bacon slowly until crisp; remove from the pan and mix with spinach. Add flour to bacon fat and blend thoroughly. Add hot water and cook over low heat until thick, stirring constantly. Add sugar, vinegar, and seasonings. Slice hard-cooked eggs and add to the spinach mixture. Combine with the sauce just before serving, and toss until the spinach is wilted and well mixed.

Red Cabbage and Apples

Serves 4

2 slices bacon, chopped
2 tart apples, sliced
1 small red cabbage, shredded
1 cup boiling water
1 small onion, thinly sliced

¼ cup vinegar
3 tablespoons brown sugar
1 teaspoon salt
Dash of pepper

FRY bacon until crisp. Add remaining ingredients. Simmer until the cabbage is tender. Serve hot.

Olie Bollen (Dutch Fritters)

Makes 4 dozen

4½ cups sifted flour
1 tablespoon salt
2 cups milk, scalded
1 teaspoon sugar
1 yeast cake

3 eggs
1 15-ounce package seedless raisins
3 tablespoons light corn syrup

SIFT flour and salt together. Combine ¾ cup lukewarm milk and the sugar with the yeast cake. Let stand in a warm place for 30 minutes. Beat eggs, add the remaining milk, the softened yeast, raisins, and syrup. Add flour and stir 2 or 3 minutes. Cover tightly and let stand in a warm place for 2 hours. Spoon the dough by tablespoonfuls into hot fat (365 degrees) and fry until nicely browned. Drain on absorbent paper. Roll in sugar if desired.

Minnesota

Mary Hart

THE MINNEAPOLIS STAR AND THE MINNEAPOLIS
TRIBUNE
MINNEAPOLIS, MINNESOTA

When we think about typical Minnesota cooking, we are likely to begin with Scandinavian dishes, for our large Norwegian, Swedish, and Danish populations have greatly influenced our eating habits. Of course the wild duck, pheasant, and deer that are hunted in our fields and forests have conditioned most of us, too, as has the availability of wild rice.

Krumkake

Makes about 6 dozen

You must have a krumkake iron to bake these Scandinavian goodies.

4 eggs	1 cup sifted flour
¾ cup sugar	½ cup cornstarch
¼ cup melted butter	½ teaspoon vanilla

BEAT eggs with sugar; add butter, flour, cornstarch, and vanilla. Mix well. Drop a large teaspoonful on the krumkake iron and bake to a light brown. Roll quickly into the shape of an ice-cream cone.

Wild Rice Hot Dish

Wild rice grows in swamps in the northern part of the state and is harvested by the Indians, who for centuries used it much as we do.

Serves 8 to 10

1 stewing chicken
2 cups raw wild rice
2 cups chopped celery
1 cup chopped onions

1 small can mushrooms
1 small pimiento, chopped
Salt and pepper to taste

COOK the chicken in water until tender. Save the broth (about 1½ quarts) to use later. Remove meat from bones. Put all the ingredients, except ½ cup of the chicken broth, into a large greased casserole. Bake 1½ hours at 375 degrees. If the food becomes too dry in baking, add the remainder of the broth.

Dolores I. Elliott

ST. PAUL DISPATCH-PIONEER PRESS
ST. PAUL, MINNESOTA

Prune Tarts

1 cup water
2 eggs
4 cups flour, approximately

Butter
1 tablespoon water

MIX together water, 1 beaten egg, and flour, using enough flour to make a stiff dough. Knead until well mixed. Let stand 15 minutes in a cold place. Weigh dough, or approximate the weight, and use enough butter to equal the weight of the dough. The salt should be washed out of the butter, or use unsalted butter. Shape butter into a round patty about ¼ inch thick and lay on a cloth to dry.

Roll out dough on lightly floured board to about twice the size of the butter patty. Fold the two ends over the butter patty to meet in the center. Roll out to ¼ to ½ inch thick. Fold in thirds one way and in thirds again crosswise, making nine layers in all. Let stand 15 to 20 minutes in a cold place. Roll out, fold, and chill in the above manner five or six times or until the butter is well blended. Be sure to fold in the same directions each time, as this is what gives the flakiness. (Part of the dough can be baked, and the rest stored in the refrigerator for later use.)

Roll the dough to ⅛-inch thickness or thinner. Cut in 2½-inch squares. Add about 1 teaspoon of filling in the center of each square.

Bring the two opposite corners together and pinch. Repeat with the other two corners, making a four-pointed star. Brush with the other egg, which has been beaten with 1 tablespoon of water. Put on ungreased baking sheet and bake 10 minutes at 450 degrees. Brush with powdered sugar.

Prune Filling:

THIS filling is simple to make. Cook dried prunes with water. Stone prunes and mash. Add sugar to taste. Use 1 teaspoon for each tart.

Fried Walleyed Pike

Serves 3 generously

1 3-pound pike	2 teaspoons salt
¾ cup flour	½ pound bacon

CUT pike into steaks from head to tail. Mix flour and salt in a paper bag. Fry bacon in a heavy frying pan until crisp and brown; remove the bacon. Flour the fish steaks by shaking well in the paper bag. Drop fish into the hot bacon fat; cover. Turn once during cooking to brown both sides. Cook 15 to 20 minutes over low heat. Place on absorbent paper to drain. Serve with the bacon and with lemon slices.

Swedish Rye Bread

2 cups milk	2 tablespoons shortening, melted
2 tablespoons sugar	
1 cake yeast or 1 package dry granular yeast	1 tablespoon salt
	2 cups sifted, enriched flour
½ cup molasses	3 cups medium rye flour

SCALD milk, add sugar, and let cool to lukewarm. Add yeast and let stand about 5 minutes. Add molasses, shortening, and salt, and blend well. Add the white flour and beat well to make a smooth dough. Add the rye flour and mix well. If the dough is not stiff enough to handle, add a bit more white flour. Knead on a lightly floured board until smooth. Put in a greased bowl, cover, and let rise until doubled in bulk (about 1½ to 2 hours). Punch down and let rise again for about 45 minutes. Divide into two loaves and let rise until light. Bake in a moderately hot oven (375 degrees) for 10 minutes, then reduce heat to 350 degrees and bake 35 to 40 minutes longer. The dough may be shaped into braids or twists. Glaze by brushing the top with beaten egg. Sesame seed may be sprinkled over the glaze.

Note: If dry granular yeast is used, follow the directions on the package.

Pheasant Baked in Cream

SKIN pheasants and cut into pieces; brown well in butter. Put into a buttered casserole or baking dish and season with salt and pepper. Cover with sweet or sour cream. Cover dish and bake in a moderate oven (350 degrees) until tender. This usually takes from 1 to 1½ hours. The cover may be removed for the last few minutes of baking.

Note: Do not oversalt the pheasant because this may curdle the cream.

Wild Rice to Serve with Duck

(Ed. note: This can, of course, be served with other game or poultry, but is a traditional accompaniment to wild duck.)

Serves 6 to 8

1 cup wild rice
Salt
1 cup medium thick white sauce

1 3-ounce can button mushrooms
1 small onion, grated

PICK over and wash rice. Soak 24 hours, changing water several times. Boil rapidly for 15 minutes in salted water. Drain, add white sauce, mushrooms, and onion. Mix lightly. Place in a buttered casserole and bake about 25 minutes in moderate oven (350 degrees).

Sour-Cream Pie

Unbaked 9-inch pie shell
1 cup brown sugar
¾ teaspoon cinnamon
¼ teaspoon nutmeg
¼ teaspoon allspice
1 cup raisins

1 cup sour cream
2 egg yolks, slightly beaten
1 tablespoon melted butter
1 teaspoon vanilla
2 egg whites
2 tablespoons sugar

MIX dry ingredients and raisins together. Add eggs, butter, and vanilla to sour cream. Combine ingredients, mixing lightly. Pour into the unbaked pie shell. Bake for 10 minutes in a hot oven (400 degrees), then reduce the heat to 350 degrees and bake for another 30 to 35 minutes. Top with meringue made with stiffly beaten egg whites and sugar. Bake in a slow oven (325 degrees) for 25 to 30 minutes, or until meringue is delicately browned.

Mississippi

Mary Alice Bookhart

THE CLARION-LEDGER
JACKSON, MISSISSIPPI

In this particular section of the South, many of our recipes have been borrowed from neighboring regions where certain foods are especially plentiful—such as seafood. To suit local tastes, however, many of the more exotic of these have been added to or subtracted from, so that, for example, the gumbo one enjoys in Jackson may not have exactly the same flavor as that served in French restaurants in New Orleans, but it is equally delicious.

These recipes for popular dishes are selected from a cookbook compiled by the women of Saint Andrew's Episcopal Church under the title Let's Cook Somethin' Nice.

Black-Bottom Pie

Makes 2 pies

Crust:

20 graham crackers   5 to 10 tablespoons melted
                            butter

CRUSH crackers and mix thoroughly with butter. Line two 9-inch piepans with the mixture. Bake in a hot oven for 10 minutes.

Filling:

1 tablespoon gelatin
4 tablespoons cold water
4 egg yolks
1 cup plus 2 tablespoons sugar
2 tablespoons cornstarch
1 pint milk, scalded

1½ squares bittersweet chocolate
4 egg whites
Pinch of cream of tartar
1 teaspoon vanilla
1 cup whipped cream
Grated bitter chocolate

DISSOLVE gelatin in cold water. Mix together egg yolks, ½ cup sugar, cornstarch, and scalded milk; add gelatin and cook to custard consistency. Melt chocolate in a double boiler with 2 tablespoons sugar, and mix with 1 cup of the custard. Beat egg whites stiff, add ½ cup sugar, fold in remaining custard, and add cream of tartar and vanilla. Pour the chocolate custard into the piecrust, then cover with plain custard. Several hours before serving, whip cream and spread over the pie. Grate bitter chocolate over the top.

Corn-Bread Dressing

This can be served with fowl or meat, or used as a stuffing for fowl, if desired.

3 cups coarsely crumbled corn bread
2 slices day-old wheat bread
3 stalks celery, diced
1 large onion, diced

Salt and pepper
2 cups chicken broth (about)
2 eggs
Bacon

CRUMBLE corn bread and bread into a large bowl; add celery, onions, salt, and pepper to taste. Add enough chicken broth (or bouillon cubes dissolved in hot water) to make the mixture very moist. Add eggs and mix thoroughly. Place in a baking pan; cover with several strips of bacon. Bake in a 400-degree oven until bacon is crisp.

Heidelberg Hotel Remoulade Sauce

1 pint mayonnaise
½ cup Creole mustard
2 tablespoons French mustard
Salt
1 tablespoon horseradish
1 teaspoon Worcestershire
sauce

½ cup chopped celery
½ bell pepper, chopped
⅓ cup chopped onion
1 clove garlic, minced
Juice of ½ lemon
Dash of Tabasco sauce

MIX all ingredients together. This makes a wonderful sauce for shrimp cocktails.

Missouri

Nell Snead

THE KANSAS CITY STAR
KANSAS CITY, MISSOURI

Black Walnut Pie

This is an Ozark favorite.

2 eggs
1 cup sugar
1 cup light corn syrup or
 sorghum
2 tablespoons butter, or
 2 tablespoons heavy cream

1 teaspoon vanilla
¼ teaspoon salt
1 cup coarsely chopped black-
 walnut meats
1 9-inch unbaked pie shell

BEAT eggs well. Add sugar gradually, beating constantly until very light. Add syrup, softened butter, vanilla, salt, and nuts. Pour into an unbaked pastry shell. Bake 10 minutes in a hot oven (450 degrees), then reduce heat to moderate (350 degrees) and bake another 35 minutes.

Spinach Ring

Serves 6

3 cups cooked spinach
½ cup crumbs
1 teaspoon onion juice
1 tablespoon chopped celery

¼ teaspoon salt
¼ teaspoon pepper
2 tablespoons butter
3 eggs, beaten

MIX all ingredients and pour into a buttered ring mold. Set in a pan of hot water and bake 30 minutes in a slow oven (300 degrees). Unmold and fill center with creamed cauliflower. Make a border of buttered carrots.

The Star's Banner Fruit Cake

¼ pound candied citron
¼ pound mixed candied orange and lemon peel
½ 12-ounce package seeded raisins
¼ pound almonds, blanched
½ pound mixed nuts
Butter
3 cups sifted flour
2 teaspoons baking powder
½ teaspoon salt
½ teaspoon nutmeg
½ teaspoon allspice
½ teaspoon cloves

2 teaspoons cinnamon
1 teaspoon ginger
½ cup powdered, unsweetened cocoa
½ cup butter
1 cup brown sugar
3 egg yolks, well beaten
1 cup cold black coffee
1 glass homemade preserves (strawberry or blackberry are especially good)
1 cup well-drained, homemade mincemeat

POUR boiling water over the citron, orange, and lemon peel. Let stand 5 minutes, drain, and dry on cheesecloth. Stand a few minutes in a warm place to dry and become soft. Slice finely or put through a coarse food chopper. Cut the raisins in small pieces, and chop the almonds and other nuts.

To the sifted flour add baking powder, salt, spices, and cocoa; sift together.

Place butter in a bowl, and cream the brown sugar with it until light and fluffy. Add well-beaten egg yolks and beat together until frothy. Add the sifted dry ingredients and coffee, and beat to a smooth batter. Add the previously prepared fruits, the preserves, and mincemeat. Mix all together thoroughly.

Line one large pan or two loaf pans with a double thickness of heavy unglazed paper. Butter well and dust with flour. Pour the batter into the pans and bake in a slow oven (325 degrees), for 2 hours or until done. Let the cake stand until cool. Remove from the pan and remove the paper. Place on a flat board or tray (a plate will not do, as it is usually not absolutely flat). Wrap and store in a closed container to ripen (at least 1 month).

(Ed. note: Aluminum foil protects fruit cake very well if tins are not available.)

Smothered Pheasant

CLEAN and cut pheasant in serving pieces. Roll in flour seasoned with salt and pepper. Brown slowly on both sides in ½ cup hot shortening. Add 1½ cups cream, and cover tightly. Bake in a slow oven (325 degrees) until tender (about 1 hour). Serve with gravy made from the drippings.

Note: One pheasant will serve three to four persons, according to the size. Allow about a pound per person.

Frances Dawson

ST. LOUIS POST-DISPATCH
ST. LOUIS, MISSOURI

Baked Beans

Serves 12

4 cups dried pea beans
½ pound salt pork (not too fat)
1 apple
1 teaspoon ground black pepper
½ teaspoon celery salt

1¼ teaspoons dry mustard
2 cups hot beef stock or bouillon
1 cup tomato juice
1 tablespoon Worcestershire sauce
1 cup sorghum molasses

SOAK beans overnight in cold water, being careful to allow room for expansion. Drain next morning and cook in fresh water, simmering only until the skins curl back when a spoonful is blown upon. Cut salt pork in cubes; scald and drain. Peel, core, and dice the apple. Put a layer of drained, cooked beans in the beanpot, then a layer of salt pork and diced apple, and continue until all the beans have been used.

Mix the seasonings, stock, tomato juice, Worcestershire sauce, and molasses into a sauce and pour over the beans. Cover and place in a moderate oven (375 degrees) until the beans begin to cook. Then reduce the heat to 275 degrees and bake for about 7 hours. Mix up a fresh batch of sauce and add to the beans from time to time during the baking if they seem to dry out.

Nebraska

Marie Dugan

THE JOURNAL
LINCOLN, NEBRASKA

Corn Salad Relish

The recipe for this wonderful relish came to me from an aunt who was a fine cook. It is a favorite of our family and friends, who make it during the canning season when corn is at its best, fresh from the garden.

Makes at least 16 pints

2 dozen large ears corn
4 heads cabbage, chopped
6 large onions, chopped
6 green peppers, cleaned and diced
2 cups sugar
1 tablespoon celery seed
2 tablespoons mustard seed
2 tablespoons dry mustard
2 tablespoons turmeric
2½ quarts vinegar
1 cup salt

SCRAPE kernels from cob. Cook ingredients together 3 minutes. Make a paste of ½ cup flour and a little water, and add to it; cook 10 minutes longer. Put in sterile jars and seal while hot.

Spiced Peach Jam

Almost every year since we first printed this recipe from a Journal *reader, someone asks us to reprint it.*

Makes about 7 or 8 pints

8 cups sliced fresh peaches   ½ teaspoon nutmeg
7 cups sugar   ⅛ teaspoon salt
2 teaspoons cinnamon   1 tablespoon lemon juice
1 teaspoon cloves

MASH ingredients together. Cook slowly, stirring frequently, until the mixture thickens, about 25 minutes. Pour into sterilized jars or glasses. Cool; seal with melted paraffin.

Maude Coons

THE WORLD-HERALD
OMAHA, NEBRASKA

If you are coming to Omaha, get set for the best steak you've ever tasted. If you come during the summer, you can enjoy an added treat—corn on the cob. Corn-fed beef is as different in flavor from grass-fed beef as night from day. It is well marbled with fat—and succulent.

Steaks are slashed around the edges of the fat to make them lie flat on the broiler rack. Place the rack so that the steaks—no thinner than 1½ inches—are 2 to 3 inches from the source of heat. Broil each side 6 minutes if you like yours rare, 7 minutes for medium, and 8 for the uninitiated who like their steaks well done.

Corn on the cob Nebraska-style requires freshly picked corn. After cleaning, drop it into rapidly boiling water and boil 4 or 5 minutes. Nebraskans would never think of cooking corn in boiling salted water; it toughens the product. When the corn is tender, remove it from the water, steaming hot, and serve with plenty of butter, salt, and pepper.

Cabbage Relish Salad

Serves 8

2 cups shredded cabbage	½ cup chopped celery
¼ cup chopped pimiento	⅓ cup grated raw carrots
2 tablespoons chopped pickles	½ teaspoon salt
¼ teaspoon paprika	⅓ cup French dressing

MIX ingredients together, except dressing, and chill. Combine with dressing and serve.

Cucumber Salad

Serves 4 to 6

2 slender cucumbers, peeled and sliced	2 tablespoons vinegar
4 or 5 green onions, chopped	¼ cup sour cream
½ cup finely chopped green peppers	2 tablespoons sugar
	1 teaspoon salt
	⅛ teaspoon pepper

COMBINE cucumbers, onions, and green peppers. Mix together vinegar, sour cream, and seasonings. Combine mixtures. Chill and serve.

Succotash

Serves 6 to 8

1½ cups corn	2 tablespoons butter or margarine
3 cups cooked lima or green beans	1 teaspoon salt
½ cup light cream	⅛ teaspoon pepper

COMBINE corn and beans. Reheat with cream, butter, and seasonings. Serve at once.

Tossed Green Salad

Serves 8

1 head lettuce
1 clove garlic
3 medium tomatoes, peeled
and sectioned
½ cucumber, sliced
1 stalk celery, diced

1 dozen small radishes, sliced
Salt
1 4-ounce package bleu
cheese
French dressing
2 hard-cooked eggs

BREAK lettuce into pieces. Put in a bowl that has been rubbed with a cut clove of garlic. Add tomatoes, cucumber, celery, and radishes. Season. Toss together lightly. Break cheese into small pieces and add. Mix with salad dressing and garnish with slices of hard-cooked eggs.

Club Steak with Mushrooms

Serves 4

4 club steaks
1 tablespoon flour
1 tablespoon butter
1 cup mushroom stock or
meat stock

1 cup button mushrooms
1 tablespoon caramel (white
sugar browned and melted)
1 tablespoon catsup
Salt and pepper

BROIL steaks, with the broiler rack 2 inches from the source of heat. Broil each side 6 minutes for rare meat, 7 minutes for medium, and 8 minutes for well done.

Combine flour and butter; gradually add meat or mushroom stock. Cook until thickened, then add button mushrooms, caramel, catsup, and seasonings. Place the broiled steaks on a large platter and pour the mushroom sauce over them.

New Jersey

Mary M. Leaming

CAMDEN COURIER-POST
CAMDEN, NEW JERSEY

Lemon Butter

If you go on a picnic here, you'll discover lemon butter is a "must" —and it's unlike any other lemon butter you ever tasted. You eat it as a sweet relish, much as you would applesauce with pork. Incidentally, it's not recommended if you're trying to reduce, but is it good!

4 eggs
1½ cups sugar
Juice of 4 lemons

2 tablespoons butter
Grated rind of 2 lemons

BEAT eggs well and set aside. Heat sugar and lemon juice in the top of a double boiler. When this gets hot, add beaten eggs slowly. Beat with a Dover beater until the mixture thickens. Remove from fire, add butter and lemon rind, and beat a few minutes longer. Let cool before placing in the refrigerator. Use within a week.

Cape May Clam Chowder

You'll not be a guest in New Jersey, especially South Jersey, many hours before you'll have had Cape May Clam Chowder made according to the following recipe (Heaven forbid that anyone suggest it contain tomatoes!).

Serves 6 generously

¼ pound lean salt pork
4 onions, sliced fine
6 raw potatoes, diced

25 hard clams, drained and chopped fine

DICE pork, put in a frying pan, and cook slowly until light brown. Remove pork; put onions in fat and fry until soft but not brown. Mix clams, pork, onions, potatoes, and enough water to show through the mixture but not cover it. Cook slowly; simmer a little beyond the time when the potatoes are soft.

This clam chowder, which is like a thick stew, is better on the second day than the first. A generous bowlful served with a crisp salad, crispy rolls, and a piece of apple pie makes a very filling and delicious meal.

(Ed. note: The juice from the clams can be used as part of the liquid, though this might not be typical of Cape May.)

Boiled Salad Dressing

1 tablespoon sugar
1 tablespoon flour
½ teaspoon mustard
Salt and pepper
3 eggs

½ cup vinegar
½ cup water
1 to 3 tablespoons butter or margarine

BLEND together sugar, flour, mustard, and seasonings. Beat in eggs; add vinegar and water. Place over the fire in top of double boiler and stir constantly until thickened. Remove from the fire and while still hot beat in butter or margarine.

Cold Catsup

Makes 4 or 5 pints

½ peck tomatoes, skinned, cut fine, and drained

1 pint freshly grated horse-radish (do not use the bottled variety)

¼ cup salt (more if desired)

1 cup mustard seed

2 sweet red peppers, chopped

2 green peppers, chopped

5 stalks celery, chopped fine

1 cup chopped onions (about 3 medium onions)

1 teaspoon cloves

2 teaspoons cinnamon

1 cup sugar

1 tablespoon black papper

1 pint vinegar (more if desired)

MIX cold and put away cold in pint jars. Do not cook! Delicious as a relish with cold meats.

Helen L. Manning

THE JERSEY JOURNAL
JERSEY CITY, NEW JERSEY

New Jersey is not noted for any one product, for New Jersey, the garden state, has everything—eggs, poultry, and all kinds of fruit and vegetables, as well as seafood and dairy products.

Steamed Lettuce

Serves 3 or 4

WASH one head of lettuce. Drain and steam, covered, in the water that clings to the leaves. Cook until tender. Chop; add butter, salt, and pepper to taste. Use as a regular cooked vegetable.

Vegetable Slaw

Serves 8 generously

1 small head cabbage, or ½ medium head	2 small green peppers, or 1 large
2 to 3 carrots	2 small green onions
1 to 2 celery hearts	Salt
1 large tomato	Salad dressing

CUT vegetables into small pieces, or chop coarsely in a food chopper. Season to taste with salt. Add mayonnaise, French dressing, spiced vinegar, or any other dressing. Mix thoroughly. Serve cold. Chopped sweet pickle and/or herb seasoning may be added if desired.

Boiled Radishes

WASH and peel as many radishes as are desired (generally two bunches). White ones are best, but not essential. Boil in salted water until soft. Mash, adding butter and seasonings as desired.

Anna Guenther Petz

NEWARK NEWS

NEWARK, NEW JERSEY

Fish in great variety and abundance is caught throughout the year in New Jersey's many fresh-water lakes, located largely in the northern section of the state, and in the salt waters of the Atlantic Ocean, which laps and lashes the extensive shore line of this small but food-important state.

Strawberry-Topped Pancakes

2 cups pancake mix
2¼ cups milk
1½ cups cottage cheese

1 quart fresh strawberries or
12-ounce box of frozen
strawberries

ADD milk to unsifted pancake mix all at once; stir lightly. For each pancake, pour a scant ¼ cup of batter onto a hot, lightly greased griddle. Bake to a golden brown, turning only once. Put two pancakes together with cottage cheese. If the cheese seems dry, mix it with 1 to 2 tablespoons top milk. Top with sweetened fresh or frozen strawberries.

Spiced Apple Balls

This is easy to make, festive, and delicately flavored with spice and the tang of lemon—a light dessert as a perfect ending to a hearty dinner.

Serves 4 or 5

6 green cooking apples
1 cup sugar
1½ cups water
6 whole cloves

1-inch stick of cinnamon
6 allspice berries
Grated rind and juice of
1 lemon

PARE apples, core, and cut into balls, using a French ball cutter. Combine sugar, water, and spices; boil 10 minutes. Add grated lemon rind and juice; lower the heat. Add half the apple balls and simmer very briefly, until barely tender; remove. Add the remaining apple balls and repeat. Strain the syrup and pour over the apple balls. Chill thoroughly. Serve with whipped cream, if desired.
Note: After the balls are made, cook apple bits, cores, and parings with very little water. Put through a food mill or sieve; sweeten to taste—applesauce!

Nut-Crusted (Baked) Apples

Serves 6

6 Rome Beauty apples
4 tablespoons rich preserves (apricot, peach, etc.)
1 egg white, lightly beaten
½ cup soft bread crumbs

¼ cup brown sugar
¼ cup Brazil nuts, finely chopped
1 cup water

CORE apples, removing a strip of skin about 1 inch wide from around top of each. Place on a heavy baking pan. Fill the centers with preserves. Coat apples with the egg white. Combine crumbs, sugar, and nuts, and use to top the apples. Pour water into the pan, and bake in a 350-degree oven until tender.

New Mexico

Vera Busch

THE ALBUQUERQUE TRIBUNE
ALBUQUERQUE, NEW MEXICO

New Mexico has developed its own distinctive type of cookery through an amalgamation of its Indian, Spanish, Mexican, and American inhabitants. In recent years New Mexican foods have acquired increased popularity; as you try the recipes, think of red chili drying in the Southwestern golden sun, outdoor ovens, and adobe houses on the New Mexican landscape.

Sopaipillas (Sweet Fried Cakes)

4 cups flour	4 eggs
1 teaspoon salt	½ cup sugar
2 teaspoons baking powder	Water or milk
4 tablespoons shortening	Deep fat for frying

SIFT flour with salt and baking powder. Cut shortening into flour. Beat eggs, add sugar, and add to the flour mixture. Add enough milk or water to make a medium dough, neither stiff nor soft. Let dough stand 30 minutes. Roll out ¼ inch thick, cut into 1½-inch squares, and fry in hot deep fat until brown. Drain. While the sopaipillas are still hot, roll them in a mixture of 2 teaspoons cinnamon to ½ cup sugar, or serve with butter, jam, or honey.

Ensalada Mexicana (Mexican Salad)

3 large green sweet peppers
1 medium onion
4 medium ripe tomatoes

4 slices bacon
1 teaspoon chili powder
½ cup vinegar

CUT vegetables in small chunks and combine them. Cut bacon in small strips and cook crisp in a hot skillet. Stir in chili powder and add vinegar. As it boils up, pour over the vegetables. Serve on lettuce.

Hot Mexican Chocolate

1 quart milk
1-inch stick cinnamon
3 tablespoons strong coffee
2 squares sweet chocolate

½ cup boiling water
1 tablespoon vanilla
⅛ teaspoon salt
½ teaspoon nutmeg

HEAT milk to boiling with cinnamon and coffee. Remove cinnamon; add chocolate, dissolved in boiling water. Heat again to boiling. Remove from the fire; add vanilla and salt. Beat with an egg beater until foamy. Serve with nutmeg sprinkled on top.

Frijoles (Beans)

1 cup pinto beans
5 cups water
1 clove garlic
1 teaspoon sugar

¼ pound salt pork, diced
4 tablespoons fat (¼ cup)
Salt to taste

WASH beans and soak overnight. Cook in boiling water, adding the garlic and sugar at the beginning. It takes about 1½ hours to cook them, starting with cold water. Add salt pork after 30 minutes. When the beans are done, drain, add fat and salt, and cook a few minutes more to bring out the flavor.

New York

Harriet Cooke

BUFFALO EVENING NEWS
BUFFALO, NEW YORK

Western New Yorkers live on the fat of the land. Eden Valley farmers, their lands protected from harsh spring winds, supply home-grown produce from early spring until late fall. From Lake Erie we take perch, pickerel, and whitefish. A fish fry in this section is a real treat. Fruits and berries are of excellent quality, and from our grapes are produced some of the country's best wines and champagnes. Western New York has large maple groves, and the state is second in the production of maple sugar products.

There's only one food that seems to be pretty much Buffalo's own—the Kimmel Weck. This is a hard-crusted roll with a cross in the center dividing it so it may be easily broken in fours. Each roll is glazed to hold a generous sprinkling of coarse salt and caraway seeds. The rolls were developed, we are told, to accompany beer, much of which is made and drunk in our fair city. Unfortunately, they are too difficult to make at home.

Overnight Strawberries

This recipe, which is made in almost every home in western New York, may be used equally well with raspberries, but in this case the berry is not scalded.

Makes 4 pints

WASH 2 quarts of large, firm, ripe strawberries and scald, leaving them in boiling water for 2 minutes. Drain. Add 4 cups sugar and 2 tablespoons lemon juice. Boil 2 minutes, counting the time after the entire contents boil. Remove from the fire. After the bubbling stops, add 2 cups sugar, return to the fire, and boil 5 minutes. Skim, then pour the mixture into a shallow pan. (It should not be more than ½ inch thick.) Let stand overnight. Next morning pour into jars and seal with paraffin, then place jar rubbers and seal as usual.

Irish Pickles

If you have time and patience, I recommend this pickle, which ends up as green as the Isles of Ireland from which it takes its name!

WASH 150 3- to 4-inch cucumbers. Put in a crock and add 2 cups salt. Cover with cold water. Let stand a week, stirring each day. Pour off this brine and cover the pickles with boiling water. Next day drain and add 2 tablespoons powdered alum. Cover with boiling water. Drain again the next day, and again cover with boiling water. Let stand, and the next day drain and cut in halves lengthwise.

Make a syrup with 12 cups granulated sugar, 6 cups vinegar, 4 ounces cassia buds, and 1 ounce celery seed. (Tie seeds in a bag.) Bring this to a boil and pour over the pickles. Next day drain, reserving the syrup. Bring syrup to the boiling point, add 1 cup sugar, and pour over the pickles. Let stand overnight. Again the next day drain, bring the syrup to a boil, and pour it back over the pickles. Place in jars, filling them not too full, and store until plump. (These will shrink but come back to normal size in time.)

Applesauce Bread

This loaf of bread uses some of our apples, many of which find their way to applesauce processors or to cider mills and vinegar factories.

½ cup shortening	2 cups sifted all-purpose flour
⅔ cup light brown sugar, packed in cup	1 teaspoon double-action baking powder
2 eggs	1 teaspoon soda
1 cup thick applesauce, sweetened or unsweetened	½ teaspoon salt
	½ cup broken nut meats

MIX shortening, sugar, and eggs very thoroughly. Stir in applesauce, then flour, baking powder, soda, and salt sifted together, and last the nuts. Pour into a well-buttered pan (5 by 10 by 3 inches) and bake in a 350-degree oven for about 55 minutes, or until the loaf tests done. Turn from the pan to cool.

Jane Nickerson

THE NEW YORK TIMES
NEW YORK, NEW YORK

New York City has more than 21,000 restaurants, according to that wizard on the subject, Lawton Mackall, author of Knife and Fork in New York *(Doubleday, 1949). They serve to the city's residents and guests foods in so many languages as to rob the city of any one set of distinctive dishes.*

True, one may not be able to dine here in the Polynesian manner, but one can eat in Polish (Polish Inn, 163 East 66th Street), Roumanian (Greenberg's Roumanian Casino, 286 Broome Street), Basque (Jai-Alai, 82 Bank Street) and in French, Italian, Chinese, German, and plain-American fashion in too many establishments to mention. One delightful little restaurant (Les Trois Moineaux, 317 West 46th Street) even invites one once weekly to savor couscous, a wonderful North African sort of stew spooned over semolina.

So what we lack in "regionality" in cooking, we make up for in variety. Home cooks (New Yorkers don't live out their lives in theaters and night clubs, despite what the out-of-towners claim) can and do duplicate some of the national specialties in their own kitchens.

Special ingredients are obtained more easily here than in probably any other city in the world at the present time. Chinatown, the French section (on Ninth Avenue in the Fifties), Italian districts (too many to list), Spanish neighborhoods (one is on the upper East Side), Near Eastern communities (one around Lexington and Third Avenues in the Twenties) are among the sections that help supply the call for unusual ingredients. Whether a recipe demands shark's fin, Spanish sausage, or squid, one can find it in this culinary-conscious city. As we New Yorkers like to say, "New York has everything."

Recipes from a few of the city's foreign restaurants, translated into terms for home kitchens, follow.

FRENCH
(From Du Midi, 311 West 48th Street)

Coq au Vin

Serves 4

1 3½-pound frying chicken
or two 2-pound broilers
Salt and pepper
½ cup diced salt pork
2 tablespoons butter
½ pound small onions
½ pound mushrooms
2 to 3 shallots, or ½ cup chopped scallions

1 clove garlic, minced
2 tablespoons flour
2 cups red table wine
3 sprigs parsley
Few celery leaves
½ bay leaf
⅛ teaspoon thyme
2 tablespoons chopped parsley

CUT fryers into quarters or broilers into halves and season with salt and pepper. Parboil salt pork 5 minutes, drain, and sauté in butter until brown. Remove pork and reserve.

Sauté chicken in the fat until brown on all sides. Add onions and mushrooms. Cover the pan and cook slowly until the onions are partially tender and beginning to brown. Remove chicken to a platter. Pour off all but 2 to 3 tablespoons fat. Add shallots (or scallions) and garlic and cook 1 minute. Blend in flour. Add wine and cook until boiling, stirring continuously. Return chicken to the pan. If the wine does not cover it, add water.

Tie parsley, celery, bay leaf, and thyme in cheesecloth and add to the chicken. Add the reserved diced pork. Simmer on top of the stove; or cook, covered, in a moderately hot oven (400 degrees) until the chicken is tender, 30 minutes or longer. Remove the herb bag, skim fat from the surface if desired. Arrange attractively on a platter and cover with sauce and chopped parsley.

BALKAN

Imam Byeldi (Eggplant Appetizer)

Serves 4

3 large onions, sliced	Salt
3 cloves garlic, sliced	Pepper
½ cup olive oil	1 medium eggplant
4 small tomatoes, sliced	2 cups water
½ cup chopped parsley	

SAUTÉ onions and garlic in oil. When soft, add tomatoes, parsley, salt, and pepper. Cook about 2 minutes.

Pare eggplant, cut in quarters, and arrange in a baking dish. Pour sautéed vegetables over eggplant. Add water to the dish and bake in a moderate oven (350 degrees) about 1 hour. Cool.

FRENCH-ITALIAN
(*From the Little Club, 70 East 55th Street*)

Lobster in Shell Borrini

Serves 4

¼ pound butter
2 live lobsters, about 1 pound each
1 tablespoon finely chopped onion
3 ounces sherry

2 cups light cream, into which has been blended
1 tablespoon cornstarch
Salt and white pepper
1 small can pimiento, sliced
½ tablespoon chopped parsley

LET butter melt and brown slightly in a frying pan. Meanwhile, lay lobsters on a wooden board and cut in halves lengthwise. Arrange lobsters and onion in the butter and cook about 5 minutes over moderately high heat. Add sherry; slowly pour in cream. Cook over low heat, stirring, 3 or 4 minutes. Season to taste with salt and pepper; add pimiento. Cover and let simmer slowly about 10 minutes. Sprinkle with parsley and serve.

ITALIAN

Frittata Cinta

Serves 2 generously

6 tablespoons olive oil
2 tablespoons butter
2 cups sliced or chopped zucchini
4 eggs

3 tablespoons chopped parsley
¼ teaspoon salt
Dash of pepper
1 tablespoon grated Parmesan-type cheese

HEAT 2 tablespoons oil and 1 tablespoon butter in a frying pan. Add zucchini and cook slowly, stirring often, until the vegetables are limp and lightly browned, or about 5 minutes. Cool thoroughly.

Beat eggs until fluffy. Add parsley, salt, pepper, cheese, and cooled zucchini. Heat the remaining oil and butter in a clean pan. Add the egg-zucchini mixture and cook over a moderately high flame, lifting the mixture around the edge, until only the center remains uncooked. Place under a very low broiler flame and cook until the center is firm. Turn out on a platter and cut into pie-shaped wedges to serve.

CHINESE
(From the Chinese Rathskeller,
125 West 51st Street and 45 Mott Street)

Almond Dice Chicken

Serves 4

3 tablespoons thinly sliced water chestnuts

3 tablespoons snow peas, cut into ¾-inch pieces

2 tablespoons bamboo shoots, cut into small cubes

3 tablespoons canned or fresh button mushrooms

½ cup sliced stalks of Chinese cabbage

4 tablespoons salad oil

1 cup cubed raw chicken

⅓-inch piece of ginger root

1¼ cups chicken stock (water and bouillon cubes may substitute for stock)

½ teaspoon sugar

1 tablespoon soy sauce

¾ tablespoon cornstarch

Salt

½ cup blanched almonds

SAUTÉ vegetables in 3 tablespoons of the oil for 5 to 6 minutes. Add chicken and ginger root, and cook about 5 minutes.

Blend stock with sugar, soy sauce, and cornstarch. Add to chicken and simmer until the poultry is tender (5 to 10 minutes). Season to taste with salt. Brown almonds in the remaining oil and add to chicken-vegetable mixture. Serve with rice.

Clementine Paddleford

NEW YORK HERALD TRIBUNE
and THIS WEEK MAGAZINE
NEW YORK, NEW YORK

The following recipes have appeared in the "How America Eats" series in "This Week Magazine," and were gathered from exceptional cooks in various parts of the country.

Gumbo d'Herbes

From New Orleans, Louisiana.

Serves 6

½ pound mustard greens
1 bunch water cress
½ small head green cabbage
½ head lettuce
½ pound turnip greens
1 bunch radish tops
1 pound beet tops
½ bunch roquette or parsley
1 pound spinach
2 onions
2 slices bacon, diced

1 pound pickled pork or ham pieces, diced
2 tablespoons shortening
2 tablespoons flour
Salt and pepper to taste
1 bay leaf
Pinch of marjoram
Pinch of thyme
1 clove
9 whole allspice
Dash of Tabasco sauce

WASH greens well. Tear off coarse stems, and boil in 2 quarts water; reserve the water. Finely chop them with the onions. Brown pork and bacon in shortening. Remove; add chopped greens and cook 10 minutes, stirring frequently. Blend in flour. Return meat to pan and pour in water in which the greens were cooked. Season with salt and pepper to taste, add herbs, spices, and Tabasco sauce or other hot Louisiana pepper sauce. Cook 1 hour. Serve with rice.

Red Beans and Rice

From New Orleans, Louisiana.

Serves 4

¾ pound large, dried red kidney beans
½ pound salt pork, pickled pork, or ham hock
1 tablespoon fat
1 tablespoon flour
1 large onion, chopped
1 carrot, scraped and sliced
3 pints stock, or water with 6 bouillon cubes
3 sprigs parsley
1 bay leaf
Pinch of powdered thyme
Pinch of sage
2 stalks and leaves of celery
Salt and pepper to taste (be careful about salt if bouillon cubes are used)
Cooked rice

SOAK red beans overnight in cold water. Brown meat in fat. Remove meat and stir flour into fat in the pan; brown lightly, add onion, and cook 3 minutes. Add beans, carrot, and meat, and cover well with stock. Cook slowly 1 hour. Then add herbs, celery, salt, and pepper. Cook until the gravy is thick and dark. Serve with rice.

Syrup-Custard Pie

From Atlanta, Georgia.

Serves 6

1 9-inch unbaked pie shell
4 eggs
¾ cup sugar
1½ cups cane syrup
1 tablespoon flour
2 tablespoons melted butter or margarine
¼ teaspoon salt
1 teaspoon vanilla

BEAT eggs lightly. Add sugar, then the remaining ingredients, mixing well. Pour into the piecrust and bake 10 minutes in a hot oven (450 degrees). Reduce the heat to moderate (350 degrees), and bake for 25 minutes, or until firm. Serve cold.

Howard Frye's Indian Pudding

From Cohasset, Massachusetts.

Serves 10

1 quart milk	1 teaspoon salt
5 tablespoons yellow corn-meal	½ teaspoon ginger
	½ teaspoon nutmeg
2 tablespoons butter or margarine	½ teaspoon cinnamon
	2 eggs, well beaten
½ cup dark molasses	1 cup cold milk
½ cup dark brown sugar	

SCALD milk in a pot over low heat; add cornmeal bit by bit, sifting it in from a little bowl in almost invisible amounts, stirring hard all the while. Never a lump! Cook 20 minutes in the top of a double boiler, over hot water; add butter or margarine, molasses, sugar, salt, spices, and eggs. Turn into a buttered baking dish. Pour the cold milk over (don't stir); as the pudding cooks the milk settles through. Bake about 50 to 60 minutes in a moderate oven (350 degrees). Serve warm with plain cream or ice cream.

Angel-Food Cake

This is a favorite of Oregon's first lady, Mrs. Douglas McKay, one of the state's best cooks.

Serves 12

1½ cups egg whites (about 13 large)	1½ cups sugar
Pinch of salt	1 cup plus 1 tablespoon sifted cake flour
1¼ teaspoons cream of tartar	1 teaspoon vanilla

TURN egg whites onto a large platter, dust with two shakes of salt. Beat with a wire whip until the whites are frothy. Add cream of tartar and continue beating until the mixture makes little mountains but is not too stiff. Sift sugar six times and add to eggs, 1 tablespoonful at a time, folding it in gently, so gently. Next add the flour, this too sifted six times, 1 tablespoonful at a time. At the very last, add vanilla. Pour the batter into a 10-inch, flour-dusted aluminum tube pan used for angel food only.

Start the cake in a cold oven; set at 150 degrees for 10 minutes, then to 200 degrees for another 10 minutes (Mrs. McKay has a new electric range and it's very fast heating). Next increase the temperature 25 degrees every 10 minutes until the oven is at 300 degrees. Now give the cake another full 10 minutes, and at this point increase the temperature to 350 degrees and leave it 10 minutes longer to take on that delicate macaroon color. After a total baking time of 70 minutes, out comes the cake to be turned upside down on a rack and let cool for 2 hours, then removed from the pan and either frosted or left plain.

(Ed. note: If you do not have an electric oven or a reliable temperature control, put the cake into a cold oven and heat oven slowly to 300 degrees (low moderate heat). Bake about an hour, or until top is golden brown and sides shrink from the pan.)

Elsa Steinberger

BROOKLYN EAGLE
BROOKLYN, NEW YORK

The section of Long Island that is now Brooklyn was first settled by the Dutch, who found a plentiful variety of game, fish, nuts, berries, and wild grapes, which they hunted and cultivated eagerly. Two items frequently mentioned in enthusiastic terms in letters to Holland were beautiful peaches, as fine as any at home, the trees bearing so heavily that the branches touched the ground; and Gowanus oysters "big as a man's hand." Every household had a bucketful roasting on the hearth.

Our choice of typical recipes includes a modern version of baked oysters (Long Island is still famous for them, though Brooklyn itself

*is far too industrialized these days to produce them), a Long Island
clam pie, and a peach dessert that may well have been made originally in a kettle hanging on a crane in the fireplace.*

Baked Oysters in the Shell

Serves 6

36 shell oysters   6 tablespoons melted butter

CLEAN oysters thoroughly. Place on a baking sheet and roast in a
hot oven (450 degrees) for about 15 minutes, or until shells begin
to open. Serve in the shells with melted butter. If desired, remove
the top shells when the oysters begin to open, add butter, pepper,
and chopped chives, and bake another 2 or 3 minutes.

Clam Pie

Serves 4 to 6

2 dozen small clams, in their   ½ teaspoon salt
  liquor   Pepper
1 large onion, sliced   Nutmeg
4 small cooked potatoes,   ½ cup rich milk
  sliced   Rich pastry
2 tablespoons butter

DRAIN clams, reserving the liquor. Arrange alternate layers of clams,
onions, and potatoes in a buttered casserole until all three ingredients are used. Dot with remaining butter. Season by sprinkling
with salt, pepper, and a dash of nutmeg. Add milk and 2 tablespoons clam liquor. Cover with flaky pastry, pressing the edges
firmly to the rim of the casserole. Cut gashes in the crust to let steam
escape. Bake in a hot oven (450 degrees) 15 minutes, or until the
top is golden brown. Serve hot.

Oysters may be used in place of clams, or half clams, half oysters may be used. Another version omits potatoes and onions and calls for mushrooms and celery. For this version, flour will be required to thicken the sauce.

Peach Roly-Poly

Serves 4 to 6

1 recipe for biscuit dough	½ cup sugar
3 tablespoons butter	½ teaspoon cinnamon
1½ cups sliced peaches	

KNEAD the dough lightly, then roll to ½-inch thickness. Spread with softened butter, then peach slices. Sprinkle with combined sugar and cinnamon. Roll as a jelly roll, moistening the edges to hold them firmly together. Be sure the ends are also sealed. Place on clean muslin or on vegetable parchment and wrap loosely to allow room for expansion. Tie the roll firmly. Place on a rack in boiling water to cover; cover pan and cook about 1½ hours. Remove from wrapping and serve hot with lemon, nutmeg, or hard sauce. Other fruit or berries may be used. Pastry dough is sometimes used in place of biscuit dough but the texture is not as light.

Agnes Adams Murphy

NEW YORK POST-HOME NEWS
NEW YORK, NEW YORK

A request for "typically New York recipes" makes people associated with the New York Post think of the days when the founder of this paper, Alexander Hamilton, and his wife Elizabeth, one of the famous hostesses of her generation, gave some of the most elaborate and gala parties of the time in their home at 52 Wall Street. It was a simple, and at the same time sophisticated, dessert custom at the time that, after the main dinner, the table was cleared, and bowls of red cherries, with stems left on, and strawberries still wearing their green petal caps were brought in and strewn lavishly across the gleaming white tablecloth. Guests picked them up with their fingers. (Ed. note: Hostesses who wish to copy this today have the benefit of plastic tablecloths—since if ripe strawberries or cherries are really "strewn" with any spirit, their scarlet juices will stain a linen cloth.)

Another picture of domestic tranquillity, as well as of the educational methods of the day, is revealed in Mary Gay Humphries' book Catherine Schuyler (Scribners'). Catherine, wife of the Revolutionary War General Philip Schuyler, was Mrs. Hamilton's mother. "Mrs. Hamilton was sitting, as was her wont, at the table, with a napkin in her lap, cutting slices of bread and spreading them with butter for the younger boys, who, standing by her side, read in turn a chapter in the Bible or a portion of Goldsmith's Rome."

Old-Fashioned Gingerbread

Many of the old cake recipes called for spices and molasses, and special mention is made of gingerbread—the moist, rich kind, made with sour milk. (In those pre-mechanical refrigeration days, milk undoubtedly soured readily.) This old-time recipe has been tested in the kitchens of the American Molasses Company.

2½ cups sifted enriched flour	½ cup lard
1 teaspoon salt	½ cup sugar
1 teaspoon ginger	1½ teaspoons soda
2 teaspoons cinnamon	1 cup unsulphured molasses
½ teaspoon nutmeg (optional)	2 eggs, unbeaten
½ teaspoon cloves	1 cup sour milk

SIFT the flour, salt, ginger, cinnamon, nutmeg, and cloves together. Cream together lard, sugar, and soda until fluffy. Add molasses to the sugar mixture, then stir ½ cup of the dry ingredients into this mixture. Add eggs, one at a time, beating well after each is added. Now add sour milk and the rest of the dry ingredients alternately, beating after each addition. Pour the batter into a well-buttered and lightly floured pan (9 by 9 by 2 inches, or 8 by 12 by 2 inches) and bake in a 350-degree oven for 45 minutes, or until done.

Isabella Beach (Janet Cooke)

NEW YORK JOURNAL-AMERICAN
NEW YORK, NEW YORK

New York food probably represents every national group in the world, and the New Yorker each year grows more cosmopolitan in his food preferences. At home, though, he enjoys dishes that belong to family tradition and heritage.

Barra Bread Pudding

Our family's Barra Bread Pudding came from the Hebrides, where my mother was taught to make it by a MacNeil of the island of Barra. We've changed it here and there—for instance, we think that evaporated milk gives it a better flavor than fresh milk does.

Serves 6 to 8

8 slices whole wheat bread
½ to ¾ cup firmly packed brown sugar
2 eggs
12 halved, pitted dates

1½ to 1¾ cups evaporated milk diluted (before measuring) only half as much as usual
3 tablespoons butter

BREAK bread into a bowl and sprinkle brown sugar over it. Scald milk, pour it over the bread and sugar, and cover tightly until the bread is very soft. Beat well until the mixture is batterlike in texture. Add eggs, one at a time, beating after each addition. Mix in the dates and pour into a well-buttered baking dish. Dot with butter on top and bake in a moderate oven (350 degrees) nearly an hour, or until very crusty but not too dark. Serve with cream.

Hot Cheese Appetizer

These cheese patties are the easiest to make, yet the most delicious hot appetizer I know of.

Makes 20 small patties

1 8-ounce package sharp
   process cheese

½ cup flour
¼ cup butter

USING the fingers, combine the ingredients into a paste and roll between the hands into balls about the size of a large marble. Flatten between the palms of the hands and place on an ungreased cooky sheet. Chill at least 1 hour, then bake in a hot oven (500 degrees) about 7 minutes, or until light brown. Serve hot.

Dixie Oliver

NEW YORK WORLD-TELEGRAM AND SUN
NEW YORK, NEW YORK

Cranberries, we're told, were growing in America when Columbus arrived. The red man gathered the berries for food, using them while in season and saving some for the long, lean winter months, in sacks hung outside his tepee to freeze. Then colonial women came along and discovered the bright red berries. They gathered them in early fall to serve with wild turkeys.

Cranberry Compote

Serves 6

2 cups fresh cranberries
2 oranges, peeled and sectioned
9 whole cloves
3 1-inch sticks of cinnamon

4 fresh pears, peeled, cored, and halved or 1 No. 2 can pears, drained
1½ cups light corn syrup

PLACE all ingredients in a 1½-quart casserole. Bake in a moderate oven (350 degrees) for 20 minutes. (If fresh pears are used, bake until tender.) Baste occasionally with syrup. Serve chilled.

Cranberry-Apple Punch

Makes about 25 cups

2 cups fresh cranberries
2 cups water
1 cup sugar
3 cups apple juice, chilled
½ cup lemon juice, chilled
1 lemon, sliced thin

1 package frozen pineapple cubes, or 1 cup canned pineapple cubes
1 quart club soda or ginger ale

COMBINE cranberries, water, and sugar in a saucepan. Bring to a boil and cook until soft. Strain and chill. Pour into a punch bowl. Add the remaining ingredients. Serve thoroughly chilled. To make the punch extra pretty, try freezing two cranberries in each ice cube in your refrigerator tray. It adds a nice touch to see them floating around in the punch.

Prudence Penny

NEW YORK DAILY MIRROR
NEW YORK, NEW YORK

Cheese Appetizer Roll

1 pound American cheddar or process cheese
1 3-ounce package pimiento cream cheese
5 tablespoons good sherry
2 tablespoons mayonnaise

½ cup finely chopped walnuts
2 tablespoons chopped parsley
¼ to ⅓ teaspoon very finely minced garlic
Dash of cayenne
Paprika

LET cheeses stand outside the refrigerator until they are at room temperature. Grate the American cheese, blend in cream cheese, sherry, mayonnaise, nuts, parsley, garlic, and cayenne. Mix and blend thoroughly. Divide into two equal portions and shape into rolls about 1½ inches in diameter. Wrap each roll in waxed paper or aluminum foil and refrigerate overnight. At serving time, lightly dust rolls with paprika and slice. Serve with crisp salted crackers.

Spiced Short Ribs

Serves 6

3 pounds beef short ribs
¼ cup flour
2 tablespoons bacon drippings
1½ teaspoons salt
¼ teaspoon pepper
1 cup beef bouillon (if well salted, reduce above amount of salt)

1 cup dried prunes
1 cup dried apricots
½ cup sugar
½ teaspoon cinnamon
½ teaspoon allspice
¼ teaspoon cloves
3 tablespoons vinegar

DREDGE meat with flour; brown in bacon drippings. Season and add bouillon. Cover; simmer for 1 hour. Add prunes, apricots, and sugar blended with the spices. Add vinegar. Bring to a boil, reduce to a simmer, and cook, covered, for an hour—or longer if necessary.

Fruit Lamb Curry

Serves 4

1 tablespoon butter or margarine
3 medium apples, peeled, cored, and sliced

2 small onions, sliced
1 clove garlic
1 tablespoon flour
1 tablespoon curry powder

Juice and grated rind of
½ large lemon
1 12-ounce can condensed
bouillon
1 teaspoon kitchen bouquet

½ cup seedless white raisins
2 or 3 whole cloves
2 cups cooked lamb, cut in
small cubes

MELT butter or margarine in a skillet and in it sauté apples, onions, and garlic to a golden brown. Remove garlic. Blend in flour, mixed with curry powder. Combine lemon juice with bouillon, kitchen bouquet, and grated lemon rind; add raisins and cloves. Mix this with the contents of the skillet. Cover and simmer 30 minutes. Add lamb cubes. Simmer 15 minutes. Serve with rice.

Nancy Dorris

NEW YORK DAILY NEWS
NEW YORK, NEW YORK

Manhattan Clam Chowder

Serves 4

3 tablespoons fat
½ cup chopped onions
¼ cup chopped carrots
1½ cups diced, raw potatoes
1 pint boiling water (about)
1 pint minced clams and juice

1 pint canned tomatoes or
tomato juice
1 teaspoon salt (or more)
¼ teaspoon thyme
¼ teaspoon celery seed
⅛ teaspoon pepper

SAUTÉ onions and carrots in the fat in a kettle over a low flame for 10 minutes. Add diced potatoes and enough boiling water to cover all. Cook, covered, until the potatoes are almost tender (about 10 minutes). Add the tomatoes or tomato juice; bring to a boil. Add the clams and juice and the seasonings; reduce the heat. Simmer gently 10 to 15 minutes. Check the seasoning. Serve in heated soup plates, with toasted pilot crackers.

Roast Long Island Duckling

Serves 4 to 6

1 duckling (5 to 6 pounds), drawn and rinsed
2 teaspoons salt
¼ teaspoon ginger
⅛ teaspoon black pepper
3 to 4 cups bread or fruit stuffing

SINGE the duckling; rinse quickly and wipe dry. Sprinkle the inside with the mixed seasonings. Fill the body cavity two-thirds full of stuffing, or omit the stuffing if desired. Sew or skewer the edges together. Truss the duck. Place, breast up, on a rack in an open roasting pan. Roast in a moderate oven (350 degrees) until well done, allowing 25 to 30 minutes to the pound. Baste with the pan fat unless the duck is very fat. Pour off the fat that accumulates in the pan. Turn breast side down for the last 30 minutes.

Lift the duck to a heated platter; discard the fastenings. Serve hot or cold. If cold, the duckling should chill about 12 hours for the best flavor. It is very good served with guava jelly, mixed with prepared mustard, or with cranberry sauce, fresh or canned.

New York-Style Beans

Serves 8 or more

1 pint navy or marrow beans
3 cups lukewarm water
4 cups cold water (about)
2 onions, sliced
½ pound salt pork, sliced
4 to 8 tablespoons sugar
¼ teaspoon pepper

WASH beans, place in a saucepan with the lukewarm water; cover. Let stand 12 hours. Do not drain. Add enough cold water to cover the beans well. Slowly bring to a boil, reduce the heat, and cook below the boiling point until partly tender (about 2 hours), adding water as needed. Add the sliced onions and salt pork; cover; simmer until tender (about 1 hour). Drain, reserving the liquid. Transfer to a greased, shallow baking dish (1½ quarts), covering the pork with the beans. Pour in enough bean liquid to cover. Sprinkle with mixed sugar and pepper. Bake, uncovered, in a slow oven (300 degrees) until soft and a brown crust forms on the top and along the sides (2 to 2½ hours). As the beans dry out, moisten with the reserved bean liquid or hot water. Serve hot with vinegar. The beans reheat successfully.

Sautéed or Fried Long Island Scallops

Serves 4

1¼ pounds scallops	¼ cup fat
½ teaspoon salt	2 tablespoons butter
⅛ teaspoon pepper	½ tablespoon lemon juice
3 tablespoons flour (about)	1 teaspoon minced parsley

RINSE the scallops; drain and dry. If large, slice across the grain to a thickness of about ⅝ inch. Sprinkle with salt and pepper; coat lightly with flour. Heat 2 tablespoons fat in a large, heavy skillet; when hot but not smoking, add the floured scallops. Pan-fry slowly 4 to 6 minutes until tender and brown on all sides, adding more fat if needed. Keep the flame low to prevent toughening. Arrange on a heated platter. Brown the butter lightly in a small pan; add lemon juice and parsley and pour over the scallops. Serve immediately.

To French-fry scallops: Egg and crumb them, and fry in hot deep fat (375 degrees) until brown, 3 to 4 minutes. Drain on soft paper and serve with lemon wedges or tartar sauce.

Pan-Fried Swellfish

Serves 2 or 3

1 pound (8 to 12) swellfish
1 teaspoon salt
⅛ teaspoon pepper
1 cup salted-cracker crumbs

1 egg, beaten with 2 tablespoons cold water
¼ cup fat, or less

WIPE the swellfish, which are bought skinned and dressed, with a damp cloth; season. Beat egg in a small bowl; add water. Dip the fish, one at a time, first into the egg and then into the crumbs, set apart from one another on waxed paper. Heat enough fat in a heavy skillet to cover the bottom ¼ inch deep. When hot but not smoking, put in as many egged and crumbed swellfish as can be turned easily. Pan-fry to a delicate brown on all sides. Cover; reduce heat; cook more slowly until the flesh can be flaked from the center bone. Place on a heated platter and keep hot while cooking the remaining fish. Serve with lime or lemon wedges.

Agnes D. Gillette

SYRACUSE HERALD-JOURNAL
SYRACUSE, NEW YORK

Milk is one of the most important foods we know. Cool milk punches, milk shakes, and eggnogs in summer; milk for hot chocolate, main dishes, and puddings in winter; any time of year, milk is a good food.

You might like to create strawberry milk shakes at home. Combine a glass of milk, a couple of scoops of ice cream, and some crushed strawberries. Shake them together in a covered glass until the result is a pink, frothy milk shake. What better way to give yourself a real treat!

Lemon-Cheese Pie

1½ cups cottage cheese
½ teaspoon salt
Grated rind of 1 lemon
¾ cup syrup

¼ teaspoon nutmeg
3 eggs
⅓ cup raisins (optional)

PRESS the cottage cheese through a fine strainer. Add salt and lemon rind. Beat syrup, nutmeg, and eggs together until light. Combine with cheese. Stir in raisins. Pour into a piepan lined with graham-cracker, bread-crumb, or cooky-crumb piecrust. Bake in a moderate oven (325 degrees) for 1 hour, or until a delicate brown.

Crust:

1⅓ cups crumbs
2 tablespoons melted fat

½ teaspoon cinnamon

MIX together and use to line a buttered 8-inch piepan.

Frozen Cheese Salad with Fruit

Serves 8

1 cup cottage cheese
½ cup mayonnaise
1 teaspoon salt
2 tablespoons lemon juice
2 bananas
½ cup light cream

½ cup chopped nuts
½ cup chopped cherries
   (fresh or maraschino)
½ cup diced fruit (fresh,
   canned, or dried)

MIX cheese, mayonnaise, and salt. When well blended, add lemon juice. Mash bananas and mix with cream. Add with nuts and fruits to the cheese mixture. Pour into a refrigerator tray and freeze. When frozen, cut in pieces and serve on salad greens.

Colonial Custard

Serves 5 or 6

2 cups milk	1 teaspoon vanilla
3 eggs	⅛ teaspoon salt
¼ cup molasses	Butter

SCALD milk. Beat the eggs, molasses, vanilla, and salt together lightly. Slowly add the scalded milk to this mixture, stirring constantly. Pour into buttered custard cups. Place on a rack in a pan of hot water, with the water not quite as deep as the custard in the cups. Cover the pan and turn the flame low, as the water must not boil. Cook until set.

Cottage Cheese Appetizers

1 pound cottage cheese	3 tablespoons chopped parsley
3 tablespoons chopped onions or chives	Few grains of salt
	Potato chips or crackers

COMBINE cheese, onions, parsley, and salt. Chill. Serve surrounded by potato chips or crackers. This mixture may also be used to fill a tomato or green pepper and served as a salad.

North Carolina

Elizabeth Hedgecock

WINSTON-SALEM JOURNAL AND SENTINEL
WINSTON-SALEM, NORTH CAROLINA

In North Carolina, even the older cooks are becoming "mix-happy."
That means the old recipes are pushed a little farther back into
sideboard drawers each year. Some exist only in the memory of old
cooks, colored and white.

Prior to the popularity of private clubs, friends were always entertained in the home, the table loaded with food until there was
no space for another dish. When the group was too large for the
dining room, the party moved outdoors for a fish fry, barbecue,
chicken stew, or oyster roast, the counterpart of the New England
clambake.

The typical menu for a fish fry consists of fresh fish coated with
a mixture of cornmeal and flour and fried in about an inch of hot
fat in a heavy black skillet. In addition, corn bread or corn dodgers
are fried in another pan. Coleslaw is the usual accompaniment.

"Barbecue" refers to any portion of a pig or hog cooked over the
low heat of slowly burning logs. The meat is brushed with a pungent mixture of butter, vinegar, and pepper. A favorite by-product
of a barbecue is the crisp, brown pork skins.

A chicken stew may be held in the home, at a school or church,
but the most picturesque spot is at a tobacco barn. Tobacco is one
of the leading crops of the state, and when curing time comes, men

have to remain at the tobacco barns night and day, firing the fur-naces with logs. Their "womenfolk" and friends plan chicken stews at the tobacco barns to keep the curers company. The increasing use of oil, instead of wood, for curing tobacco means less attention is required; therefore, fewer tobacco-barn chicken stews.

Possum hunts, threshin's, and Lovefeasts are three additional practices in which groups participate. Opossums are trailed over fields, after the first frost, and trapped by forcing them out on a limb of a tree. A bright light in the opossum's eyes blinds him and makes his capture possible. The opossum is placed in a "tow sack," which is a burlap bag, and carried away to his slaughter. (Ed. note: In parts of the South, the opossum is allowed to gorge himself for a week or so before slaughtering.)

The animal is quite fat. It is prepared like roast pork, and the flavor of the two is similar.

A wide variety of North Europeans settled colonial North Caro-lina. The Moravians, a group of persecuted Protestants from Mo-ravia, in Czechoslovakia, who settled in western North Carolina, practice distinctive food customs. One such is the Lovefeast. On Christmas Eve, New Year's Eve, Good Friday, and on other religious holidays, Moravians have ceremonial Lovefeasts in their churches. The meal served at the Lovefeast consists of a slightly sweet yeast bun and a large white mug of coffee containing cream and sugar.

Moravian Sugar Cake

Makes 2 cakes

1 cup hot mashed potatoes
1 cup granulated sugar
4 tablespoons butter
½ cup shortening
1 teaspoon salt
1 yeast cake
½ cup lukewarm water

2 eggs
4 cups sifted all-purpose flour, or enough to make a soft dough
2 cups brown sugar
4 to 6 tablespoons butter
Cinnamon

ADD sugar, butter, shortening, and salt to hot mashed potatoes. Dissolve yeast cake in lukewarm water and add to potato mixture. Set aside and allow to rise until spongy. Add slightly beaten eggs. Add flour to form a soft dough. Allow to rise overnight, or at least 5 hours. Spread out evenly in flat, buttered pans after kneading lightly on a floured board. Allow to rise again. When light, make holes in the dough, into which put combined butter and brown sugar. Sprinkle surface liberally with cinnamon. Bake in a moderate oven (375 degrees) for 20 minutes, or until golden brown.

Moravian Christmas Cookies

Makes about 12 dozen cookies

7½ cups sifted all-purpose flour
4 tablespoons ground cloves
4 tablespoons ground cinnamon
4 tablespoons ground ginger
1 teaspoon salt
1 tablespoon soda
¼ cup boiling water
¾ cup butter and shortening, mixed
¾ cup brown sugar
1 pint black molasses

SIFT flour together with spices and salt. Put soda in a bowl and pour boiling water over it; cool. Cream shortening and butter; add sugar and molasses.

Add flour and soda mixtures. Work well together with the hands. Cover and allow to stand overnight. Roll very thin on a lightly floured board covered with tightly stretched white material. Some of the old cooks like to cover their rolling pins with stockinet.

Cut out the cookies; place on buttered cooky sheets and bake in a moderate oven (375 degrees) for a very few minutes, or until they begin to brown. Cool and store in a tightly covered can.

Muscadine and scuppernong grapes were once widely grown, but the supply has diminished. Old jam and jelly makers still seek dew-

berries far and wide. A dewberry looks like a blackberry but is larger and redder. The flavor, according to the old-timers, is superior to that of any other berry. Dewberries are also used for pies.

Pork and poultry are served more frequently than other meats because they are produced in greater abundance. Fried chicken is most often floured and fried in a mixture of shortenings, with butter added to facilitate browning. It may be served crisply browned, or steamed by pouring boiling water over the browned pieces and covering tightly. Chicken potpie and chicken with dumplings are two other favorites.

The flavor of North Carolina cured ham differs from the Smithfield of neighboring Virginia and the peanut-flavored ham of Georgia. There is no uniform way of curing North Carolina hams —some are hickory-smoked, others are dry-salt-cured. Ham is usually fried and served with natural "red" gravy. Though grits (coarsely ground hominy) actually belong to South Carolina, they are served in North Carolina with ham and other dishes.

In addition to ham, hog killin' produces other foods—chitterlin's, liver pudding, souse meat, hog jowl. Societies have been formed for the preservation of this practice of eating chitterlings, the entrails of hogs served crisply fried. Liver pudding, made from heads, tails, livers, and hearts, might be called a regional liverwurst. Souse meat is a gelatinous loaf made of the heads, ears, and feet of pigs.

The fat of hogs is rendered into lard. Those crisp bits of fat remaining after the fat has been extracted are called cracklin's. They are added to corn-bread batter to make Cracklin' Corn Bread.

Corn, which when fresh is referred to as "roastin' ears," reaches the table in many forms. It may be water-ground into cornmeal; served as creamed corn, corn on the cob, corn pudding; made into lye hominy; and, though stills have long been outlawed, fruit jars of still-made corn "likker" ("white lightnin'") are smuggled down from the hills. Tarheels want their corn bread made without sugar, but prepare corn pudding with almost as much sugar as in a baked custard.

Corn bread, hot biscuits, and hot rolls lead the bread field. Hot biscuits are still made with soda and buttermilk as often as with baking powder. "Light" bread refers to a loaf of yeast bread, home-

made or store bought. The smell of salt-risin' bread rising and bak-ing is one not easily forgotten.

Salt-Rising Bread

This recipe proves that the old folks had more time to spend in their kitchens than do the 1952 vintage of homemakers.

Makes 3 to 4 loaves

3 medium white potatoes	2 cups lukewarm milk
2 tablespoons sugar	¼ teaspoon soda
3 tablespoons cornmeal	Flour—be sure you have plenty
1 teaspoon salt	4 tablespoons shortening
4 cups boiling water	

PEEL and slice potatoes and place in a large mixing bowl. Add sugar, cornmeal, and salt. Pour boiling water over the mixture. Cover with a dish towel and place in a pan of hot water. Keep the water hot under the bowl by keeping on the lowest heat of the stove for 24 hours. Near the end of this time, the odor of fermenta-tion will be evident and little bubbles will form on the surface.

At the end of the 24 hours, remove the potatoes. Add lukewarm milk, soda, and enough sifted flour to make a stiff sponge. A large amount of flour is required. Put the mixture back into the large mixing bowl over hot water for 2 to 2½ hours, or until light.

In another large bowl cut shortening into 2 cups sifted flour. Add previous mixture and sufficient additional flour to make a soft dough. Knead lightly and quickly so that the dough will stay warm.

Shape into loaves and place in greased pans (four small loaf pans or three large ones). Grease tops. Allow to remain in a warm place until doubled in bulk. Bake at 375 degrees for 10 minutes, then reduce temperature to 350 degrees and bake until the crust is golden brown and shrinks from the sides of the pan.

"Soppin' " is a favorite table exercise. Both 'lasses and ham gravy are sopped with bread. " 'lasses" usually refers to sorghum, a honey-

blond-colored syrup with a malty flavor, made from sugar cane, which is a member of the maize family. The sorghum cane differs from that used for commercial syrup and sugar.

Greens of all kinds, except beet and dandelion, are served. The list includes turnip greens (turnip "salat"), collards, mustard, kale, poke, and "cressies" (cress that grows on land instead of water).

Greens, dried beans, fresh and dried black-eyed peas, cabbage, corn, and green beans (snaps) are seasoned with fat back (salt pork). With cabbage and corn, for instance, the salt pork is fried slowly and the drippings are poured over the cooked vegetables, with the crisp pork served separately. Cabbage is frequently served fried in drippings. Vegetables requiring long cooking are boiled with a hunk of salt pork.

The art of cooking vegetables with salt pork for several hours, until only a small quantity of liquid (pot likker) remains, is one lost to young cooks; for the sake of vitamin content, this may be just as well. Old folks claim that weak babies fare well on pot likker.

Green beans (field beans) or black-eyed peas are often planted in the same hills with corn. The corn stalks provide poles for the running beans or peas. When both are mature, they are cooked together. "Succotash" includes green beans and corn, as well as lima beans (butter beans) and corn. Green peas are still called "English" peas, and "creamed" potatoes are mashed potatoes.

Fried apple rings, especially early May and June green apples, are browned in drippings and served as a vegetable or meat accompaniment. Fried tomato slices with cream gravy are also popular.

Okra and yellow summer squash or patty-pan squash are stewed or fried. Hubbard squash is infrequently seen on the market, and zucchini never appears. Garden lettuce is served wilted with bacon drippings and vinegar or a mixture of vinegar and sugar.

Persimmon pudding is the dessert most characteristic of the region. Our fruits are much smaller than the Japanese variety. Persimmons are deep orange in color and only about 1½ inches in diameter. They cannot be eaten until after the first killing frosts. Before this time, they pucker the insides of the mouth.

Other regional desserts include strawberry pie, muscadine grape pie, dewberry or blackberry pie, hypocrite pie, rhubarb (pieplant) pie, and fried or halfmoon pies.

A hypocrite pie is one in which an unbaked pie shell is partially filled with cooked dried peaches or apples, mashed and sweetened. Over the fruit is poured a mixture of milk, sugar, and eggs, which, when the pie is baked, becomes a custard.

Fried or halfmoon pies are also made from cooked dried peaches or apples, mashed and sweetened. One half of a circle of uncooked pastry is covered with the fruit pulp. The other half is folded over the fruit and the edges pressed together with the fingers or a fork. The pie is fried in fat about 1 inch deep, in a heavy skillet until brown on both sides. It is best served hot.

An old-fashioned cook never sets her table without adding an assortment of sweets to spread on hot breads, and pickles to accentuate the flavors of other foods. The favorite sweets are honey served in the comb, sorghum, damson plum preserves, strawberry jam, and dewberry jam or jelly. Pickles include sweet pickled peaches, pickled root artichokes, green-tomato pickles, pickled green peppers stuffed with raw pickled cabbage, watermelon rind sweet pickles, chowchow, and grape-leaf pickles.

North Dakota

Sally Glein

GRAND FORKS HERALD
GRAND FORKS, NORTH DAKOTA

Norwegian Julekake

Makes 3 or 4 loaves (serves 15 to 20 or more)

⅓ cup sugar
1 teaspoon salt
1 teaspoon crushed cardamon seed
2 cups milk, scalded
1 yeast cake mixed with ¼ cup warm water

4 cups flour
¼ cup butter or margarine
1 cup raisins
1 cup currants
1 cup finely cut citron
Flour
Melted butter

PLACE sugar, salt, and cardamon seed in a bowl, and add the scalded milk. When lukewarm, add yeast cake mixture and flour, and beat thoroughly. Cover and let rise until doubled in bulk. Beat again, add butter, the fruit drenched with flour, and enough flour to knead. Let rise again until doubled in bulk. Shape into round loaves and place in greased tins. Brush loaves with melted butter or milk. Let rise again until doubled in bulk, and bake in a moderate oven (350 degrees) about 45 minutes.

Bord Stabler (Lumber Pile)

Makes about 50 cookies

1 cup butter	3 tablespoons cream
1 cup sugar	4 cups sifted flour
3 eggs, beaten	

CREAM the butter, add the sugar gradually, then the beaten eggs, cream, and sifted flour. Roll as for cookies, very thin, cut into strips 1¼ inches by 4 inches. Place on a greased and lightly floured cooky sheet. Bake in a slow oven (about 325 degrees). Do not overbake, as these are put into the oven a second time. Spread with a thin layer of almond paste and return to the oven just long enough to dry out the paste.

Almond Paste:

3 egg whites	1¼ cups blanched, ground
1¼ cups sugar	almonds

BEAT egg whites until stiff and dry. Add almonds and sugar, and mix well. Spread on the cookies as directed.

Kris Kringle Cookies

Makes about 50

1 cup shortening	1 teaspoon baking powder
⅔ cup white sugar	1 teaspoon vanilla
1 egg	½ teaspoon salt
3 cups flour	

CREAM shortening, add sugar and egg, and beat well. Add remaining ingredients. Make into a roll. Chill. Slice ¼ inch thick and place on an ungreased cooky sheet. Bake in a hot oven (375 to 400 degrees) for 15 minutes or until light brown.

Fattigmann

Makes 50 to 60

10 eggs, separated
4 tablespoons sugar
5 tablespoons thick sweet
cream

Cardamon to taste
Pinch of salt
3¾ cups flour (about)
Powdered sugar

BEAT egg yolks until light, add sugar, cream, cardamon, and salt.
Add stiffly beaten egg whites and enough flour to make a dough.
Chill; roll thin; cut into pieces 4 by 1½ inches with a fattigmann
cutter, pastry wheel, or knife. Cut a gash through the center of
each strip, pull one end through the gash, and fry in deep hot fat
like doughnuts. Drain; sprinkle with powdered sugar while warm.

Norwegian Fruit Soup

Serves 6 to 8

2 quarts water
1 cup sugar
1 cup dried prunes

½ cup sago
½ cup raisins
2 cinnamon sticks

BOIL slowly for 1 hour, or until prunes are well done. Serve either
hot or cold with small sweet rusks.

Rullepolse

Serves 8 generously

5 pounds beef or mutton
flank
2 pounds lean pork
Salt, pepper

Ginger
Allspice
Onion
Bouillon or stock

CUT sinews and fat from the flank and divide into convenient
pieces. Cut the pork into strips. Lay them on the flank and sea-

son with the spices and chopped onion. Roll tightly, sew up with strong cord, and wind a cord around to hold it together when being cooked. Simmer in bouillon or stock 1 to 1½ hours. Place under a heavy weight while cooling. Cut into thin slices for serving.

Norwegian Fish Soup

Serves 4

2 carrots	1 tablespoon flour, mixed
1 onion	with a little cold milk
2 parsnips	1 tablespoon butter
Salt	½ cup sour cream
1 pound fish (salmon is good)	Pepper

BOIL carrots, onion, parsnips, and salt in 3 pints water for 20 to 30 minutes, then put in fish. Let boil a few minutes. Remove fish and save it for a salad or entrée. Add flour to soup, cook a few minutes, then add butter. Place on a low flame and beat in sour cream and pepper.

Berliner-Kranser

4 egg yolks, well beaten	1½ cups (3 ¼-pound sticks)
1 cup sugar	butter
3 hard-boiled egg yolks,	2 egg whites, slightly beaten
crumbled	Crushed loaf sugar or chopped
6 cups flour	almonds

MIX beaten egg yolks with sugar and hard-boiled egg yolks. With your hands work in the flour and the butter alternately, a little bit at a time. Chill the dough. Roll into rolls about the thickness of a pencil and 5 inches long. Form into wreaths. Dip into slightly beaten egg whites and sprinkle either with crushed loaf sugar or chopped almonds. Bake in a medium oven (350 degrees) until light brown.

Ohio

THE CINCINNATI ENQUIRER

CINCINNATI, OHIO

Cincinnati is neither East nor West, North nor South, but just on the borderline. There was a time when Cincinnati was noted for its typically German food, originating with the many Germans who settled here in the mid-nineteenth century. But even this strong influence has faded out, and we find that Cincinnati's food likes and dislikes are comparable to those of most urban centers.

Sour Noodles

Serves 6

1 8-ounce package finely cut noodles
1 pint sour cream
1 pint cottage cheese
2 eggs, beaten
Salt and pepper to taste
Butter

COOK noodles until just tender in 1 quart of boiling, salted water. Drain. Combine with sour cream, cottage cheese, well-beaten eggs, and seasonings. Place in a buttered baking dish and dot with small pieces of butter. Set dish in a pan of water and bake in a moderate oven (350 degrees) 1 hour. Traditionally served with stewed chicken.

Stuffed Cabbage Leaves

Serves 8

1 large head cabbage	1 tablespoon chopped parsley
6 mushrooms	2 cups fresh bread crumbs
Butter	Few chopped chives
2 pounds sausage meat	1 teaspoon thyme
1 onion, chopped	2 teaspoons salt
1 or 2 eggs	1 pint chicken broth

REMOVE heart from the head of cabbage and steam for a few minutes, until the leaves become loosened. To make the stuffing, brown mushrooms in a little butter and combine with other ingredients. Season large leaves of cabbage with salt and pepper. Put 3 tablespoons of stuffing on each leaf—you will need about twenty-four leaves. Roll, secure with toothpicks, and put in a baking pan. Bake in a hot oven (450 degrees) for 45 minutes to 1 hour, and serve with brown sauce.

Yorkshire Lamb Hotpot

Serves 6

6 shoulder lamb chops	½ teaspoon salt
3½ tablespoons butter	⅛ teaspoon black pepper
4 cups milk, scalded	2 tablespoons flour
12 small white onions	Parsley for garnish
12 small potatoes	

TRIM off excess fat from chops and brown in 1½ tablespoons butter in a heavy frying pan; add milk, onions, potatoes, salt, and pepper. Cover and simmer about 30 minutes, or until vegetables are soft.

Arrange chops, onions, and potatoes on a hot platter, and serve with gravy made by thickening liquid in the pan with a *roux* of 2 tablespoons butter and flour. Garnish with parsley.

Sauerbraten and Noodles

Serves 6 to 8

4 pounds beef: chuck, rump, or round
Salt and pepper
1 onion, sliced
3 bay leaves
1 teaspoon peppercorns
¼ cup raisins

Vinegar and water (equal parts if vinegar is mild; 1 to 2 if vinegar is strong)
4 to 6 gingersnaps
1 cup thick sour cream (optional)
¼ cup sugar

SPRINKLE meat well with salt and pepper and rub in thoroughly. Place in deep earthen dish, with onion, bay leaves, and peppercorns. Heat enough water and vinegar to cover the meat, and add salt and sugar to taste. Pour hot over the meat. Cover dish well, put in a cool place or a refrigerator, and let stand 8 days.

Put meat in a kettle, add onion and a little of the spiced vinegar, and place in a hot oven to brown all over. Then put on a tight-fitting cover and cook slowly about 3 hours, or until tender. Add more of the spiced vinegar if the meat starts to dry out. Take out the meat, slice for serving, and keep hot. Strain liquid in the kettle, skim off fat. Let ¼ cup sugar melt in an iron skillet, add the strained liquid very gradually, then the raisins and gingersnaps; cook until thickened and smooth, and pour while hot over the meat. For added flavor, add thick sour cream to the gravy. Serve with buttered noodles.

Elizabeth S. Collis

THE CINCINNATI POST
CINCINNATI, OHIO

Cheese Cake

Cheese Cake is one of the most popular recipes from this vicinity. This recipe appeared in the Post's *"The Male in the Kitchen" column, written weekly by Jerry Ransohoff, a member of our staff.*

Serves 10

30 single graham crackers	¾ cup sugar
¼ pound butter or margarine, melted	½ cup milk
1 pint cottage cheese	3 eggs, separated
Pinch of salt	1 teaspoon vanilla
1 teaspoon lemon juice	Graham crackers

GRIND the thirty graham crackers to a fairly fine powder. Add melted butter or margarine, working resulting mixture into a dough. Place dough in the bottom and along the sides of a low, rectangular baking dish.

Mash cottage cheese until curds are broken up. Add salt, lemon juice, sugar, and milk. Beat ingredients together until the cheese has been reduced to the consistency of whipping cream.

Beat egg yolks slightly; add to cheese mixture; add vanilla. Whip whites of eggs until stiff. Fold whites into cheese mixture. Pour on top of graham-cracker crust. Sprinkle with a handful of crushed, dry graham crackers. Bake in 350-degree oven for 1 hour.

When cake is baked, remove from the oven and cool slowly so that it will not fall. When cool, place in the refrigerator to chill thoroughly.

Spoon Bread

Cincinnati inevitably shares some of the food preferences of nearby Kentucky.

Serves 6 to 8

1 pint boiling water
1 pint cornmeal (Kentuckians use only white, water-ground meal)
½ teaspoon salt

1 large tablespoon butter or margarine
2 eggs, separated
1 pint sweet milk

POUR boiling water over cornmeal. Add salt, then butter or margarine. Add beaten yolks of eggs to milk. Blend thoroughly and turn into cornmeal mixture. Beat whites of eggs until stiff. Fold into mixture. Pour into buttered pan or casserole and bake 30 minutes in a moderate oven (350 degrees), or until spoon bread is firm in the center. Serve from the pan.

Transparent Pudding

Makes 2 puddings

1 cup butter or margarine
2 cups sugar
2 tablespoons flour
1 cup rich milk

4 eggs, separated
1 teaspoon vanilla
½ cup jelly or preserves
Rich, unbaked piecrusts

CREAM butter and sugar together. Add flour and milk. Beat yolks of eggs and add to mixture. Beat vigorously. Add vanilla and jelly or preserves. Beat egg whites until stiff and fold into mixture last. Pour into unbaked pie shells and bake in a moderate oven (350 degrees) until firm and browned on the top.

These may be baked as individual puddings by lining shallow muffin tins with piecrust.

Sarah MacDuff Austin

CINCINNATI TIMES-STAR
CINCINNATI, OHIO

Goette

This is sometimes spelled ghetta, or getta. It's a form of scrapple popular in Cincinnati; nice for breakfast.

Serves about 10

3 pounds lean pork
3 quarts water
1 pound rolled oats

1 teaspoon salt
⅛ teaspoon pepper

ADD water to meat and simmer until tender. Remove meat and chop it very fine. Slowly add oats to boiling broth, with more water if the mixture gets thick. Add meat and seasonings. Cook slowly for about an hour. Turn into a loaf pan; chill; slice in ½-inch slices. Roll in flour and brown both sides on a greased griddle.

Pineapple Cheese Cake

Serves 10

4 eggs, separated
1 cup sugar
¼ teaspoon salt
2½ cups fine cottage cheese
1 cup light cream

1 cup crushed pineapple
2 tablespoons lemon juice
2 teaspoons grated lemon
   rind
Zwieback crust

BEAT egg yolks until thick and light-colored. Add sugar and salt gradually, beating thoroughly. Fold in cottage cheese, cream, and pineapple. Add lemon juice and rind. Fold in stiffly beaten egg whites. Pour into prepared crust and bake at 325 degrees about

1 hour. Let cool in oven with door open and heat off to prevent falling.

Zwieback Crust:

2 cups zwieback crumbs
¼ cup sugar

¼ cup melted butter or margarine

MIX crumbs with sugar and melted butter. Pat into a well-greased spring form, to form a crust.

Helen Robertson

CLEVELAND PLAIN DEALER
CLEVELAND, OHIO

Dishes made from maple sugar and syrup are among Ohio's specialties. The early spring of the year sees buckets hanging from trees, steam rising from great pans where the sap is being cooked down to syrup and to sugar.

Maple wax was one of the treats of sugar making in the early days. To make it: "Boil maple syrup until thick and waxy, or until it spins a thread. Drop by spoonfuls onto blocks of ice or pans of clean snow. Let stand a few minutes, and you have a waxy, chewy delicacy.". . . Guess what went with this sweet? Dill pickles and/or doughnuts.

There was great rivalry among the guests at a sugaring-off party as to who could make the smoothest maple cream. The syrup, cooked to soft-ball stage, was ladled into saucers or saucedishes, one for each guest. Then came the fun. With small wooden spatula or spoon, each guest stirred her syrup in the manner she thought would give the creamiest candy. Dill pickles were served with this, too.

Maple syrup is perishable, if it is not sealed in sterile jars. Nowadays it is often put into food freezers. There are two definite and iron-clad rules with regard to using maple sugar or syrup in dishes. First, it must never, never be combined with brown sugar; and second, no other flavoring should be used in the recipe. Modern methods have shown that a drop or two of tarragon vinegar added to the maple sauce or other maple dish will enhance the maple flavor.

Maple Dumplings

Serves 4 to 6

1 cup sifted flour
1½ teaspoons baking powder
½ teaspoon salt
⅓ cup milk

3 tablespoons butter or margarine
1 cup maple syrup
½ cup water

SIFT flour, baking powder, and salt, into mixing bowl. Blend in 2 tablespoons butter with a pastry blender or the tips of the fingers. Add milk gradually. Have maple syrup, water, and 1 tablespoon butter boiling in a kettle with a tightly fitting cover. Drop dough into the kettle by small spoonfuls. Cover and cook gently 15 minutes. Serve dumplings with syrup.

Baked Maple Custard

Serves 4

2 cups milk
3 eggs

½ teaspoon salt
1 cup maple syrup

SCALD milk, pour slowly onto eggs beaten with salt and maple syrup. Turn into four or five custard cups that have been rinsed with cold water. Set them in a pan containing 1 inch of hot water. Bake in a moderate oven, 350 degrees, until firm, about 1 hour. If a silver knife inserted into one of the custards comes out clean, the custard is done.

Maple Gingerbread

Makes 1 pan of gingerbread

¼ cup shortening	½ teaspoon soda
1 cup maple syrup	1 teaspoon ginger
1 egg	½ cup sour milk
2 cups sifted flour	½ lemon, rind and juice
½ teaspoon salt	

CREAM shortening until of whipped-cream consistency. Add maple syrup slowly, blending it in well. Add beaten egg. Sift flour with salt, soda, and ginger. Add to first mixture alternately with sour milk. Add lemon juice and grated rind. Turn into a well-greased, shallow pan 8 by 12 inches, or into individual cupcake pans, and bake in a moderate oven, 350 degrees, 50 minutes for the large cake or 25 minutes for the cupcakes. Remove from oven, let stand a few minutes, then remove from pans. Frost with a cream-cheese frosting.

Frances LaGanke Harris

THE CLEVELAND PRESS
CLEVELAND, OHIO

When the sons of early settlers in New England felt cramped and closed in and the men decided to "go West," many of them settled in northern Ohio, the part called Western Reserve for many years. Thus we acquired New England and Old England dishes.

Kentucky settlers were restless, too. They migrated to Ohio, bringing with them Southern cooking.

Germans too, found the land around Cincinnati to their liking. French people came up as far as Marietta, bringing combinations of the delicious Creole and the subtle French foods.

Indians taught us, as well as people in other regions, to enjoy succotash, pumpkins, and parched corn. We still use variations of the recipes they gave us.

Southern European families came over to work in the mines of Pennsylvania. They wandered across the border to Ohio to work in our mines and steel mills. They brought myriads of foreign recipes.

And so it goes. Ohio, like most Midwestern states, has been the stopping-off place for people from so many lands that we have made our cooking a nationality hash. But by and large it's good!

Vanocka (Christmas Twist or Braid)

½ cup butter
4 cups flour
½ cup sugar
½ teaspoon salt
1 teaspoon grated lemon rind
1 cake yeast
2 tablespoons flour
1 tablespoon sugar
3 tablespoons milk

2 egg yolks
1 cup milk
⅓ cup raisins
¼ cup blanched almonds
2 tablespoons citron, cut fine
1 egg
Additional almonds for
    topping

WORK butter into 4 cups flour, as for piecrust. Add ½ cup sugar, salt, and lemon rind.

Mix crumbled yeast with 2 tablespoons flour, 1 tablespoon sugar, and 3 tablespoons milk. When bubbles form, add to the first mixture. Add egg yolks to 1 cup milk. Combine with first ingredients.

Knead the dough on a bread board about 20 to 30 minutes. Add raisins, almonds, and citron. Put the dough in a pan, cover, and let rise for 2 hours.

Divide the dough into nine parts. Make of each part a strand about 14 inches long. Make a braid with four pieces and put it on a baking sheet covered with a buttered piece of paper. On this braid put another braid made of three pieces; and finally the two remaining pieces of dough, twisted together.

Beat the egg well and brush the dough with it. Let rise 1½ hours. Brush again with beaten egg and sprinkle with more chopped almonds. Bake in a moderate oven (350 degrees) for 75 minutes.

Raspberry Shrub

A refreshing, old-fashioned drink that has long been popular during hot Cincinnati summers.

4 quarts red raspberries   2 cups cider vinegar
Sugar

PUT berries in a colander, wash lightly with cold water; drain. Spread on a large enameled tray. (The enameled drip pan of the stove is excellent.) Set in a cool oven, not more than 250 degrees. After the berries have been in for 10 minutes, pull the tray out and mash them lightly with a spoon. Put tray back in the oven for 30 minutes. The heat should be so low that it does nothing but set the juice to running.

Put fruit in a jelly bag. Squeeze out juice; measure. Measure one-quarter as many cups of sugar as of juice. Boil sugar and juice for 15 minutes. Add vinegar. Boil 10 minutes longer. Pour into hot, clean jars, capping with sterilized rubber rings and tops.

Before serving, dilute the juice with cold water and chipped ice, using one-third shrub and two-thirds water. Serve in 8- to 10-ounce glasses.

Hasenpfeffer

Serves 2 or 3

Hare or rabbit   1 large bay leaf
Vinegar   Salt
Water   Pepper
3 slices onion   Shortening
12 whole cloves   Sour cream

SKIN rabbit; clean well. Rub with a damp cloth and cut into serving pieces. Arrange pieces in an earthenware bowl. Cover with equal parts of vinegar and water. Add onion slices, cloves, bay leaf, salt, and pepper. Leave the pieces of rabbit in this liquid for 2 days, turning frequently and keeping them covered with the liquid.

Remove meat. Sear in fat, turning meat to brown it on all sides. Pour off the fat. Pour in just enough of the spice mixture to cover the meat. Allow it to simmer, covered, for about 1 hour, or until the meat is tender. When ready to serve, remove the bay leaf, stir in sour cream and bring to a rapid boil.

Cumberland Sauce for Roast Duck

Sauce for one duck

¼ cup currant jelly
2 tablespoons orange juice
1 tablespoon lemon juice
1 teaspoon prepared mustard
1 teaspoon paprika
1 teaspoon ginger
Grated rind of 1 orange
2 tablespoons sherry

MIX ingredients. Heat over low fire until the jelly melts. Serve cold. Add sherry just before serving.

Betty Montei

THE COLUMBUS DISPATCH
COLUMBUS, OHIO

Columbus, Ohio, doesn't seem to have any typical foods—our dishes are just good eating (at least we like them) and have been gathered from all parts of the country and world. We love our fresh corn on the cob—but then there are states more typically corn-raising than Ohio. Dairy products are abundant—yet we're not a famous dairy state. And so the list goes.

Chicken and Rice Casserole

We like casserole dishes—and of course chicken is an all-time favorite.

Serves 6

3 cups cooked chicken, cut
  into medium-sized pieces
1 cup cooked rice
1½ tablespoons chopped
  parsley
1½ tablespoons chopped
  pimiento
1 teaspoon salt

⅛ teaspoon pepper
3 eggs, slightly beaten
1½ cups seasoned chicken
  stock
1 tablespoon melted butter or
  margarine
1 cup oven-popped rice cereal

COMBINE chicken, rice, parsley, and pimiento. Stir in salt, pepper, and slightly beaten eggs. Mix carefully. Heat chicken stock and add to chicken mixture, stirring constantly. Pour into a greased casserole. Mix melted butter and cereal together and sprinkle over top of dish. Bake in moderate oven (350 degrees) for 50 minutes.

Cherry-Coconut Cake

Makes 2-layer, 8-inch cake

½ cup shortening
1½ cups sugar
2⅓ cups flour
3 teaspoons baking powder
¼ teaspoon salt
¼ cup maraschino cherry
  liquid

½ cup milk
½ teaspoon vanilla
16 maraschino cherries, cut
  fine
½ cup chopped walnuts
4 egg whites

CREAM shortening and sugar until fluffy and light. Sift together flour, baking powder, and salt. Combine cherry liquid, milk, and vanilla. Add the flour mixture in thirds, alternating with the milk mixture, to the creamed shortening and sugar, beating smooth after each addition. Fold in cherries and nuts. Beat egg whites until stiff and fold into cake mixture. Bake in two greased 8-inch layer-cake pans in a moderately hot oven (375 degrees) for 30 to 35 minutes.

Fluffy Boiled Frosting:

1 cup sugar	1 teaspoon vanilla
⅓ cup water	¼ teaspoon salt
⅛ teaspoon cream of tartar	Shredded coconut
2 egg whites	

MAKE a syrup of sugar, water, and cream of tartar, cooking until it spins a thread. While this is cooking beat egg whites until stiff. Pour syrup slowly over egg whites and beat until frosting holds its shape. Add vanilla and salt. Frost the cooled cake and sprinkle with coconut.

Soft Gingerbread

In our recipe collection is a well-thumbed and very tattered little book that has a most important role as a source of good recipes. It was published by the old First United Presbyterian Church, probably about 35 years ago. Above the name "Mrs. J. S. Quigley" is the soft-gingerbread recipe that we have used for years. Only the list of ingredients is given, but at the Dispatch kitchen we have worked out these directions.

Serves 8 to 10

½ cup shortening	½ teaspoon salt
½ cup sugar	1 teaspoon ground cinnamon
2 eggs, well beaten	1 teaspoon ground cloves
1 cup dark molasses	1 teaspoon ground ginger
2½ cups sifted all-purpose flour	2 teaspoons baking soda
	1 cup boiling water

CREAM together shortening and sugar until light and fluffy. Stir in eggs and molasses. Sift together flour, salt, and spices. Dissolve baking soda in boiling water; add to the molasses mixture alternately with the sifted flour and spices. Stir well.

Pour into a well-greased pan 12 by 7½ by 2 inches, and bake in a 350-degree oven for 50 to 55 minutes, or until done. Cut into squares and serve hot with lots of rich, fluffy, whipped cream.

Marj Heyduck (Mrs. E. C. Heyduck)

THE DAYTON JOURNAL HERALD
DAYTON, OHIO

Folks in Dayton like plain, but good, food. They order seafood, Chinese, Hungarian, or Italian foods when they eat out. But at home they choose fried chicken or steak, with buttermilk pineapple ice for dessert. Youngsters, in for television or dancing, or Pop's poker club favor Mom's open-face hamburgers.

The whole family likes creamed onion soup with croutons, the way Mom makes it. Or, if they're cooking for themselves, they open a can of tomato soup, add a can of whole milk, serve it in mugs, and eat handfuls of popcorn on the side. Mom also uses cream of tomato soup for quick company luncheons, with popcorn sprinkled on top instead of croutons.

Pineapple Ice

And you can't taste the buttermilk in it!

Serves 4

2 cups buttermilk	1 teaspoon vanilla
1 cup sugar	1 egg white
1 small can crushed pineapple	

MIX together all ingredients but egg white. Freeze until mushy. Fold in stiffly beaten egg white. Return to freezing unit for 1 hour or more.

Open-Face Hamburgers

Serves 4

1 pound ground beef	1½ teaspoons Worcestershire
⅓ cup chili sauce	sauce
1½ teaspoons horseradish	1 teaspoon pepper
1½ teaspoons dry mustard	1 teaspoon minced onion
1 teaspoon salt	

MIX together all ingredients. Spread on buns. Place under broiler for 5 to 6 minutes.
(Ed. note: These will be hot—very hot.)

Elizabeth Alden

THE TOLEDO BLADE
TOLEDO, OHIO

Pumpkin—squash, how many people know the difference between the two? There is only one means of differentiation, by the stem. The pumpkin stem is serrated and hard, that of the squash, round and soft. Strange as it may seem, most of the canned pumpkin purchased for pie is really squash.

Because of the rich, black, sandy loam soil of Ohio, and the longer growing season created by the proximity of Lake Erie, this state is one of the largest squash-growing centers of the country. Of the more than sixty known varieties of squash and pumpkins, Ohio farmers grow twenty-five. Blue Hubbards, Butternuts, and Delicious are the three types most popular with consumers.

Baked Stuffed Acorn Squash

Serves 6

3 acorn squash
2 cups ground, cooked ham
2 cups cooked rice
3 tablespoons minced onion

2 drops Tabasco sauce
1 teaspoon Worcestershire
sauce
Buttered crumbs

SPLIT squash and remove seeds. Combine all of the above ingredients except buttered crumbs. Fill cavities of squash with mixture and sprinkle with buttered crumbs. Bake in a 400-degree oven for 45 minutes.

Note: Hubbard squash can be baked in this same way, first cutting the squash in six pieces.

Squash Pie

Makes 2 medium-sized or 1 large pie

Pastry
3 eggs
1½ cups mashed, cooked
squash
⅔ cup brown sugar
½ teaspoon salt

½ teaspoon ground cloves
¼ teaspoon ground ginger
1¼ teaspoon ground cinna-
mon
½ teaspoon ground nutmeg
1¼ to 1½ cups milk

PARTIALLY bake pastry crust. Beat eggs slightly. Mix squash with sugar and spices and add to beaten eggs. Add milk and pour into partly cooked crust. Bake in a slow oven (300 to 325 degrees) until the center of the filling is firm. Cool; serve with whipped cream.

The consistency of this pie may be varied by separating egg yolks and whites. Beat egg whites until stiff and fold into mixed ingredients just before pouring into pastry crust. This makes a lighter pie filling.

Oklahoma

Pearl Adsit

THE TULSA TRIBUNE
TULSA, OKLAHOMA

Lime-Milk Sherbet

Here is a simple recipe for lime sherbet that should appeal to all who are watching waistlines. Serve it plain or with sweetened sliced peaches or frozen strawberries.

Makes about 1 quart

1 package lime gelatin (or any desired flavor)
1 cup hot water
1½ cups sugar
Dash of salt
Juice of 2 lemons
1 quart milk

DISSOLVE gelatin in hot water and add sugar, salt, and lemon juice. Cool. When thick and ropy, beat with a rotary beater until foamy and fluffy. Add milk, turn into automatic refrigerator tray, and freeze. Turn control to highest point and allow the sherbet to freeze very rapidly. Stir once during the freezing process. As soon as it is frozen, lower the temperature to normal and let stand until ready to serve.

Red Chili Sauce

Chili sauce that's really red, and really a sauce instead of a relish.

Makes about 4 quarts

1 peck ripe tomatoes, peeled and diced

6 medium or 12 small onions, ground

1 large or 2 small cloves garlic, ground

2 small (2-inch) hot red peppers, ground

6 sweet red peppers, ground

3 tablespoons salt

2 cups best grade white pickling vinegar

1½ tablespoons paprika

1 tablespoon whole allspice

1 tablespoon whole cloves

2 packages red cinnamon candies (2 cups)

1 bottle favorite commercial brand chili sauce

COMBINE tomatoes with ground vegetables and cook until smooth and rather thick. Add all other ingredients, putting cloves and allspice in a cheesecloth bag large enough so spices can circulate freely. Cook to desired thickness, add commercial brand chili sauce for that hard-to-get flavor, and seal while hot.

To prevent scorching and still avoid constant stirring, cook this sauce in the oven. Regulate the oven temperature so the sauce just bubbles gently.

Oregon

Nancy Morris

PORTLAND OREGONIAN

PORTLAND, OREGON

Oregon fruits—pears, apples, and prunes—are probably the best known of our excellent foods. Equally delicious, though, are Columbia River salmon and smelt, Olympia oysters, plump razor clams, and Oregon filberts. There are wonderful wild ducks and venison to be had during the hunting season, too.

Probably our most unusual fish is the smelt. Every year there is a smelt run in the Columbia River, and most years in its tributaries, too. As the smelt swim in huge, unbelievable masses up the river, everyone goes to the banks armed with fish nets, butterfly nets, bird cages, and whatever else will hold the wriggly little fish. When the family has eaten its fill, freezing, canning, and pickling begin. To eat at the table, the fish are most often fried like small mountain trout, baked in milk, or broiled.

Though there is good salmon in other parts of the world, almost everyone agrees that Columbia River salmon is the best of all. Mostly it is eaten fried or baked, sometimes with a dill-flavored cracker stuffing, for which the recipe is given.

Our clams are unusual in size, shape, and variety. There are tiny butter clams, razor clams (so-called because they are sharp-edged and shaped like a razor hone), and geoduck (pronounced goo-y-duck) that are extra large, delicious, and shaped rather like a duck. For all-around good eating the razor clams are most popular because they are just the right size for frying whole and can be obtained easily at fish markets. They make wonderful fritters and casserole dishes.

Oregonians love their fruits, most of which are available in one variety or another all year long. Probably the best of all are the tart, crisp, and juicy summer apples that make applesauce a dish for a king. Winter apples, while not as crisp, are delicious and find their way into wonderful-to-eat things such as Raw-Apple Cake.

Pears are so plentiful that not only are they a favorate fruit eaten whole or in salads, but they are used in cooking, much as apples are. Prunes—we all call them that, though they are really the Italian plums that are familiar the world over in their dried stage—are a delicacy used in cakes, pies, jams, butters, and even pickles.

Oregon can claim filberts almost exclusively. They are similar to the hazelnut but are bigger and have a more buttery flavor. We enjoy them not only in nut bread, nut cakes, nut tortes, but in practically everything.

Orange Sugared Filberts

These candy-coated nuts are usually made at Christmas, but taste good any time.

1½ cups sugar
3 tablespoons orange juice
½ teaspoon grated orange
  rind

¼ cup water
2½ cups blanched or toasted
  filberts or other nuts

COMBINE sugar, orange juice and rind, and water. Stir until sugar is dissolved. Cook slowly over low heat until a small amount tested in cold water forms a soft ball (236 degrees). Stir occasionally to prevent burning. Remove from heat. Add filberts and stir until the coating is creamy and loses its gloss. Turn out immediately on waxed paper and separate nuts from one another very quickly.

Baked Stuffed Salmon

Serves 10 or more

1 large piece fresh salmon, about 5 pounds	1 bay leaf, crushed
Salt	½ teaspoon Worcestershire sauce
Lemon juice	2 tablespoons chopped dill pickle
3 cups cracker crumbs, coarsely crushed	2 tablespoons chopped celery
4 tablespoons melted shortening	1 onion, chopped
½ teaspoon salt	1 clove garlic, chopped
2 tablespoons dill pickle juice	1 blade dry sage, crushed, or ½ teaspoon dried sage

RUB fish well inside and out with salt. Sprinkle with lemon juice. Combine all stuffing ingredients and pile into fish. Sew together, if desired. Place fish on a rack in a shallow pan. Bake, uncovered, at 500 degrees, allowing 10 minutes per pound.

(Ed. note: Any of this that is left over will not go to waste. It makes wonderful salads or casserole dishes.)

Clam Fritters

Serves 4 to 6

1½ cups ground clams	2 eggs, beaten
1½ cups coarsely crushed crackers	1 teaspoon salt

COMBINE all ingredients. Drop by spoonfuls into a skillet containing a little hot fat. Fry on both sides until browned.

French Pear Pie

This is a dessert known only to Westerners.

Unbaked 9-inch pie shell	½ teaspoon ginger
6 cups sliced pears	½ cup butter or margarine
Juice of 1 lemon	½ cup brown sugar
⅔ cup sugar	1 cup sifted flour

CHILL pie shell. Sprinkle pears with lemon juice. Add sugar and ginger. Place in pie shell. Combine remaining ingredients, cutting in butter with knives or a pastry blender, as for pastry. Sprinkle over the pears. Bake at 450 degrees for 10 minutes. Reduce heat to 350 degrees and bake 35 minutes.

Raw-Apple Cake

¼ cup butter or margarine	1 teaspoon nutmeg
1 cup sugar	¼ teaspoon salt
1 egg	1½ cups grated raw apples
1 cup flour	½ cup chopped nuts
1 teaspoon soda	½ cup raisins
1 teaspoon cinnamon	

CREAM butter and sugar. Add egg and sifted dry ingredients. Add apples, nuts, and raisins. Bake in a buttered cake pan, 9 by 13 inches, at 350 degrees for 50 to 60 minutes.

Cathrine C. Laughton

OREGON JOURNAL
PORTLAND, OREGON

Walnut Butter Balls

Makes 3 to 4 dozen cookies

1 cup butter
4 to 6 tablespoons sugar
2 cups sifted flour
1 teaspoon vanilla

2 cups finely chopped walnuts
Powdered sugar

CREAM butter, add sugar, and blend well. Add flour; knead to make a smooth dough. Add walnuts and vanilla. Break off small portions of dough and shape into balls the size of small walnuts. Place on a buttered cooky sheet and bake in a moderately hot oven (400 degrees) for about 10 minutes, or until done. Take from pan and roll in powdered sugar.

Filbert Kisses

Makes 1½ to 2 dozen kisses

2 egg whites
1 cup white sugar or
    1¼ cups brown sugar
¼ teaspoon salt

1 teaspoon vanilla or
    lemon juice
1½ cups filberts or walnuts,
    coarsely chopped

BEAT egg whites until just fluffy; beat in half of the sugar. Fold in remaining sugar, then salt, flavoring, and nuts. Push off tip of teaspoon onto a buttered and floured pan. Bake in a moderate oven (350 degrees) for 12 to 20 minutes, or until light yellow. Remove from the pan while warm.

Prune Cake

Serves 8

½ cup shortening
1 cup sugar
2 eggs
½ cup buttermilk or prune
  juice
2 teaspoons single-action, or
  1 teaspoon double-action
  baking powder

2 cups sifted all-purpose flour
½ teaspoon each of soda, salt,
  nutmeg, and cinnamon
1 teaspoon vanilla
1 cup cooked, drained, pitted,
  and chopped prunes
½ cup chopped walnuts or filberts

CREAM shortening, add sugar, and cream until light and fluffy. Add eggs one at a time and beat thoroughly. Add buttermilk or prune juice alternately with sifted dry ingredients. Stir in vanilla, prune pulp, and nuts. Pour into two greased layer-cake pans or a sheet-cake pan about 10 by 12 inches. Bake in a moderate oven (350 degrees) for 25 to 30 minutes.

Pennsylvania

Virginia Cheney

THE PHILADELPHIA INQUIRER

PHILADELPHIA, PENNSYLVANIA

Chester County, due west of Philadelphia and bordering it, is the largest mushroom-growing area in this country. Other sections of the country are now raising mushrooms, but for many years Chester has been the mushroom capital of the United States.

The first mushrooms to be raised commercially were imported from England. The industry here got its start when a local florist, who planted mushrooms in his greenhouse under the tables that held his flower plants, found that the darkness and heat, plus our special type of light soil, were all that were needed to start the mushroom growing industry.

Because mushrooms are very sensitive to heat, we used to have fresh mushrooms only during the cold months. However, some growers, who have air-conditioned their buildings, are now producing fresh mushrooms the year round.

Fishhouse Punch

Fishhouse punch is one of the oldest and most famous of punches, as delicate as it is potent. It originated in the State in Schuylkill, the oldest social club in continuous operation. The club was organ-

ized in 1732 as the Colony of the State in Schuylkill Fishing Club, with a charter similar to that of the Colony of Pennsylvania. When the Colonies declared their independence, the club was reorganized as the State in Schuylkill.

The club's membership, limited to thirty, is distinguished and exclusive. Each member must become an expert cook and be able to prepare and serve a meal worthy of the club's tradition. A toast in Fishhouse Punch is always drunk to the State in Schuylkill, and after dinner a rising toast in Madeira is drunk to the memory of George Washington. Both Washington and Lafayette were entertained there. There is a story that Washington noted in his diary that he was on his way to Philadelphia to dine at the State in Schuylkill, after which blank pages appeared for several days.

Makes about 1½ gallons

¾ pound loaf sugar	2 quarts Jamaica rum
2 quarts water	1 quart brandy
1 quart lemon juice	1 wineglass peach brandy

SOAK loaf sugar in a punch bowl in 1 cup of water. Add more if necessary. When entirely dissolved, add lemon juice. Then add all other ingredients. Put a large lump of solid ice in the punch bowl and allow the mixture to ripen for about 2 hours, stirring occasionally. In winter, when ice melts slowly, more water may be used; in summer, less; the melting ice dilutes the mixture sufficiently.

Pepper Pot Soup

Pepper Pot varies in seasonings, but the basic ingredients remain about the same. Tomatoes are sometimes included but they have no right to be in the recipe. This soup was a favorite even in the days when tomatoes were called "love apples" and were strictly a decoration on the mantelpiece. The hot soup was hawked through the streets of early Philadelphia by Negro women; it was sold from a large milk can covered with a white towel.

There is so much work involved in making the soup, most women today buy it already prepared. It is a complete meal in itself, usually served with crusty bread on a cold winter day.

Serves 10 to 12 as a meal in itself

6 to 7 pounds raw lean honey-
   comb tripe
1½ teaspoons salt
1 knuckle of veal
3 leeks
1 large onion
3 or 4 carrots, sliced
1 large stalk celery, sliced
1 large bunch parsley
½ teaspoon salt
¼ fresh hot red pepper, or
   whole dried red pepper

1 teaspoon whole cloves
1 teaspoon whole black pepper, crushed
1 heaping teaspoon sweet
   marjoram
1 dessertspoon summer savory
1 dessertspoon sweet basil
1 teaspoon thyme
3 cups diced potatoes
3 tablespoons flour
2½ tablespoons butter
Meat or flour dumplings

WASH and scrub the tripe thoroughly. Cover liberally with cold water, about 6 quarts, to which 1 teaspoon salt has been added. Bring to a boil and boil moderately, but constantly, for 6 or 7 hours, until tripe is tender. Add more water if necessary, as tripe must cook well covered with water.

In another saucepan put the veal, leeks, onion, carrots, celery, and parsley; cover with water and add salt and the red pepper. Simmer until meat falls from the bone, about 2 hours. At the end of the first hour add the cloves, black pepper, marjoram, summer savory, sweet basil, and thyme tied in a cheesecloth. Strain, allow to cool, and remove all grease.

Remove tripe from its liquor, saving the liquid. Dice the tripe in ¼-inch pieces and combine it with the tripe and veal stocks, which have been heated.

Put potatoes on in cold salted water and boil 10 minutes. Drain; add to the stock and tripe. Season if necessary. Make a *roux* of the flour and butter, mix slowly with a little of the boiling soup, then add to the soup, stirring constantly. Serve with dumplings if desired.

Fried Oysters

One of our very popular luncheon dishes, a combination often served at church suppers, is fried oysters and chicken salad. Usually three large, well-breaded oysters constitute a serving.

Serves 4 (8 for lunch)

2 dozen oysters
Salt, pepper, and cayenne
3 eggs

Stale bread crumbs, for crumb-
ing
Oil for deep frying

SELECT the finest oysters you can get. Drain them in a colander and dry one by one on a piece of soft linen. Do not lift them with a fork but with the fingers, carefully. Season on both sides with salt, pepper, and cayenne. Beat the eggs in a saucer, add 1 tablespoon boiling water and ½ teaspoon salt. Season the bread crumbs with salt and cayenne. Dip oysters one by one first in the crumbs, then in the egg, then again in the crumbs, covering every part carefully and pressing lightly with the hand. Put on a platter and allow crumbs to harden. Fry in deep, hot oil, 365 degrees or hot enough to brown a crumb of bread quickly. Fry six oysters at a time in a frying basket. As soon as they are golden brown, remove and drain on absorbent paper. Serve at once on a hot dish. Oysters should never be fried until just before they are to be eaten. Serve with pickles, Philadelphia relish, or coleslaw.

Stuffed Mushrooms

Serves 4 as a lunch dish

½ onion, chopped fine
2 tablespoons butter
12 large chicken livers (or chopped ham)
½ cup thick cream sauce

Few drops Worcestershire sauce
6 slices toast
12 large mushroom caps, sautéed

COOK onion in butter until soft but not brown. Add chicken livers and cook slowly until tender. Mash with fork until smooth. Add cream sauce and Worcestershire. Spread toast with part of the mixture, and fill mushroom caps with the remainder. Place two caps on each slice of toast. Brush with melted butter and reheat just before serving.

Philadelphia Pepper Relish

Pepper relish is almost always served with fried oysters, and occasionally with crabmeat. When the relish is made properly, the vegetables stay crisp and full of flavor.

Makes about 3 pints

1 cup minced green pepper
½ cup minced sweet red pepper
4 cups minced cabbage
1 cup minced celery

2 tablespoons salt
2 tablespoons mustard seed
2 tablespoons brown sugar
½ cup vinegar

COMBINE the minced vegetables and salt and let stand overnight. Drain thoroughly; add mustard seed and brown sugar to vinegar and heat to a boil. Pour over drained vegetables, placed in an earthen jar. Cool and serve within 3 days.

Frances Blackwood

THE PHILADELPHIA BULLETIN
PHILADELPHIA, PENNSYLVANIA

Some of Philadelphia's regional dishes are distinctive because they are unique. Snapper soup, for instance, is the only one of its kind. Other dishes earn their distinction from the way in which they are made in this locality. Other places have cinnamon buns, for in-

stance, but Philadelphia's cinnamon buns are noted for their very special sticky tops and are found only hereabouts.

Some Philadelphia cooking feels the influence of our Pennsylvania Dutch neighbors, while some still retains the English influence of our early settlers.

Philadelphia Cinnamon Buns

The genuine Philadelphia cinnamon bun is a thin, light, delicious ribbon of yeast-raised dough spiraled around raisins, sugar, and spices. It is brown on the bottom and oozing with luscious stickiness on top. It may be a tiny bite-sized morsel, or it may be foursquare and huge. But it has to be sticky if it's to be the real thing. At its very best it is eaten hot from the oven.

Makes about 3 dozen

¾ cup milk	¾ cup sugar
¾ cup water	2 eggs
1 yeast cake	Butter, brown sugar, cinnamon, raisins, and syrup for spreading on the dough
5 cups flour	
1 teaspoon salt	
1 tablespoon sugar	Molasses or syrup
½ cup shortening	

PUT milk in a saucepan and let it heat to a scald (until a thin skin forms on it, but before it is hot enough to boil). When milk has scalded, add water and cool to lukewarm. Crumble the yeast cake into a cup and slowly stir the lukewarm liquid into it, dissolving the yeast cake completely.

Measure 2 cups of flour into a mixing bowl, together with salt and one tablespoon of sugar. Make a well in the center and slowly pour the yeast mixture into it, stirring as you pour. Stir from the inside of the well toward the outside, until the flour is all mixed in; then, grasping the bowl in one hand and the beating spoon in the other, beat the whole mixture until it is velvety smooth. A good beating is very important at this point in the procedure. Next, cover the bowl with a cloth and set it aside out of any draft.

Beat shortening as light as a feather. Gradually beat in the ¾ cup sugar. Add eggs one at a time, beating well after each addition.

At this point the first mixture should be light and bubbly. Add to it the shortening mixture, 1 tablespoon at a time, beating it in well. Be thorough about the beating here, too. When it is all beaten in, start adding the remaining 3 cups flour. Don't beat these, just stir them in smoothly, a small amount at a time. Cover the bowl again, set out of a draft, and let the dough rise until doubled in bulk.

Next, take a part at a time, roll it out on a floured board to a rectangular sheet ¼ inch thick. Spread generously with butter, sprinkle thickly with brown sugar and cinnamon, then with raisins. Trail syrup over it, snail fashion. Roll up like jelly roll. Cut in 1- or 1½-inch slices. Lay them in cake pans that have been generously buttered and filled ¼ inch deep with molasses or syrup. Cover, let rise again until doubled in bulk. Place in a preheated moderate (350-degree) oven, and bake until nicely browned.

As soon as the pans are taken from the oven, turn out the buns, sticky side up. Remember, generous buttering of the pans and a ¼-inch coating of syrup are the secrets of that much-to-be-desired sticky topping.

Snapper Stew

Still famous in the old eating places are Philadelphia Snapper Stew and Snapper Soup.

(Ed. note: Miss Blackwood gave detailed directions for preparing the stew from a live snapper. These have been omitted as the problem is most unlikely to confront housewives today.)

WHEN you buy snapper in the market, usually the raw meat is displayed on the top shell, all cleaned and ready to cook. It is all good to eat, with two exceptions: the white inner tubing; and the gall sac, located in the liver. If these have not been removed by the butcher, they should now be discarded. Take great care not to break the gall sac, since the bile will make inedible anything it touches. The sac is deep in one side of the liver. Cut the liver carefully until the sac is located; remove it, together with any discolored liver in its vicinity.

Snapper eggs are good, if you are lucky enough to find them. The fat is delicious, as is the liver itself.

Put the shell and meat into a pot. Add water to barely cover, 2 tablespoons salt, and 1 or 2 tablespoons vinegar. Bring to a simmer, covered, and simmer until tender. Don't let the water boil, as this will toughen the meat. The length of cooking time depends on the snapper's age, and nobody has ever discovered how to tell a turtle's age. It may take 45 minutes . . . or 3 or 4 or even 5 hours. The meat is done when you can pierce body or legs easily with a fork. About 30 minutes before the meat is tender, add the liver to the simmering liquid; cook the eggs, if any are present, about 20 minutes. (The white of a turtle egg does not coagulate as a chicken's egg does.)

Lay the meat on a large platter. Search for, and remove, every tiny bit of bone and cut the meat into bite-sized pieces. Slice the liver and add it to the meat, together with the eggs. Put everything in a bowl, pour over it some of the liquid in which the meat was cooked, and add ¼ to ½ cup sherry. Keep covered in the refrigerator until dinnertime.

At dinner, put the snapper meat (which is probably jellied by now) in the top of a double boiler and heat carefully over hot water. (If the stew boils again, it will be stringy, tough, and will taste fishy.)

In a separate saucepan make your very best cream sauce, well seasoned, and add 1 or 2 beaten egg yolks to give a rich color. Combine hot snapper meat and highly seasoned cream sauce. Add a dash of cayenne, and serve garnished with toast points or mashed potato.

Philadelphia Scrapple

Another famous Philadelphia dish is scrapple. Sometimes, in the Pennsylvania Dutch regions, this is given the Indian name "Ponhaus."

Makes 2 loaf pans of scrapple

2 pounds lean, bony pork	½ teaspoon sage (or poultry
1½ quarts cold water	seasoning)
1 tablespoon salt	1 cup fine cornmeal
Pepper, to taste	½ cup buckwheat flour
¼ teaspoon mace (or nutmeg)	2 cups cold water

PUT meat in a saucepan and add the 1½ quarts cold water. Add salt and pepper; heat slowly to boiling. Lower heat, and simmer gently until meat is very tender. Remove the meat, and skim the grease from the surface. Remove bones and chop the meat very fine; return to the broth in the pan. Add the sage (or poultry seasoning) and mace (or nutmeg). Mix together the cornmeal and buckwheat flour. Slowly add the 2 cups of cold water, making a paste free from any lumps. Bring the broth with the meat and seasonings to a boil. Spoon the cornmeal paste mixture into it without stopping the boiling. When all is stirred in, continue stirring until it has thickened to the consistency of a soft mush. Then lower the heat almost as much as possible and let the mixture cook 1 hour, stirring occasionally. (Or do this part of the cooking over boiling water.) Pour the mixture about 3 inches deep into loaf pans. Let stand until cold. Turn out of the pans, slice, and fry slowly in a heavy skillet. Let one side get crisp and brown, then turn and brown the other.

Josephine Gibson

PITTSBURGH PRESS
PITTSBURGH, PENNSYLVANIA

In Pennsylvania we can be justly proud of our special dishes known as Pennsylvania Dutch, from the Palatinate in Germany, many of them so good that they have become nationally famous.

The very names Schnitz un Knepp, Sauerbraten, Ponhaus, Shoo-Fly Pie, or Apple Strudel seem to conjure the aroma of a good, old-time Pennsylvania German dinner, the table high with from thirty to forty dishes.

One of the quaintest traditions of the Pennsylvania Dutch is the celebrated custom known as the "seven sweets and seven sours." It is the custom for guests to look for, and even count to see that there are, exactly seven of each.

A typical Pennsylvania Dutch dinner might include Sauerbraten with Kartoffelkloesse (potato dumplings); red cabbage; lettuce salad, Dutch style, or Dutch string bean salad; hard rolls with apple butter or jelly; Apfel Kuchen or Shoo-Fly Pie for dessert, and lots of coffee.

Sauerbraten

Serves 5 or 6

3 pounds beef pot roast	2 bay leaves
½ cup cider vinegar	3 whole cloves
½ cup water	2 teaspoons salt
1 small onion, thinly sliced	⅛ teaspoon pepper

PLACE meat in a small bowl and pour over it the remaining ingredients, which have been mixed together. Cover and set aside for 18 to 24 hours. Remove meat from vinegar and brown it in beef fat or drippings. When thoroughly brown, pour over it the liquid in which it was soaked, adding 1 cupful water. Simmer for 3 hours, or until tender. Remove meat and thicken gravy. If too much liquid evaporates, it may be necessary to add more water.

Kartoffelkloesse (Potato Dumplings)

Serves 6

2 cups mashed, cooked potatoes (leftover potatoes may
be used)

1 tablespoon butter

1 tablespoon finely minced
onion

1 egg

¾ cup sifted all-purpose flour

1½ teaspoons salt

⅛ teaspoon pepper

1 cup bread cubes, ¼ inch
thick, fried in butter or
bacon fat

TO hot mashed potatoes add butter, then cool. Add onion and egg, and mix thoroughly with a fork. Sift in flour, salt, and pepper, and blend well. Make into twelve balls the size of an egg, forming each around four or five cubes of bread. Cook tightly covered for 7 minutes in gently boiling water. Lift out the dumplings and place them on a large platter, sprinkling them with fine bread crumbs or corn flakes that have been browned in the frying pan in a small amount of butter or bacon fat.

Shoo-Fly Pie

¼ cup sifted flour

½ cup sugar

⅛ teaspoon salt

3 tablespoons shortening

1 egg

⅓ cup molasses

2 tablespoons boiling water

½ teaspoon soda

1 unbaked, 9-inch pie shell

MIX flour, sugar, salt, and shortening together to form crumbs. Beat egg until light and fluffy. Add to it the molasses, boiling water, and soda, and beat until soda is dissolved. Add all but ¼ cup of crumb mixture to molasses mixture, and stir until well blended. Pour into unbaked pie shell, sprinkle top with reserved crumbs, and bake in a moderate oven (375 degrees) for 35 minutes.

Schnitz un Knepp

Serves 8

3 pounds ham	¼ teaspoon pepper
4 cups dried apples	1 egg, well beaten
2 tablespoons brown sugar	Milk enough to make fairly
2 cups flour	moist, stiff batter
4 teaspoons baking powder	3 tablespoons melted butter
1 teaspoon salt	or margarine

PICK over and wash dried apples. Cover with water and let soak overnight or for a number of hours. In the morning, cover ham with cold water and let boil for 3 hours. Add apples and the water in which they have been soaked; continue boiling for another hour. Add brown sugar. Make dumplings by sifting together the flour, baking powder, salt, and pepper. Stir in the beaten egg, milk, and butter. Drop the batter by spoonfuls into the hot liquid with the ham and apples. Cover kettle tightly and cook dumplings for 15 minutes. Serve piping hot on a large platter.

Old-Fashioned Cider Apple Butter

Apple butter is a dish of Pennsylvania Dutch origin, and its goodness has become widely known. A really thick layer of spicy, creamy-smooth, rich apple butter on hot biscuits, muffins, or rolls provides eating that defies description!

Apple butter may recall fall days when huge kettles of apple butter were being stirred over an open fire in the back yard at your farm home or at the neighborhood gathering of a relative or friend. Apple-butter making, in those days, was a social occasion.

Today the big iron and copper kettles used in the past are practically gone, but the liking for good apple butter is not. Today it is made in kitchens and in smaller amounts, and part of the cooking is done in a slow oven to reduce the time required for stirring.

Some stirring is needed, however, to get the smooth texture, creaminess, and richness necessary for a really good product.

Makes about 4 quarts

1 peck apples	6 cups sugar
(10 or 12 pounds)	1 tablespoon cinnamon
1 gallon sweet cider	½ tablespoon cloves

WASH and slice apples. Add cider and cook until soft, then press through a sieve. Boil the strained pulp until it is thick enough to heap in a spoon, then add sugar mixed with spices and boil until it is again thick enough to heap in a spoon. Pour while hot into jars. Process 10 minutes in a hot-water bath, and seal.

Note: A less rich sauce may be made using 1 or 2 quarts cider.

Marion G. Leslie

PITTSBURGH SUN-TELEGRAPH
PITTSBURGH, PENNSYLVANIA

We went to Mrs. Isabel Bewick Smith, home economics extension representative for Allegheny County, for recipes based on some of the products grown in the Pittsburgh district. Many of these recipes originated with homemaker groups in the county.

Pennsylvania Pudding

(From the Brookside Farms group)

Serves 6

6 tart apples	¾ cup sugar
1¾ cups sifted flour	1 egg, well beaten
3 teaspoons baking powder	¾ cup water
½ teaspoon salt	2-ounce bar of milk chocolate
¼ cup shortening	

PEEL and slice apples. Place in a greased baking dish. Mix and sift together flour, baking powder, and salt. Cream shortening and add sugar; beat until light and fluffy. Add egg and beat again. Add flour mixture, alternately with water, until smooth. Pour batter over apples. Grate chocolate and scatter over top of batter. Bake in 350-degree oven for 1 hour.

German Potato Pancakes

(From the School of Agriculture, Agricultural Extension Service, Pennsylvania State College)

Makes 24 cakes

3 eggs, separated
1 teaspoon salt
1 tablespoon sugar
3 cups milk
2½ cups sifted all-purpose flour

1 tablespoon melted shortening
3 cups grated raw potatoes
Onions, finely grated (optional)

TO well-beaten egg yolks add salt, sugar, and milk. Gradually add flour and shortening, beating well. Stir in grated potatoes, then fold in stiffly beaten egg whites. Bake at once on a hot, greased griddle. Finely chopped onions may be sprinkled on top of the batter. Serve hot.

Grated-Apple Cake

(From the Deer Creek Homemakers group of Allegheny County)

Serves 6 to 8

½ cup shortening
1 cup granulated sugar
½ cup brown sugar
2 eggs, beaten

½ teaspoon lemon rind or extract
1 teaspoon soda
½ teaspoon salt

2 cups chopped or grated
  apples
2½ cups sifted flour
1 teaspoon baking powder

½ cup chopped nuts
2 tablespoons brown sugar
Cinnamon

CREAM together shortening and sugar (white and brown); add eggs and lemon rind. Next add soda, salt, and apples. Add flour and baking powder which have been sifted together. Place in a buttered baking dish and sprinkle top with nuts and brown sugar mixed with cinnamon. Bake 1 hour at 350 degrees.

Rhode Island

Mildred Emery

THE PAWTUCKET TIMES
PAWTUCKET, RHODE ISLAND

New England Boiled Dinner

From the smallest state in the forty-eight, Rhode Island, come recipes that remind us of the thrifty New England idea of an all-in-one-pot meal.

Serves 6

4 pounds corned beef
1 small head cabbage, quartered
6 carrots

2 small turnips, quartered
6 potatoes
6 parsnips
6 medium onions (optional)

WASH the corned beef in cold water; if very salty, soak in cold water for 30 minutes or bring to a boil and remove from water. Place meat again in cold water and cook for 3 to 4 hours, until tender. About 1½ hours before serving, add the cabbage, carrots, turnips; and 30 minutes before serving, add potatoes and parsnips. Place on a large platter and serve. Onions may also be cooked with the meat if desired.

Violet B. Higbee

PROVIDENCE JOURNAL & EVENING BULLETIN
PROVIDENCE, RHODE ISLAND

Jonnycakes

Rhode Island jonnycakes, as unusual as is their spelling, have won fame wherever they have been served. The South County variety is not like the Newport, nor is either like the northern kind. But for each you must have Rhode Island flint corn, stone-ground, which makes a fine, ivory-colored meal. The coarse yellow meal in most markets will not do at all.

Serves 4

2 cups Rhode Island cornmeal   ½ teaspoon salt
2 tablespoons sugar

SCALD the meal, mixed with sugar and salt, by pouring boiling water over it until thick enough to drop from a spoon. Bake in little cakes on a well-greased hot griddle. When browned on one side, turn over. Serve with meat or fish.

Mina's Huckleberry Jonnycake

Serves 4

1 cup sour milk
1 cup molasses
1 teaspoon soda
½ teaspoon salt

1 cup sifted flour
1 cup Rhode Island cornmeal
1 cup huckleberries

MIX sour milk and molasses. Sift soda and salt with flour. Add cornmeal. Add dry ingredients to liquids, and lastly the huckleberries. Put in a buttered baking dish. Bake in a moderate oven (350 degrees) about 25 minutes.

Cornmeal Dumplings

Serves 4

1 egg	½ teaspoon salt
¼ cup milk	1 teaspoon baking powder
½ cup sifted flour	½ cup cornmeal

BEAT egg and add to it the milk. Sift flour, baking powder, and salt together. Add cornmeal. Add liquids to dry ingredients and drop by spoonfuls into hot soup or stew. Cover tightly and cook 12 to 15 minutes.

K. Eileen Doyle

THE WOONSOCKET CALL

WOONSOCKET, RHODE ISLAND

As popular in Woonsocket as their traditional song, "Alouette," are the dishes handed down to French-Canadian residents by their forefathers. They are not to be found in most cookbooks, but the residents, of whom 90 per cent are of French extraction, are happy to pass them along to others.

Leek Soup

Serves 4

2 bunches leeks	2 tablespoons flour
3 tablespoons butter or mar-garine	2 quarts water

WASH and cut up leeks in 1-inch pieces. Melt butter or other fat in a soup kettle, put in leeks, add flour, and brown lightly. Gradually add water; let simmer 1 hour. Variation: Many use onions in addition to leeks, and thicken with vermicelli instead of flour.

Pea Soup

Serves 8

1 pound dried yellow peas	½ pound salt pork
1 large onion, chopped	Salt and pepper

COVER peas, onion, and salt pork with water. Cook slowly until peas are well done. Salt and pepper to taste. For variety, add a little parsley and crisp bacon just before serving.

Tourtière (Meat Pie)

It wouldn't seem like Christmas or New Year's in a French home if Tourtière weren't on the menu. It is eaten both as a main dish and for breakfast.

Makes 3 pies

3 pounds ground fresh pork	Cracker or bread crumbs
2 pounds hamburger	1 tablespoon cinnamon
1 large onion, chopped fine	1 tablespoon cloves
1½ tablespoons salt	Double crust for three pies
1 teaspoon pepper	

COVER meat, onion, salt, and pepper with water and boil 20 minutes. Thicken with cracker or bread crumbs. Remove from stove and add cinnamon and cloves. Place between two crusts and bake in a hot oven (450 degrees) until crust is brown. These pies may be kept in the refrigerator for several weeks and reheated as wanted.

French-Canadian Dessert

TO make a simple and delicious French-Canadian dessert, slice fresh white bread, pour maple syrup over it, and then thick cream; or soak bread in syrup, fry in butter, and serve with cream.

Blade-Meat Dressing

The Canadians here use Blade-Meat Dressing almost exclusively.

1½ pounds blade meat for a 12-pound turkey (1 pound is enough if you do not care for any leftovers). Have meat ground, and be sure there isn't too much fat with it

Onions (1 to 3)
Cracker crumbs
1 egg, beaten
Salt, pepper, and poultry seasoning

PLACE the ground blade meat in a saucepan; add boiling water until it comes to the top of the meat. Cook 20 minutes; allow to cool. Add onions, the number depending on one's preference. Add enough cracker crumbs to absorb the juice; add beaten egg and season to taste.

South Carolina

Bessie R. Murphy

ARKANSAS DEMOCRAT
LITTLE ROCK, ARKANSAS

CHARLESTON EVENING NEWS
CHARLESTON, SOUTH CAROLINA

SHREVEPORT TIMES
SHREVEPORT, LOUISIANA

(Ed. note: Bessie R. Murphy is the versatile food editor for three papers, each in a different state. We have placed her contribution under South Carolina, as she is the only member of the group writing in that state.)

Southern Fried Chicken and What Goes with It

Southern fried chicken, like Southern biscuit, needs no introduction. We spend a great deal of time today fixing fancy dishes, dressing them up, and trying various and sundry ways to make them appealing to the eye. But why all this bother, when the most famous company will sing our praises after just such a simple dinner as: Southern fried chicken and gravy (and plenty of it), with snowy rice, sweet-potato pudding of 1828, and lots of hot biscuits; then charlotte russe or ambrosia for dessert.

Southern Fried Chicken

This dish seems very simple, but simple things are often the hardest to do.

FOR frying, select young chickens, from 1½ to 2 pounds. Dress and disjoint; chill. Sift flour (about 1½ cups), add salt and pepper, and roll each piece of chicken in this mixture. Place in a heavy frying pan with a close-fitting top. The fat should be deep enough to cover the pieces when it boils up (about 2 inches deep in the pan). The shortening must be very hot when the chicken is first dropped in. Always put in the larger pieces first, flesh side down, and in the hottest part of the pan. Do not place too many pieces in the pan at one time; they should not touch in frying. Then lower the heat, so the chicken will not cook too fast. The skillet must remain covered to keep the steam in. When the chicken is tender and golden brown, remove it and make the gravy. Pour from the pan all the fat but 2 tablespoons, add to this 2 tablespoons flour, mix smooth, and add 1 cup milk. Stir until the gravy boils and is thick and rich. Add salt and pepper. Never pour gravy over the chicken; serve it in a separate dish.

Famous Sweet-Potato Pudding of 1828

Most delicious to serve at Thanksgiving or Christmas, but welcome at any time.

Serves 6 to 8

1 pound boiled, peeled sweet potatoes (about 3 to 4 medium)

1 cup granulated sugar

½ cup melted butter or margarine

6 egg yolks, well beaten

Grated rind of 1 lemon

¼ teaspoon mace

1 cup orange juice

6 egg whites

Citron

PRESS the cooked potatoes through a colander, then add sugar and melted butter or margarine, mixing well. Add egg yolks, lemon rind, mace, and orange juice, beating well after each addition. When all is well mixed, fold in the egg whites, beaten to a stiff froth. Butter a pudding dish, pour in the pudding, sprinkle the top with granulated sugar and bits of sliced citron. Bake in a moderate oven (350 degrees) until the top springs back when touched gently.

Charlotte Russe

Serves 12 to 15

2 tablespoons unflavored gelatin
¼ cup cold water
1 cup boiling water

6 eggs, separated
1½ cups sugar
1 quart heavy cream
Flavoring

SOFTEN gelatin in cold water, then dissolve in boiling water. Keep hot by placing over hot water until ready to use. Beat egg yolks, add sugar, and mix thoroughly. Add the gelatin. Beat egg whites until stiff; fold into the egg-yolk mixture. Whip the cream until stiff and fold in lightly but thoroughly. Flavor as desired, and place in the refrigerator until firm.

Tennessee

Virginia Chumley

CHATTANOOGA NEWS-FREE PRESS
CHATTANOOGA, TENNESSEE

Po'k Chop Casserole

Chattanooga's cookery, these days, is taking on a less stereotyped "Southern-innity" than it once knew. For example, everybody knows how Southerners love pork. Well, in the past few years, pork has popped out on local tables with a Northern (or perhaps Creole?) accent.

Serves 6

6 loin pork chops	1 teaspoon sugar
1 package frozen lima beans	1 teaspoon salt
1 No. 2 can whole tomatoes	Dash of pepper
1 small green pepper	Pinch of thyme
1 medium onion	

BROWN chops well on both sides in a skillet. Mix thawed limas, tomatoes, pepper, onion, and seasonings, and put into a casserole dish. Arrange chops on top. Cover and bake in a 350-degree oven for 35 minutes.

"Cheese-Quick" Dish

This is a popular concoction for warm-weather luncheons or cool-weather Sunday night suppers.

Serves 6

6 slices bread   6 slices bacon
Butter   1 large egg
6 slices American cheese   Milk

SPREAD bread slices with butter and arrange on a baking sheet. Then cover each bread slice with one of cheese. Cut each bacon strip in half, and, allowing one strip per bread slice, arrange the strips crisscross atop the cheese. Break the egg into a cup and add enough milk to fill the cup. Beat egg and milk 1 minute, then pour the mixture over the bread slices. Broil for 20 minutes, or until the egg mixture has puffed evenly and is a golden-brown color.

Blanche Grace Davis

KNOXVILLE NEWS-SENTINEL
KNOXVILLE, TENNESSEE

The true Tennessean, home-grown or transplanted, comes to dote on green beans. But our native dish of green beans is a country cousin of the crisp, light-green, buttered product. Ours are over-cooked to a hue of dark-greenness and slowly heat-tortured to a state of delicious limpness. Every bean packs a rich pork flavor derived from a slice of fat back in the center of the pot.

The serious Tennessee green-bean cook remembers to offset the pork flavor with a bit of dried red pepper pod. A handful of dried beans, or "shellies," are also cooked amid the broken green beans. Such a dish seems more meat than vegetable, and is frequently served as the main dish of an all-vegetable dinner. For contrast, ac-companying foods are seasoned lightly and cooked briefly, or are raw. There is always a generous platter of sliced ripe-red tomatoes and green onions, and perhaps raw cucumbers.

Cracklin' Bread

Corn bread in all its variations is served daily at most Tennessee tables. One of these is "Cracklin' Bread." Cracklings are those chewy bites made from the skin of the hog, fried very crisp.

Serves 6

1½ cups cornmeal
2 tablespoons flour
½ teaspoon salt
3 teaspoons baking powder

1 egg, well beaten
1¼ cups milk
1½ cups cracklings

COMBINE cornmeal, flour, sugar, salt, baking powder, egg, and milk. Add cracklings and beat thoroughly. Bake in a well-oiled, shallow pan in a 450-degree oven for about 20 minutes. Or drop by teaspoonfuls on a hot, well-oiled griddle and fry until golden brown.

Mountain Ham with Red-Eye Gravy

The flavor of Tennessee Mountain Ham goes right down to your toes and is like no other. It has a smoky, sweet-bitter taste, and both tender and chewy qualities. The best sauce to serve with it is "red-eye gravy."

CAREFULLY trim the rind off a slice of ham. Rub a heated skillet with ham fat. Fry ham over low heat until brown; turn and brown on the other side. A sprinkle of sugar on each side, before cooking, intensifies the flavor.

Pour 2 tablespoons of ham grease into a gravy boat. Brown the residue in the skillet. Add ½ cup water and bring to a boil. Pour into the grease in the gravy boat. To make a redder gravy, before adding the water, add to the skillet 1 tablespoon of brewed coffee or ½ teaspoon sugar.

Green Beans, Tennessee Style

Serves 4 to 5

IF you plan to add a few shellies, select green beans with plenty of green pod. Wash 3 pounds thoroughly in several waters; remove ends and any strings. Break in 1- or 1½-inch pieces. Place the beans in a large covered pot or deep-well cooker, with a generous slice of salt pork, or fat back, in the center. Add 1 cup water, 2 scant teaspoons salt, and a small piece of dried red pepper pod.

Cover and bring to the steaming point; then reduce heat to low for 2 to 2½ hours, or until the pork is completely tender, through and through. If the pot becomes dry, add very small amounts of water during the cooking period.

Eloise Hunter Womack

THE NASHVILLE TENNESSEAN
NASHVILLE, TENNESSEE

Virginia is credited with being the mother of Tennessee cooking. The early settlers came through the mountains and valleys from Virginia into what is now Tennessee and Kentucky, bringing with them many of the old English utensils and recipes from the Old World.

The typical foods in the mountainous regions are somewhat different from the foods we eat in the middle and western parts of our state, so I will try to give you recipes from both sections. One of the recipes that originated in Tennessee is Spiced Beef Round (Spice Round, we call it). We are so familiar with this wonderful dish that we find it hard to realize that it is so little known in other parts of our country.

Tennessee Country Ham is eaten and enjoyed the year round. Another meat we are rightly proud of is our smoked sausage, which is smoked right along with the hams and has a flavor not found in sausage anywhere else in the world.

Spiced Beef Round

Serves 24 or more

10 to 12 pounds beef, top round
½ teaspoon saltpeter
2 cups salt
2 cups brown sugar
1 tablespoon pepper
1 tablespoon ginger
1 tablespoon grated nutmeg
1 tablespoon cinnamon
1 tablespoon allspice
¼ teaspoon cayenne pepper
2 cups minced onions
2 cups minced celery
4 cups minced beef suet

MIX saltpeter, salt, and brown sugar, and rub well into the meat. Mix the spices and rub over the meat. Lay on a large platter or in a big dish in a cool place and turn every day for 2 weeks; drain off the juices and save. Mix the dregs of the spices with onions, celery, and suet. Make incisions all over the beef and stuff with the mixture. Sew up in a cloth to keep the stuffing from escaping. Put on a rack in a kettle, add juices and sufficient water to cover, and boil like a ham until tender and well done. Cool and slice. Serve cold.

Country Ham

15- to 20-pound country ham
2 cups sugar
2 cups vinegar
Mixed whole spices (cloves, cinnamon, allspice) tied in a bag
Pickled peaches

WASH the ham well and cut away the rough spots. If much salt has been used in its curing, soak it overnight. Put into a large kettle and cover with water. To this add 1 cup sugar, 1 cup vinegar, and the bag of spices. Boil hard for 1 hour. At the end of this hour add 1 cup sugar and 1 cup vinegar; cook several hours, until tender. Remove from the water and skin. Cover the scored fat with crushed pickled peaches and bake in a 375-degree oven until golden brown. Baste occasionally with the drippings. Serve hot or cold.

Hog's Jowl and Turnip Greens with Potlikker

This is one of the dishes that we are truly devoted to, but to make it at its best the jowl must come from a private supply and not from a store. The jowl must have that special smoke and cured flavor about it, or you will miss a great deal.

Serves 4 to 6

CLEAN the jowl, then put it into boiling water to cover. Cook 45 minutes, or until the jowl is almost done. Now add a panful of well-washed and drained young turnip greens. Cook gently for another hour or more. Serve the jowl in the center of a platter with the greens around it. Garnish with poached eggs. Serve the potlikker in a separate dish, to be used as gravy with corn bread. Give everyone a slice of the tongue and a bit of the cheek. Pass a cruet of wine vinegar in which a hot pepper pod has been soaked.

Corn Light Bread

Serves 4 to 6

2 cups water-ground cornmeal	1 cup sugar
2 cups boiling water	1 tablespoon salt
1 cup buttermilk	1 pint warm water
1 cup flour	1 scant quart cornmeal
1 teaspoon soda	

MOISTEN 2 cups cornmeal with cold water. Add boiling water and allow to work in a warm place (at 82 degrees) overnight. In the morning add buttermilk, flour, soda, sugar, salt, warm water, and enough more meal to make a batter that will streak the spoon. Let this rise until light (about 1 hour or more). Bake in a well-greased loaf pan in a 375-degree oven for 1 hour. Cover and leave for 24 hours, then eat cold. This is a favorite for picnics.
(Ed. note: Ordinary cornmeal is degerminated and therefore will not "work" as the water-ground meal will.)

Chess Pie

3 whole eggs
1 cup sugar
Pinch of salt
1 tablespoon cornmeal (or 2 tablespoons grated almonds)

¼ cup heavy cream
1 teaspoon vanilla
¼ pound butter, melted
Unbaked 9-inch pastry shell

BEAT eggs until thick and lemon colored; add sugar and salt and mix well. Add cornmeal and cream alternately, blending until smooth. Add vanilla. Add butter, mixing well. Pour into the unbaked pastry shell and bake in a 325-degree oven until done.

Texas

THE DAILY TIMES HERALD
DALLAS, TEXAS

Texans generally, and Dallasites specifically, have formed a cosmopolitan attitude toward food. Typical Texas food as known a few years ago reflected many influences, yet "chuck-wagon fare" managed to creep in. Nowadays, although chili and barbecue are still popular dishes, they by no means dominate the culinary scene.

Texas Barbecue Sauce

Makes 2¼ cups sauce

5 tablespoons vinegar
3 tablespoons tomato catsup
2 tablespoons Worcestershire sauce
3 bay leaves
1 clove garlic, minced
2 tablespoons chopped onion

1 cup canned tomatoes
3 stalks celery and leaves, chopped
½ lemon, thinly sliced
1½ cups water
½ cup butter or margarine

SIMMER for 15 minutes everything but butter. Strain. Add butter.

Chili Con Carne

6 to 12 pods dried chili peppers

2 pounds center cut round steak

1 pound center cut fresh ham

2 onions, chopped

4 cloves garlic, chopped

½ to 2½ cups fat rendered from beef suet

1 teaspoon comino seed

1 teaspoon orégano

1 tablespoon salt

WASH, stem, and carefully remove seeds from the dried chili pods. Add 2 to 4 cups cold water and bring to a boil. Reduce heat to a slow boil and cook until the skins slip easily—usually about 45 minutes to 1 hour. Rub pulp through a colander or sieve to make a smooth paste. This yields about ½ to ¾ cup pulp. If commercially prepared chili powder is used instead of the chili-pod pulp, substitute 1 tablespoon chili powder for each pod. This will make the flavor a bit harsher.

Trim meats; cut into cubes less than ½ inch. Sauté onions and garlic in fat; add meat; cook until gray in color. Add 2 cups water and simmer 1 hour. Rub comino seeds and orégano to powder, roasting first if necessary. Add chili pulp (or powder), comino and orégano powder, and salt to meat, and cook slowly for 1 hour. This makes a highly condensed chili that will keep for quite a while. Cut off pieces as desired and cook in boiling water until a stewlike consistency is obtained. Chili is usually served with kidney beans. These may be added when the chili is reheated.

May Del Flagg

THE HOUSTON POST
HOUSTON, TEXAS

Hot breads always win praise among Houstonians or residents of the Gulf Coast area. Newcomers quickly take up the habit of indulging in hot breads, and soon they, too, rate them tops in the food line.

Since the introduction of the packaged ready-mix breads, home-makers use them often. But continuing favorites, especially among the men of the households, are hot biscuits made by the buttermilk-and-soda recipe, and hush puppies, the traditional accompaniments for a vegetable dinner.

Corn Sticks

Serves 4 to 6

2 cups cornmeal
1 cup boiling water
1 tablespoon butter
1 teaspoon salt

3 eggs, separated
1 cup milk
4 teaspoons baking powder

SCALD cornmeal with boiling water; cool. Add butter, salt, beaten yolks, milk, and baking powder. Beat well, then add stiffly beaten whites. Pour in corn-stick pans that have been heated and greased. Bake in a hot oven (450 degrees).

Texas Fig-Bran Muffins

Makes 12 muffins

1 cup flour
2 cups bran cereal
3 tablespoons baking powder
½ teaspoon salt
2 eggs, well beaten
1 cup milk

4 tablespoons melted butter
½ cup fig syrup or ½ cup brown sugar
¾ cup fig preserves, cut in small pieces

SIFT together dry ingredients. Combine with eggs, milk, and butter. Add fig syrup and fig preserves. Bake in buttered tins in a hot oven (450 degrees) for 20 minutes.

Buttermilk Biscuits

Serves 4 to 6

2 cups sifted flour
1 teaspoon salt
2 teaspoons baking powder

4 tablespoons shortening
½ teaspoon soda
1 cup buttermilk

SIFT together flour, salt, and baking powder. Cut in shortening. Add soda to milk and beat until the mixture foams. Stir into other ingredients and mix quickly. Toss on a lightly floured board, roll gently, cut, and bake in a hot oven (425 degrees) for 12 minutes.

Sally Lunn

Serves 6 to 8

3 cups flour
1 cup sugar
1 teaspoon soda dissolved in
    ½ cup warm water

2 teaspoons cream of tartar
1 cup sweet milk
1 tablespoon butter

STIR all ingredients briskly, put in two buttered pans, and let rise for 15 minutes before baking. Bake in a medium-hot oven (425 degrees) for 30 minutes. Sprinkle powdered sugar and cinnamon on top before serving.

Hattie Lewellyn

SAN ANTONIO EXPRESS AND
SAN ANTONIO EVENING NEWS
SAN ANTONIO, TEXAS

In San Antonio, it is not difficult to demonstrate how interesting and appetizing Mexican foods are, and how easy to serve.

One cannot still buy Mexican food in the open plaza, as in earlier years, but many places serve delightful Mexican dishes, and it does not take too much experience to prepare them in one's own kitchen. With chili powder as a flavor basis, plus tortillas, the most popular dishes can be made quite easily.

Because of the many good canned Mexican foods now available, it is easy to serve this type of food in almost any part of the United States.

The tortilla is the national bread of Mexico, used as a basis for many dishes. Tortillas can be purchased here by the dozen and can also be found in most of our larger cities. Very good ones can now be bought in cans.

Here is a popular, typical Mexican dinner menu: Guacamole Salad; Enchiladas or Tacos; Frijoles; Chili con Carne; Tamales; Mexican Rice; Tortillas; Pralines; and iced tea or coffee.

Guacamole Salad

Serves 8

4 avocados
1 teaspoon minced onion
½ teaspoon chili powder
½ teaspoon salt

3 tomatoes
Lettuce
French dressing

MASH avocados, add minced onion, chili powder, and salt. Halve tomatoes; pile with the mixture. Serve well chilled on lettuce, with French dressing. Garnish with dashes of chili powder.

Tacos

PLACE sliced, cooked meat or chicken on a tortilla; spread with pickle relish, and fold over; fasten each with two toothpicks. Fry in deep, hot fat (390 degrees), or toast on a hot griddle until thoroughly heated and golden brown in color. Have ready a salad of shredded lettuce and chopped tomatoes; pile this in each open end of the taco, and sprinkle with French dressing.

Enchiladas

Serves 6

18 tortillas
½ cup shortening
1 No. 2 can chili con carne
½ cup grated cheese

1 onion, sliced
½ teaspoon salt
½ teaspoon chili powder

HEAT tortillas in hot fat until soft; spread with chili con carne and roll. Stack rolls parallel on a hot, ovenproof platter; pour over them the remainder of the chili con carne. Sprinkle with grated cheese, and place in the oven to melt the cheese. Cover with thinly sliced onion; sprinkle with salt and chili powder. Serve at once.

Mexican Rice

Serves 4

1 cup uncooked rice
2 tablespoons fat
1 small onion, minced
½ green pepper, chopped

1 cup canned tomatoes
2 teaspoons salt
2 teaspoons chili powder
2 cups water (about)

WASH rice well, dry, and brown in hot fat. Add onion, green pepper, tomatoes, salt, and chili powder. Mix well and add just enough water to cover. Allow to simmer, covered, until the rice is tender, about 30 minutes. Remove the lid to allow the mixture to dry out. Do not stir after the cooking starts.

Utah

Winnifred Cannon Jardine

THE DESERET NEWS
SALT LAKE CITY, UTAH

Although many inhabitants of Utah are third- and fourth-generation descendants of the original Mormon pioneers (as I myself am), it is amazing to see pioneer influences that have carried over to present-day homemaking. Folks out here are homebodies. They love their homes and their kitchens, and they spend a good deal of time in them, making them happy, pleasant places for their families.

In a sense, this heart of the Mormon country is a melting pot, for church converts migrate to Utah constantly from all parts of the world; thus we find favorite pioneer recipes including split-pea soup from Holland, pie from Switzerland, cake from Denmark, and pastry from Scotland, as well as those recipes evolved by the pioneers themselves.

These recipes are only a handful from a most successful pioneer recipe contest just completed by the Deseret News. *They have all been tested and approved.*

Old-Fashioned Whole-Wheat Bread

The only flour those early pioneers knew anything about was straight whole-wheat flour. This recipe has been revised to use the modern yeast cake, but it retains the old-fashioned ingredients. Certainly no loaf of bread could be made more quickly or easily.

Makes 2 medium-sized loaves

1 yeast cake	3 teaspoons molasses
⅓ cup cold water	3 teaspoons salt
3 teaspoons shortening	3 cups milk, scalded
3 teaspoons honey	6 cups whole-wheat flour

SOFTEN yeast in water. Melt shortening; combine with honey, molasses, salt, and scalded milk. Cool to lukewarm and combine with yeast mixture. Add enough flour to make a soft dough, and knead thoroughly, using extra flour as needed. Shape into two loaves and place in greased loaf pans. Let rise to not quite double in bulk (about 2 hours), and bake at 350 degrees for 70 minutes. Note: Whole-wheat bread that rises too long becomes a little sour.

Angie Earl's Lemon Pies

Anyone who eats at the Lion House Social Center, the home of Brigham Young, in Salt Lake City, has tasted these melt-in-your-mouth lemon pies that Angie Earl, cateress there for ten years, has made so famous. The pastry has a quality of its own—a golden-brown tenderness that's rare in a piecrust. Because of its water content, it requires longer baking time than usual. Although it's at its best in prebaked shells, it also makes delicious two-crust pies.

Serves 12

Pastry:

2 cups flour	⅔ square butter (about 2 tea-
1 teaspoon salt	spoons)
1 teaspoon sugar	½ cup ice water
¾ cup lard	

SIFT together flour, salt, and sugar. With the fingertips break butter into half-inch bits through the flour. Then break in lard, making the pieces half the size of the butter bits. With a knife cut in ice water, adding only a little at a time. When the dough forms into a ball, turn onto a floured board and knead just enough to have a smooth dough. Roll in waxed paper and let stand in the refrigerator overnight or longer, if possible. (For best results have the butter and lard very cold. The dough may be kept refrigerated 5 to 7 days.)

Bake twelve shells over the backs of individual pie or muffin tins.

Filling:

1½ cups water
½ cup lemon juice
1 cup sugar
½ square butter (about 1½ teaspoons)
⅛ teaspoon salt
4 tablespoons cornstarch

½ cup cold water
3 eggs, separated
½ cup sugar
¼ teaspoon lemon flavoring
Whipped cream or meringue (for topping)

COMBINE water, lemon juice, sugar, butter, and salt, and bring to a boil. Combine cornstarch and cold water; stir into the boiling mixture. Cook over direct heat for 2 minutes. Pour part of the hot mixture over well-beaten egg yolks, then combine with the boiling mixture. Take from the range immediately and fold the hot filling into egg whites that have been stiffly beaten and blended with sugar and lemon flavoring. When cool, fill the pastry shells and top with whipped cream or meringue.

Mormon Pancakes with Side Pork

Serves 4

8 slices salt pork
2 eggs
2 cups milk
2¼ cups flour

1 teaspoon salt
1 teaspoon sugar
4 teaspoons baking powder
Salt-pork drippings

PARBOIL salt pork, then drain thoroughly and brown on both sides in a hot skillet. Remove from the pan and keep warm. Beat together eggs and milk. Sift together flour, salt, sugar, and baking powder, and stir into milk mixture. Beat well, then beat in 2 tablespoons salt-pork drippings. Heat the griddle and grease it with salt-pork drippings. Fry the pancakes to an even brown. As each one is ready to come off the griddle, roll a slice of the fried pork into the cake. Trickle over it plenty of hot syrup.

Pioneer Syrup:

1 cup corn syrup   2 tablespoons molasses

MEASURE corn syrup into a small saucepan; blend molasses with it. Heat but do not boil. If a thin syrup is desired, add ¼ cup water.

Quilter's Potato Salad

Serves 6

3 large potatoes, or 5 small   3 teaspoons sugar
3 hard-cooked eggs, chopped   2 eggs, uncooked
4 tablespoons minced onion   3 tablespoons melted butter
Salt and pepper   ½ cup hot vinegar
1 teaspoon dry mustard   1 cup cream, whipped
1 teaspoon salt

COOK potatoes with their jackets on. Cool, skin, and dice. Add hard-cooked eggs, onion, and salt and pepper to taste. Set aside a few minutes before adding the dressing. For the dressing, mix mustard, salt, and sugar. Beat eggs with melted butter and hot vinegar, and combine with the mustard mixture. Cook over boiling water or low heat until thick. Cool thoroughly. Combine with whipped cream and mix with potatoes.

Swiss Apple-Cherry Pie

This unusual pie, which came all the way from Switzerland, combines the tang of the cherry with the good, old-fashioned apple-pie taste that's a favorite with all.

Pastry for a two-crust pie   6 tablespoons butter or mar-
4 tart apples   garine

1 cup sugar
2 tablespoons flour
2 teaspoons cinnamon

½ teaspoon nutmeg
1 No. 2 can pitted sour red cherries, drained

PARE apples, core, and slice. Place a layer of pastry in piepan and brush with 2 tablespoons melted butter. Arrange a layer of apples on the pastry shell. Mix together the dry ingredients and sprinkle a portion over the layer of apples. Arrange a layer of red cherries, sprinkle with a portion of the dry ingredients, then a layer of apples, dry ingredients, a layer of cherries, dry ingredients, and end with a layer of apples. Top with dots of butter. After the top crust is placed on the pie, brush the crust with cream or evaporated milk and sprinkle with a mixture of ½ teaspoon sugar and ¼ teaspoon cinnamon. Bake at 425 degrees for 30 to 40 minutes.

Ann Ward Sutton

SALT LAKE TELEGRAM
SALT LAKE CITY, UTAH

Game Birds

Here in Utah meat of game birds has always been a special treat, since the hunting is so fine. When properly prepared, both duck and pheasant, for which we are noted, are delicious eating.

The fat in the bird varies with the type of bird and the manner of dressing. Fat is distributed under the skin and inside the bird, rather than throughout the flesh. If the birds are skinned, all of the surface fat is removed. Dry picking is the most satisfactory way of dressing. (Local markets will do this rather unpleasant job for you at a very low cost.) Skinned birds, and those having only small fat deposits, should be larded by inserting narrow strips of fat pork into the meat.

Pineapple Duck

Serves 6

5- to 6-pound duck
4 cups water
2 teaspoons salt
½ clove garlic
1 cup drained, diced, canned
pineapple

1 medium green pepper, cut
in 1-inch squares
2 tablespoons cornstarch
1 teaspoon salt
1 tablespoon lemon juice
1 teaspoon soy sauce
Hot, cooked rice

CUT duck into quarters. Place it with water, salt, giblets, and neck in a Dutch oven or pressure cooker. Cook covered until tender (25 minutes under pressure, or 1 hour in a Dutch oven). Remove the duck. Drain off the liquid. Allow the fat to rise to the top of the liquid, then skim off and reserve. Remove the skin, and cut the duck into narrow pieces about 2 inches long.

Cook 3 tablespoons duck fat and garlic for 3 minutes over low heat. Remove garlic and add the duck pieces. Cook 5 minutes. Add 1 cup of duck broth, pineapple, and green pepper. Blend together and add cornstarch, ¼ cup water, salt, lemon juice, and soy sauce. Cook, stirring lightly, until the sauce thickens. Serve with hot, cooked rice.

Pheasant

Pheasant is a dry bird needing extra fat to make it palatable, but otherwise it may be cooked in any fashion used for chicken.

TO BROIL: Split down the back; cut into quarters. Rub well with melted butter. Broil slowly until done. Pheasant takes 30 to 40 minutes. Turn every 5 minutes, basting with additional butter. Season with salt and pepper.

TO ROAST: Season the inside with salt; stuff with dressing. Do not sew openings but cover them with thin slices of fat salt pork fastened down with toothpicks. Place on a rack in a shallow pan. Do not cover. Bake at 275 to 300 degrees for 70 to 80 minutes.

Arrange the birds in the center of a large, hot platter, surrounded by fluffy rice and topped with broiled mushroom caps. Garnish with candied red apples, green peppers stuffed with corn, and water cress.

TO FRY: Cut the bird into serving pieces and season with salt and pepper. Shake in a paper bag containing ½ cup flour. Brown slowly to a fine golden brown in ¼ cup vegetable shortening. Remove and place on a rack in a Dutch oven or roaster with a tight lid. Swish out frying pan with ½ cup water and pour over the pheasant. Steam at 275 degrees for 1½ hours. Remove the lid during the last 30 minutes of cooking to make the skin crisp.

Venison

Venison is similar in texture and conformation to lamb and mutton. The fat of young deer is thick, clear, and firm, and the meat is a very dark red. Venison is prepared like lamb or mutton, according to the age of the animal.

Tender cuts are cooked quickly (broiled or roasted) until rare or medium well done. Tougher cuts are best when cooked slowly in moist heat (braised) or until well done.

BROILING

Venison: Leg steaks, rib steaks, loin steaks, ground patties.
Elk: Sirloin, porterhouse, T-bone, club, tenderloin, ground patties.

Cut steaks ¾ to 2 inches thick. Remove from the refrigerator 30 minutes before needed, and wipe dry. Slash the fat edge of the meat in several places, to prevent curling. Rub the cut surfaces with garlic (optional), and brush generously with melted butter. Place the broiling pan so the top of the meat is 2 to 3 inches from the flame. Brown, turn, and complete the broiling; season with salt and pepper.

Venison takes 8 to 12 minutes on each side.

Elk requires 12 to 20 minutes on each side.

Since the fat congeals quickly, serve as soon as broiled.

ROASTING

Venison: Leg, loin, shoulder (boned and rolled), ribs.
Elk: Ribs (standing or rolled), rump, sirloin tip, loin section.

If desired, rub meat with a cut clove of garlic or stud it with small pieces of garlic; season with salt and pepper. Place fat side up on a rack in a pan with low sides. If the meat is lean, dot the surface with suet, bacon, or salt pork. Roast at 300 degrees. Do not cover.

Venison takes 20 to 25 minutes per pound.

Elk takes 25 to 30 minutes per pound.

POT-ROASTING

Venison: Chuck, rump.
Elk: Chuck, rump (older animals).

If desired, before pot-roasting, a 4- or 5-pound chunk of venison may be marinated for 2 to 3 days in equal parts of water and wine (preferably claret) to cover, 1½ teaspoons salt, 6 to 8 peppercorns, 1 bay leaf, 10 to 12 whole cloves, 1 onion, sliced. This marinade is used in place of other liquids when pot-roasting the meat.

Wipe the surface of the meat with a damp cloth and lard with salt pork; rub with salt, pepper, and flour. Sauté in hot fat until browned, turning frequently. This should take approximately 30 minutes. Add ½ cup water (or marinade liquid, as above) and 1 tablespoon vinegar. Cook, covered, 2 to 2½ hours, or until tender.

Thirty minutes before the meat is done, add ½ cup chopped celery; 1 onion, chopped; 1 carrot, sliced; 1 tart apple, chopped; and 1 tablespoon lemon juice.

Trout

It is important not to overcook trout. This fish, unlike meat, has very little tough connective tissue and is sure to be hard and dry if over-cooked.

In Utah there are three kinds of trout: rainbow, brook, and lake. Rainbow and brook are best fried or broiled, since they are considered medium fat. Lake trout are best baked or broiled.

BROILING

Clean, remove head and tail, wipe dry. Brush generously with melted butter and place on a broiler. Place the broiler 2 to 3 inches from the flame and broil until the fish flakes when tried with a fork (6 to 8 minutes). Season and serve with lemon butter, tartar sauce, or drawn-butter sauce.

Lemon Butter:

CREAM ¼ cup butter. Beat in, drop by drop, 1 tablespoon lemon juice.

FRYING

Clean fish and wipe dry. If fish is large, cut in small slices or fillets. Dip in cream or canned milk and then in flour. Place in a hot frying pan containing enough butter or bacon drippings to just cover the bottom of the pan (approximately 3 tablespoons). Brown on one side, turn, and brown the other. Season. This slice or small trout requires only a short cooking period, usually 2 to 3 minutes. Thicker fillets or larger fish should be browned in the pan and then placed in the oven at 350 degrees for 10 minutes to complete cooking.

DEEP-FAT FRYING

Dip fish in canned milk, then in flour, and then in beaten egg and crumbs. Place in a single layer in hot fat to cover; brown 2 to 3 minutes. Season and serve.

Vermont

Betty Sproston

THE BURLINGTON FREE PRESS
BURLINGTON, VERMONT

Of the natural sweets man has discovered, none surpasses the delicate flavor and satisfying taste of Vermont maple syrup. Maple syrup and honey were the only forms of sweetening readily available to the early settlers. With the increase of population and wealth of our country, maple products have changed from primitive articles of food to luxury items.

Maple Syrup Cake

½ cup sugar
⅓ cup butter
¾ cup maple syrup
2¼ cups flour

3 teaspoons baking powder
Pinch of salt
½ cup milk
3 egg whites

CREAM sugar and butter together. Add syrup and stir well. Sift together flour, baking powder, and salt. Add milk and flour alternately to syrup. Fold in beaten egg whites and bake 30 to 35 minutes in an oblong pan at 350 degrees. When cake is baked and cool, place it on an inverted cake pan and cover with icing.

Maple Syrup Icing:

BRING 1 cup maple syrup to a brisk boil. Beat the white of 1 egg to the frothy stage, pour the syrup slowly into the beaten egg white, stirring briskly. Cool and spread over cake.

Maple Syrup Fudge

2 cups maple syrup
1 tablespoon light corn syrup
¾ cup light cream

¾ cup walnut meats, coarsely chopped

COMBINE maple syrup, corn syrup, and cream, and place over a low flame. Stir constantly until the mixture begins to boil. Cook without stirring until a soft ball forms in cold water. Remove from fire; cool to lukewarm; then beat until it thickens. Add nuts and pour at once into a buttered pan. When cold, cut into squares.

Frances Fancher

RUTLAND HERALD
RUTLAND, VERMONT

Mincemeat

Many Vermont cooks look forward to the November deer-hunting season—and the makings for those holiday mince pies. Venison makes rich mincemeat, but if hunting is poor, the cook has to make do with beef.

A warning from the donor of this recipe: "Make it just as I've told you; you'll find that the seasoning can't be improved upon." I did—and found her advice reliable.

(Ed. note: The original recipe gave the measurements in bowlfuls, but for uniformity the quantities have been given in cups. Do not try to make the full recipe unless you have an enormous cooking pot, as well as a large crock to store the mincemeat.)

Makes over 1 gallon

6 cups chopped, cooked venison or beef
2 tablespoons cinnamon
2 tablespoons cloves
1 tablespoon salt
1 tablespoon black pepper
6 cups apples, pared, cored,
and cut up

2 cups molasses
2 cups vinegar
2 to 4 cups boiled cider
2 cups suet, chopped
4 cups raisins
10 cups sugar
Grated rind and juice of 3
lemons

PLACE venison in a covered stone crock with spices, salt, and pepper. Cook together, thoroughly, the remaining ingredients, and pour over the meat and spices. Store in a cool place.

Note: Our mincemeat, stored in this manner for two years, has kept perfectly.

Vermont Suet Pudding

If you mention "suet pudding" to a Vermont housewife, she'll tell you that her recipe came straight from her great-grandmother. The following recipe is offered with no apologies; it's delicious.

Serves 8

1 cup finely chopped beef
suet
1 cup sour milk
½ cup molasses
½ cup maple syrup
2 cups flour

1 teaspoon each: soda, salt,
cinnamon, cloves, and nutmeg
2 cups seedless raisins
1 cup broken butternut meats

MIX first four ingredients together. Blend together all dry ingredients, add raisins and nut meats, and stir into the first mixture. Fill a well-greased pudding pan one-half full. Cover and steam for 2½ hours.

Sauce:

1 tablespoon butter	1 cup maple syrup
2 teaspoons flour	1 cup milk
⅛ teaspoon salt	

MELT butter; blend in flour and salt; add syrup. Stir until mixture is smooth. Add milk gradually, stirring constantly, over boiling water, and cook until the mixture reaches the consistency of rich cream sauce. Serve hot over the pudding.

Note: This pudding will keep for several weeks if wrapped in waxed paper and stored in a cool place.

Virginia

Dorothy Robertson

RICHMOND TIMES-DISPATCH

RICHMOND, VIRGINIA

Georgian silver and handmade mahogany, rich with generations of rubbing, furnish an appropriate setting for food in the Colonial tradition, beloved of tidewater Virginians. You won't find much of this food in public eating places. But recipes for dishes that have come down from Colonial ancestors are still in proud use among many families here. This traditional cookery of eastern Virginia is the cookery of abundance, born in a very bountiful land where servants were once as plentiful as game, and seafood, and Virginia hams.

The first cookbook published in the American colonies bore a Virginia imprint. The Compleat Housewife or Accomplished Gentlewoman's Companion was printed in Williamsburg in 1742; the recipes it contained were a collection made from an earlier and much larger cookbook printed in England. To this English influence was added a French touch by Thomas Jefferson, who brought back with him from his stay in France a knowledge and love of French cooking that caused Patrick Henry to denounce him as a man who had "abjured his native victuals." Jefferson set fashion when he introduced such French dishes as blancmange, meringues, macaroons, ragouts, vanilla, and beef à la mode.

Characteristic and colorful dishes have also developed from the foods either less abundant or unknown in England and France. The wild turkeys of Virginia, the succulent oysters and crabs of her coastal regions, peanut-fed hogs, and white, water-ground cornmeal are among the distinctive native products that have inspired Virginia cooks.

Sweet-Potato Biscuits

Makes 18 to 20 biscuits

2 cups flour
½ teaspoon baking soda
1 teaspoon salt

4 tablespoons lard
½ cup sour milk
1 cup mashed sweet potatoes

SIFT together flour, baking soda, and salt. Work in the lard with the fingertips. Mix in sour milk, and add sweet potatoes. This should make a soft dough. Roll out, cut, and bake in a hot oven (450 degrees). Serve hot with butter.

Damson Pie

Serves 8

5 eggs, separated
1½ cups sugar
½ cup soft butter
1 tablespoon flour

⅛ teaspoon salt
1 cup damson preserves
8 individual unbaked pastry
  shells

BEAT yolks of eggs until light. Add slowly, while beating, ¾ cup of sugar. Beat the other ¾ cup sugar into the soft butter. Combine the two mixtures and add to them the flour and salt. Now add the preserves. Lastly fold in the beaten egg whites. Bake in pastry shells in a moderate oven about 30 minutes, or until set.

Rich as it is, damson pie is sometimes served with a topping of whipped cream.

Mary B. Armistead

ROANOKE TIMES AND WORLD NEWS
ROANOKE, VIRGINIA

Virginia Fried Chicken

CLEAN chicken thoroughly, cut into the proper pieces, and chill in the refrigerator. About 30 minutes before frying, pop the pieces into a deep bowl of rich buttermilk and let them soak well.

Do not dry the chicken after removing it from the buttermilk. Put the pieces into a paper bag containing flour, salt, and pepper, and shake thoroughly. Then fry slowly in a well-greased frying pan, and serve while piping hot. You'll love the result!

Buck and Breck

Old-fashioned pickle concoctions are coming back into their own these days. One is Cold Pickle or Buck and Breck, which needs no cooking and includes, of all things, raw vegetables. This will keep indefinitely in a sealed container.

1 gallon vinegar
1 pound brown sugar
1 cup salt
2 ounces each: black pepper, ginger, white mustard seed, ground mustard, and celery seed

1 ounce turmeric
2 ounces whole cloves
1 cup grated horseradish
Fresh, chopped, raw vegetables: onions, celery, cabbage, tomatoes, red and green peppers

PUT vinegar in a 2-gallon crock; add sugar, salt, spices, and horseradish. Then add vegetables until the crock is almost full. Be sure that the vinegar covers everything well.

Mix thoroughly, put on an airtight cover, and, as the old directions read, "Let it stand until Thanksgiving." The older this pickle gets, the better its flavor.

Virginia Ham

No list of Virginia recipes would be complete without including directions for cooking old Virginia ham.

SELECT a 3- to 5-year-old ham weighing between 12 and 18 pounds. Trim and wash it carefully and soak overnight. The following day, change the water and add 1 cup apple vinegar and 1 cup brown sugar. Add more water to cover the whole ham. Boil very slowly 5 or 6 hours, or until the end bone becomes loose. Leave the ham in the water in which it was cooked until the water is cold. Remove and skin the ham.

Cut the top fat in gashes 1 inch apart. Stuff with bread crumbs mixed with chowchow pickle, a little ham stock, and butter. Pat smooth and place cucumber pickles, cut in rings, on top. Bake until the ham is browned, basting if it dries out.

Quail on Toast

The fall season brings quail hunting, and Virginians brag about this way of fixing the juicy birds.

PLUCK and draw the birds, cleaning them thoroughly but leaving them whole.

Stuff each bird with one large oyster or two small ones, sprinkled with salt and pepper and bread crumbs. Put the birds in a pan with a little water and butter, and bake in a moderate oven (350 degrees), basting frequently, until brown and tender. Serve on toast with the essence or thickened gravy poured over them.

Washington

Maurine Kelly (Prudence Penny)

SEATTLE POST-INTELLIGENCER
SEATTLE, WASHINGTON

Cooking in the Northwest area is influenced by our large Scandinavian population and our fondness for seafood. Fishing is everyone's hobby. Father brings in the salmon, and even the children dig clams at the shore. The tiny Olympia oysters, big king salmon or the 3- or 4-pound silver salmon, clams, and wild blackberries are native foods, to be had for the fun of getting them. And since we grow such wonderful apples, we can't omit Apple Kuchen and Apple Dumplings, either.

Western Baked Salmon

Serves 6 to 8

3- or 4-pound salmon	1 onion, sliced
Prepared mustard	4 slices bacon
Salt and pepper	

HAVE the head of the salmon removed and clean the fish well. Spread inside with mustard, season with salt and pepper. Lay slices of onion in the fish. Place in a greased baking dish. **Cover with** bacon slices and bake, uncovered, in a 350-degree oven for 45 minutes, or until the fish flakes easily when tested with a fork.

Hangtown Fry

Serves 4

6 to 12 oysters, drained	6 eggs
Crumbs	¼ cup milk
1 egg, beaten	Salt and pepper
Butter	Bacon

SEASON oysters with salt and pepper. Dip in crumbs, then in beaten egg, and again in crumbs. Fry in butter until golden brown on one side. Turn oysters over and pour in eggs, which have been slightly beaten with milk and seasoned with salt and pepper. Cook slowly until the eggs are set and lightly browned. To serve, fold in half and slip onto a hot platter. Garnish with crisp bacon curls.

Apple Kuchen

Serves 4 to 6

2 cups sifted flour	¾ cup milk
½ teaspoon salt	Sliced apples
3 teaspoons baking powder	1 cup brown sugar
¼ cup sugar	¼ cup butter
2 eggs	⅓ cup raisins
¼ cup melted butter or margarine	½ teaspoon nutmeg

SIFT flour, salt, baking powder, and sugar together. Add the eggs, milk, and melted butter. Beat to a smooth, heavy batter. Spread in a buttered baking pan, cover with sliced apples, and top with a mixture of brown sugar, butter, raisins, and nutmeg. Bake in a 375-degree oven about 35 minutes. Serve with cream or hard sauce.

Apple Dumplings

Serves 4

Pastry for two-crust pie
4 medium apples, pared and cored
1 cup sugar

2 cups water
¼ teaspoon cinnamon
3 tablespoons butter

ROLL out pastry ⅛ inch thick and cut into four 7-inch squares. Set an apple on each square of pastry; pack the centers with filling. Fold pastry around the apples, envelope fashion, pinching the edges together.

Make a syrup by boiling together the sugar, water, cinnamon, and butter for 3 minutes. Place the dumplings in a shallow baking pan, pour the syrup over them, and bake at 425 degrees for about 40 minutes.

Filling:

¾ cup sugar
4 tablespoons softened butter
½ teaspoon salt

½ teaspoon cinnamon
½ teaspoon nutmeg

CREAM together the butter and sugar; add the remaining ingredients.

Wild-Blackberry Pie

3 cups fresh wild blackberries
1 cup sugar
2 tablespoons flour
2 tablespoons lemon juice

⅛ teaspoon salt
1 recipe plain pastry for two-crust pie
1 tablespoon butter

COMBINE berries, sugar, flour, lemon juice, and salt. Line a piepan with pastry, add the filling, dot with butter, and cover with the top crust. Bake in a very hot oven, 450 degrees, for 10 minutes; reduce the temperature to 350 degrees and bake 25 to 30 minutes longer, or until the berries are tender.

Miriam R. Beckes (Dorothy Neighbors)

THE SEATTLE TIMES
SEATTLE, WASHINGTON

Geoducks

The geoduck (pronounced goo-y-duck) is a native of the Pacific Coast. The Puget Sound beaches furnish the environment best suited to its propagation and growth. This giant clam, weighing 6 pounds or more, lies 2 to 3 feet deep and is submerged in water except for an hour or two at extremely low tide. The tip of the long, giraffelike neck above the silt is the guide to the digger in locating the geoduck.

WASH well in cold water. Pour boiling water over the geoduck, cut away the shell, and strip off the skin from the body. Cut the tender flesh in slices, pound, and fry as razor clams are fried but longer and more slowly. The tough necks, ground, may be used in chowder.

Olympia Pepper Pot

Serves 3

1 pint Olympia oysters	1 tablespoon butter
1 cup tomato sauce	½ green pepper, minced
2 tablespoons catsup	Salt and cayenne
2 tablespoons lemon juice	Buttered toast

HEAT oysters slowly in their own liquor. In a separate pan heat tomato sauce, catsup, lemon juice, butter, and minced pepper. When these begin to bubble, add the drained oysters and sufficient oyster liquor to thin the mixture. Season; simmer only until the oysters are plump. Serve on buttered toast.

Baked Apple Rolls

Serves 6 to 8

2 cups sifted flour	6 medium apples, grated
½ teaspoon salt	½ cup sugar
⅔ cup shortening	1½ teaspoons cinnamon
7 tablespoons ice water (about)	1 tablespoon butter

SIFT flour with salt. Cut in shortening with a pastry blender. Add just enough ice water to make a soft dough. Roll out on a slightly floured board. Cover with grated apple; sprinkle with a mixture of the sugar and cinnamon, and dot with butter.

Roll up as for jelly roll; cut in 1-inch slices. Place slices, cut side up, about 1 inch apart in a buttered baking dish and cover with the cinnamon sauce given below. Bake at 450 degrees for 7 minutes, then reduce the heat to 350 degrees and bake about 40 minutes longer.

Spicy Sauce:

¼ cup sugar	1 tablespoon butter
2 tablespoons flour	¼ teaspoon allspice
1 cup water	1 teaspoon cinnamon
3 tablespoons lemon juice	½ teaspoon nutmeg

MIX sugar and flour together. Add water and lemon juice. Cook together until thick and clear. Add butter and seasonings.

Dorothy C. Raymond (Dorothy Dean)

THE SPOKESMAN-REVIEW
SPOKANE, WASHINGTON

Spokane is the trade center of the Inland Empire, a fertile region that stretches from the Canadian boundary down into Oregon and from the Montana Rockies to the Cascades. The area produces about one-twelfth of the nation's wheat. We have cattle country, too, if that means a place where cattle are far more numerous than people. Everyone knows about our apples, which are our third most important crop. And as our canning industry develops, Washington is becoming better known for its soft fruits—pears, apricots, sweet cherries, grapes and prunes, and in recent years, freestone peaches.

Not the largest in volume but the most distinctive product of the Inland Empire is the dry pea. Many regions where green peas are grown for canning and freezing cannot grow their own seed. But the highest quality seed peas ripen on our hills, the same hills that are noted for big wheat yields, so maybe your favorite little green peas have ancestors from out our way. We also provide lots of split peas for soup. Peas for canning and freezing are grown a little to the south of the seed-pea country, down near Walla Walla in the foothills of the Blue Mountains.

The western slope of the Cascades has a climate entirely different from that of the Inland Empire. Mild temperatures and lots of rain produce different crops. Blue Lake beans, for canning, grow high on trellises. Strawberries and raspberries are picked and frozen in great quantities. Peas are grown here for canning, but there is too much moisture for ripening of seed. Green pastures are dotted with "contented" cows.

Puget Sound produces oysters, the unique variety being the tiny, sweet Olympia. Crabs, fresh salmon, and other seafoods abound. The Port of Seattle handles the Alaska salmon production. Each summer huge warehouses are filled with the canned fish.

Over by the ocean, cranberries flourish.

If variety is the spice of life, ours is a spicy life indeed.

Fairy Loaf Cake

This isn't the best cake in the world, but it is the best one I can make with the egg yolks left from angel-food cake—and that makes the recipe worth having.

8 egg yolks

1¼ cups sugar

½ cup salad oil

2¾ cups sifted cake flour

3 teaspoons double-action baking powder

½ teaspoon salt

1 cup water

Flavoring: 1½ teaspoons vanilla, or 1 teaspoon vanilla plus ½ teaspoon lemon, or what-will-you

BEAT egg yolks until fluffy. Beat in sugar thoroughly. Add oil and beat until very fluffy. Sift flour with baking powder and salt. Add the dry ingredients to the first mixture alternately with water and flavoring, beating carefully. The batter will be thin. Bake in a tube pan or in a large sheet pan (9 by 13 or even 10 by 16 inches) at 350 or 375 degrees for 35 to 50 minutes. This is a good cake to cut into small pieces and frost for *petits fours*.

Note: Sometimes I color the water with burnt sugar and have a caramel cake.

Choc-Oat Crispies

(By "Liz" Gailey, one of the assistant Dorothy Deans)

¾ cup sifted flour

½ teaspoon salt

½ teaspoon soda

½ cup soft shortening

½ cup brown sugar

½ cup granulated sugar

1 egg

½ teaspoon vanilla

¾ cup raw quick-cooking oatmeal

¼ cup chopped nut meats

1 6-ounce package chocolate bits

SIFT together flour, salt, and soda into a bowl. Add shortening, brown and white sugar, egg, and vanilla. Beat until smooth. Fold in rolled oats, nut meats, and chocolate bits. Drop from a teaspoon onto a buttered cooky sheet. Bake at 350 degrees for about 10 minutes. These cookies spread quite a bit, so give them room.

Herb Bread

This won first prize in one of our contests.

Makes 2 large or 3 medium loaves

2 cups milk	1 teaspoon nutmeg
4 tablespoons sugar	4 teaspoons dried leaf sage
1 tablespoon salt	4 teaspoons caraway seed
2 yeast cakes or 2 envelopes	4 tablespoons salad oil
dry yeast	7 or 8 cups sifted flour
2 eggs, beaten	

SCALD milk; add sugar and salt. Cool to lukewarm. Add yeast, beaten eggs, nutmeg, crumbled sage, caraway seed, salad oil, and enough flour to make a smooth dough. Knead well; let rise until doubled in bulk. Punch down, divide into two large or three medium loaves; round dough up and let it "rest" for 15 minutes. Mold loaves and place in greased pans. Let rise until doubled in bulk. Bake at 400 degrees for about 40 minutes. If you are using glass pans, set the oven at 375 degrees.

Serve this bread while fresh, cut into jaggedy slices and accompanied by plenty of butter. Watch the "heel divers," to avoid mayhem or even murder.

Washington D.C.

Violet Faulkner

THE WASHINGTON EVENING STAR

WASHINGTON, D.C.

The waters of the Chesapeake along the Maryland and Virginia shore lines produce most of the country's hard- and soft-shelled crabs. The crab leads an interesting and complex life, going through more evolutions than a butterfly. Every year between the first of June and the end of August a new generation is produced. As a young crab grows, it sheds its shell repeatedly. It starts life as a hard-shell, then undergoes various changes until it reaches the soft-shelled state—the gourmet's delight. Then, in the space of 48 hours, the cycle is completed and the crab is back where it started, a hard-shell again. Crabs molt about fifteen times before they mature, at first they molt about every 6 days, but later there is a span of some 25 days between molts. They gain about one-third in size with each molt.

Soft-shelled crabs are shipped alive, whereas most hard-shells are steamed near the place of capture, the meat then picked out and shipped in ice.

The Carolinas, Louisiana, and Georgia ship an appreciable amount of this steamed crabmeat, packed in tins in three different grades. The choicest of these is the back-fin meat, or the big "lump" crab. There are only two pieces of this choice morsel to each crab, so naturally it brings the best price on the market. The middle *grade is sold as white crabmeat, and the least expensive is the claw, which is slightly dark in color.*

In the matter of cooking the soft-shelled crab, you'll find a variety of opinions. Some say the best and only way is to dip the crabs in seasoned flour or meal and fry as you would chicken. Use only enough fat to cover the bottom of the pan. Others hold to the deep-fat method, while still others prefer the broiling process. Whatever method you choose, remember this: Soft-shelled crabs are tender enough to eat raw, so don't fry them past a light brown.

Bishop's Imperial Crab

Serves 6 to 8

2 pounds lump crabmeat	1 teaspoon capers
⅔ cup mayonnaise	¼ teaspoon pepper

PICK over crabmeat carefully, seeing that all bits of shell are discarded. Add capers and pepper to mayonnaise; mix gently with crabmeat. Pile the mixture into six to eight crab shells, depending on the size of the serving desired. Bake in a 350-degree oven for 15 minutes, or until lightly browned on top. Serve with a wedge of lemon and with Worcestershire and Tabasco sauce, if desired.

Crab Norfolk

Serves 3 or 4

2 cups lump crabmeat	Juice of ½ lemon
½ cup butter or margarine	Salt

THE finest lump meat should be used for this dish. Pick over meat carefully, discarding all bits of shell. Melt butter in individual frying pans or ramekins, add lemon juice and crabmeat. Season with salt. Sauté over medium heat until piping hot; or bake in a very hot oven (500 degrees) for 15 minutes.

Broiled Soft-Shelled Crabs

Serves 3 to 6

6 live soft-shelled crabs	Cayenne
½ cup butter	Salt, pepper
2 tablespoons lemon juice	½ cup flour

WASH crabs in cold water, clean, and dry well. (To clean, remove the spongy material under the pointed flaps on each side. Then remove the pointed "apron" underneath. Cut across the front of the crab to remove the eyes and sandbag.) Melt butter, add lemon juice and cayenne pepper. Sprinkle crabs with salt and pepper and roll in the butter sauce. Dredge with flour, shaking off any excess. Lay crabs on a broiler rack and broil under a medium flame, turning to brown both sides. Pour any remaining seasoned butter over the crabs after cooking, and garnish with lemon sections. Allow one to two crabs per serving, depending on the size.

Deviled Crabs

Serves 6

1 pound crabmeat	1 teaspoon sage
2 tablespoons minced onion	Dash of cayenne
3 tablespoons butter	1 tablespoon lemon juice
2 tablespoons flour	1 tablespoon Worcestershire
1 cup milk	1 egg, beaten
½ teaspoon salt	1 tablespoon minced parsley
⅛ teaspoon pepper	½ cup bread crumbs
1 teaspoon dry mustard	2 tablespoons melted butter

REMOVE any shell or cartilage from the crabmeat. Cook onion in butter until tender, blend in flour, add milk gradually, and cook until thick, stirring constantly. Add seasonings, lemon juice, Worcestershire sauce, and beaten egg. Blend in crabmeat and parsley. Fill crab shells or buttered ramekins and sprinkle tops with buttered bread crumbs. Bake in a moderate oven (375 degrees) for 15 minutes, or until brown.

Shad Roe

POACHED: Place shad roe in cold water with 1 tablespoon lemon juice and 1 teaspoon salt. Bring to a boil and cook for 15 minutes.

BROILED: First boil roe for 10 minutes in water containing 1 tablespoon lemon juice and 1 teaspoon salt. Plunge roe into cold water. After 10 minutes, remove and dry with a damp cloth, or drain on absorbent paper. Dip in flour, brush well with melted butter or margarine. Place in a preheated broiling compartment 2 inches from the source of heat. Broil for 3 minutes on one side and 5 minutes on the other. Garnish and serve immediately.

Sauerkraut in White Wine

It is traditional in this section to serve sauerkraut with turkey at Christmas time.
(Ed. note: So great is the variety of traditions in Washington that though we grew up there neither I nor any of my Washington friends knew about this one.)

Serves 6 to 8

1 onion, minced	1 large potato, grated
2 tablespoons butter or drippings	1 teaspoon caraway seed
	1 cup stock or water
1 quart sauerkraut	1 cup dry white wine
1 large apple, chopped	

SAUTÉ onion in butter until light brown. Add to sauerkraut with apple, potato, and caraway seed. Place in a greased casserole and pour over the stock and wine. Bake, covered, in a 350-degree oven for 1½ to 2 hours.

Poppy Seed-Cheese Wafers

Makes 50 to 60 wafers

1 cup sifted flour
½ teaspoon salt
⅓ cup shortening
3 to 5 tablespoons ice water

½ cup grated cheese
1 egg white, slightly beaten
Poppy seed

SIFT together flour and salt. Cut in shortening until the mixture resembles coarse meal. Add water gradually until all of the dough is moist enough to hold together. Roll out ⅛ inch thick on a floured pastry cloth. Spread half of the dough generously with grated cheese. Fold the other half on top. Roll again, until about 3/16 inch thick. Brush the top with slightly beaten egg white. Sprinkle again with cheese and then with poppy seed. Cut into oblongs 2 inches by 1 inch. Bake in a 450-degree oven on an ungreased cooky sheet for 10 to 12 minutes.

Lucia Brown

THE WASHINGTON POST
WASHINGTON, D.C.

Bean soup is one dish that appears every day on the menus of the Senate and House restaurants on Capitol Hill. It's a tradition of more than forty years' standing.

The late Senator Knute Nelson, Minnesota Republican, started the custom back in 1907. A bean-soup fancier, he was also Chairman of the Senate Committee on Rules. He decreed that the soup should be served daily in the Senate dining rooms. It was, and became so popular that it's never left the menu since. The Hon. Joseph ("Uncle Joe") Cannon, Speaker of the House from 1903 to 1911, who was irate because only the Senators were being stoked to daily feats of eloquence with this hearty dish, issued a similar order for the House.

The Senate's Bean Soup

*This recipe was provided by Paul C. Johnson, head of service in the
Senate dining rooms. It's made in a big brass kettle there, but Mr.
Johnson says other utensils can be used.*

Serves 10 or 12

1½ pounds small navy (pea)   1 onion, chopped
  beans   Butter
2 quarts hot water   Salt and pepper
¾ pound smoked ham hocks

WASH the beans and run them through hot water until they are
white again. Add hot water and ham hocks and boil slowly for 2½
hours. Braise onion in butter. When light brown, add to the soup.
Season to taste with salt and pepper immediately before serving.

Ozark Pudding

*White House meals have varied greatly through the years, reflect-
ing the part of the country from which the President came, the
times, and the chef's ability.*

*Mrs. Harry S. Truman has favored typically American dishes
since she has been chatelaine of the White House. Many are made
by recipes she has collected throughout her long years as a homemaker, some of them from her native Missouri. This recipe attracted
nationwide attention when it was first published in 1948. Letters
poured into the White House, questioning some of the directions,
but Mrs. Truman stuck by her guns.*

Serves 4

1 egg   ⅛ teaspoon salt
¾ cup sugar   ½ cup chopped nuts
2 tablespoons flour   ½ cup chopped apples
1¼ teaspoons baking powder   1 teaspoon vanilla

BEAT egg and sugar together for a long time, until very smooth.

Mix flour, baking powder, and salt. Stir into the sugar-egg mixture. Add nuts, apples, and vanilla. Bake in a greased pie tin in a medium oven (350 degrees) for 35 minutes. Serve with whipped cream or ice cream.

Southern Maryland Stuffed Ham

Many residents of southern Maryland, adjacent to Washington, D.C., serve ham stuffed with greens as a traditional Easter dish. The following recipe was given by Mrs. J. William Roberts, of Landover, Maryland.

1 country-cured ham	1 cup mint leaves
4 quarts shredded kale	1 teaspoon red pepper
1 cup chopped wild-onion tops	2 teaspoons salt

SIMMER the ham in enough water to cover until about half done. This will take 15 minutes to the pound for a ham of 15 pounds or under. Remove from the fire and let cool, leaving the skin on. Next, make pockets in the top of the ham by jabbing it about twenty times clear to the bone with a sharp carving knife. Work the knife around a bit to form pockets.

Mix kale, onion tops, mint leaves, red pepper, and salt. Scald with hot water. Stuff this mixture into the pockets, using fingers and the knife. Stuff in as much of the greens as possible, and arrange the rest over the top of the ham. Sew stuffed ham up in a cloth bag, return it to the pot, and simmer until done—about 15 minutes more per pound.

This ham may be eaten—skinned first, of course—hot or cold, with a little vinegar if desired. Some Southern Marylanders serve it, with plenty of good hot biscuits, for Easter breakfast, others for Easter dinner. When the ham is sliced, the effect is of green veining through the pink meat. Mrs. Roberts says the best ham to use is one cured only the fall before, so that the meat will not be too hard to stuff.

Lamb with String Beans

*(Recipe of Madame Vassili Dendramis, wife of the
former Greek Ambassador to the United States)*

Serves 4

1 pound shoulder of lamb
¼ pound butter or margarine
1 medium onion, finely
  chopped
Salt and pepper to taste

1 tablespoon tomato sauce
2 pounds fresh green beans,
  cut in halves
1 fresh tomato, chopped
1 teaspoon flour

CUT shoulder of lamb into cubes. Place in a saucepan with butter
and onion, and brown slightly. Then pour in enough water to cover
the meat, adding salt, pepper, and tomato sauce. Cover the saucepan
and allow the meat to boil for several minutes.

In the meantime place string beans in a saucepan together with
fresh tomato, adding enough water to almost cover the beans. When
the vegetables have cooked down to a fairly thick sauce, strain, and
mash through a sieve. Thicken with flour, mixed with a little cold
water, stirring constantly. Pour over the lamb before serving.

Roast Duckling with Orange Sauce

*(Recipe of Madame Henri Bonnet, wife of the
French Ambassador to the United States)*

Serves 4

1 duckling
2 oranges
Salt and pepper
1 tablespoon butter

1½ tablespoons curaçao or
  Cointreau
1 tablespoon flour
1 cup strong bouillon

PEEL one orange and cut up the pulp. Stuff the duckling with the
pulp. Cut the rind in thin strips and put it aside. Season the duckling
with salt and pepper. Roast in a 325-degree oven.

Sauce:

BOIL the cut-up rind of the orange in boiling water for 10 minutes; drain. Put the rind in a bowl with the raw liver of the duckling and mash together well, moistening with curaçao.

Melt butter, add flour gradually, stirring constantly. Add bouillon. Add the mashed liver and orange rind, also the gravy from the pan in which the duckling was roasted, having first removed the grease. Force through a strainer.

Remove orange pulp from inside duckling. Place duckling on a platter, decorating it with orange slices. Serve sauce separately.

Ruth Nicol

THE WASHINGTON DAILY NEWS
WASHINGTON, D.C.

Oyster Stew

(Recipe from Étienne Barbatini, chef at Normandy Farm and formerly chef to Madame Pandit, then the Ambassadress from India.)

Serves 4

1½ cups cream	Salt and pepper
½ cup skim milk	Dash of cayenne
1 pint small Chinchoteague oysters and juice	Dash of lemon juice
	Dash of paprika
4 tablespoons butter	

HEAT cream and milk in a double boiler, taking care not to let any skin form or let the liquids reach a boil. In a small saucepan heat the oysters and their juice, watching them carefully and removing them from the fire just as the edges begin to curl. Combine oysters and the cream mixture. Add butter, salt and pepper to taste, and cayenne. Just before serving, add lemon juice and paprika.

(Ed. note: Chinchoteague oysters are the extra large ones from the Atlantic shore of Maryland; even the small ones are large.)

Coleslaw

(From Réné Roux, chef at Olmstead's.)

Serves 4

1 medium head cabbage, well trimmed, washed, and shaved as fine as possible

2 teaspoons chopped onion

1 medium clove garlic, minced

1 small green pepper, chopped

12 anchovy fillets

6 pitted green olives, split lengthwise

½ pint mayonnaise

2 tablespoons chili sauce

1 teaspoon dry mustard

1 teaspoon chopped parsley

2 tablespoons wine vinegar

Salt and pepper to taste

MIX everything but the cabbage in a bowl. Pour over the cabbage and toss thoroughly. Serve on lettuce.

Barbara Holmes

WASHINGTON TIMES-HERALD
WASHINGTON, D.C.

Pears Baked in Ginger Syrup

Serves 4 to 6

⅓ cup sugar

½ teaspoon ginger

Juice of 1 lemon

Grated rind of ½ lemon

¾ cup water

6 to 8 fresh pears

MIX sugar, ginger, lemon juice and rind. Add water; boil 5 minutes. Peel pears, put into a buttered baking dish, pour syrup over them. Cover and bake for 30 minutes.

Oyster Crabs

(Ed. note: The first problem is to find a quart of these fantastically rare, tiny, and delicate creatures.)

Serves 4

1 quart oyster crabs
¼ pound butter
1 wineglass sherry
Paprika, salt, and pepper

1 jigger brandy
2 egg yolks
2 cucumbers

WASH oysters well, then cook in butter and sherry until they are red. Add seasonings. Stir brandy into egg yolks; add to oyster mixture and heat. Do not allow it to boil. Serve in cooked cucumber shells that have been halved and parboiled.

Wisconsin

Eleanor Shefferman

WISCONSIN STATE JOURNAL
MADISON, WISCONSIN

In Wisconsin, America's dairyland, nothing goes over quite as well as an old-time German or Scandinavian dish. Of course, the people of the state are their own best customers for our dairy products, particularly cheese.

Sauerkraut and Herb Frankfurters

This recipe reflects the German influence.

Serves 4

2 tablespoons butter
4 tablespoons minced onion
4 tablespoons chopped green pepper
1 No. 2½ can sauerkraut
1 cup canned tomatoes
½ teaspoon caraway seed
2 cups bread crumbs

2 tablespoons melted butter
1 tablespoon grated onion
¼ teaspoon thyme
Salt
2 tablespoons milk
8 frankfurters
Rich prepared mustard
8 strips bacon

MELT butter in a saucepan over low heat; add onion and green pepper. Simmer until tender. Add sauerkraut, tomatoes, caraway seed; mix thoroughly. Cover; simmer 20 to 25 minutes, stirring occasionally.

In a bowl, combine crumbs, butter, onion, thyme, salt, and milk. Split frankfurters lengthwise but without cutting them all the way through. Brush the surfaces with mustard. Fill with the dressing. Wrap with bacon, fastened with toothpicks.

Place on the broiler rack with the stuffing side down. Broil, turning once, until the bacon is done. Allow approximately 3 minutes for each side. Serve with cooked sauerkraut.

Cheese Cake with Berries

Serves 6 to 8

1¼ cups zwieback crumbs	1¼ cups creamed cottage
2 tablespoons sugar	cheese
3 tablespoons melted butter	2 eggs, separated
½ cup sugar	1 teaspoon vanilla
¼ teaspoon salt	Whipped cream
2 tablespoons flour	2 cups fresh (or frozen) rasp-
½ cup cream	berries or strawberries

COMBINE crumbs, sugar, and butter. Blend thoroughly and press evenly into a buttered 9-inch cake or spring-form pan, reserving ¼ cup of the mixture for the top.

Blend together sugar, salt, and flour. Add to cheese, which has been drained and sieved, and mix thoroughly. Stir in cream and beaten egg yolks. Fold in stiffly beaten egg whites and vanilla.

Turn into the crumb crust and sprinkle with the remaining crumbs. Bake in a slow oven, 325 degrees, for about 45 minutes, until set. Let cool in oven with heat off and door open.

When ready to serve, garnish with whipped cream and serve with sweetened raspberries or strawberries.

Dorothy Parnell

MILWAUKEE SENTINEL
MILWAUKEE, WISCONSIN

Schaum Torte

Serves 10

6 egg whites
2 cups sugar

1½ teaspoons lemon juice or vinegar

BEAT whites until stiff (hold a point), and then gradually beat in sugar about 1 teaspoonful at a time, beating after each addition. Then beat in the lemon juice or vinegar. Beat until very stiff and glossy.

The torte is usually baked as a whole, with the meringue spread in a buttered straight-sided pan, heaped up around the sides so that after baking the filling can be placed in the center for serving. It is possible to make individual servings, however, either by dropping large spoonfuls of the meringue on buttered brown paper in a circle to make a ring, the center of which is filled for serving, or by baking separate meringues, each piled high on the buttered paper and then hollowed out by pressing the spoon onto the top, to make a depression which is filled just before serving.

Bake the whole torte or the individual meringues in a very, very slow oven (225 degrees) until delicately browned and crusty; the individual shells take about 40 minutes and the large size about 60 minutes. Cool in the open oven; remove from pan. Serve filled with ice cream and fresh berries or cut-up fruit.

Welsh Rabbit

Because Wisconsin, known as the Dairy State, is famed for its cheeses, and Milwaukee is noted for its beer, the following Welsh Rabbit seems a happy combination of our "local talents."

Serves 4 to 6

½ teaspoon Worcestershire
   sauce
⅛ teaspoon paprika
½ teaspoon dry mustard
Dash of cayenne

Salt to taste
½ cup beer
1 pound sharp cheddar cheese
Toast

MIX all the seasonings to a smooth paste. Add the beer, put into a skillet, and let the mixture stand over extremely low heat until the beer is hot. Then add the cheese, crumbling it as you do so. Stir until the cheese is melted. Serve piping hot over crisp toast.

Clarice Rowlands (Alice Richards)

THE MILWAUKEE JOURNAL
MILWAUKEE, WISCONSIN

Food produced in Wisconsin includes milk and manufactured dairy foods; vegetables and fruit; meat; and poultry, and eggs. Wisconsin holds first place in the nation in the production of milk and all major manufactured dairy products with the exception of butter, ice cream, and cottage cheese.

Potato-Cheese Soup

Serves 4 to 6

3 medium potatoes
2 cups boiling water
2 to 3 cups milk
3 tablespoons butter
½ small onion, finely chopped
2 tablespoons flour

1 teaspoon salt
Pepper, cayenne
1 cup grated Wisconsin American (cheddar) cheese
1 tablespoon chopped parsley

COOK potatoes in boiling, salted water until tender. Drain; put through a strainer. Measure the liquid remaining and add enough milk to make 4 cups. Scald. Melt butter, add onion; simmer 5 minutes; then add flour and seasonings. Combine with the strained potatoes. Cook 3 minutes; strain, if desired. Add cheese and beat until smooth. Add parsley and serve very hot.

Wyoming

Louise Love

THE WYOMING EAGLE

CHEYENNE, WYOMING

When the Women's Section of the Wyoming Eagle was born in December of 1949, it included a daily column titled "Favorite Recipes of Cheyenne Women." Each day a recipe of some local housewife appeared in the column, which soon became one of the most popular features of the newspaper. Since cooking at 6200 feet is quite different from cooking at lower altitudes, these recipes, tried and tested in Cheyenne kitchens, were much more popular with local women than those in cookbooks published in other regions. The recipes were in such demand that at the end of a year they were gathered into a little book. Here are a few.

Light Rye Bread

Makes 3 loaves

9 cups white flour
3 cups Fisher's rye flour
3 yeast cakes
1½ teaspoons salt
4¼ cups lukewarm water

6 tablespoons melted shortening
3 tablespoons caraway seed
Melted butter

SIFT and measure flours; resift together. Crumble yeast, add salt, then add lukewarm water gradually, allowing yeast to dissolve.

Add shortening; add flour and stir until the dough is thoroughly mixed and ready to knead. Knead until smooth, about 20 minutes. Let rise until doubled in bulk. Work again for 5 minutes, then let rise again to double its bulk. Divide the dough in three parts; add 1 tablespoon caraway seed to each part. Shape into loaves and place in bread pans. Make five slits across the top of each loaf. Let rise in pans until doubled in size. Brush the tops with butter. Bake at 450 degrees for 15 minutes; reduce heat to 375 degrees, and bake for 30 minutes longer.

Chocolate Torte

Serves 10

½ cup butter (¼ pound)
1 cup granulated sugar
1 cup brown sugar
3 eggs, separated
2½ cups sifted cake flour

1 teaspoon soda
1½ cups milk
2 squares unsweetened chocolate, melted
1 teaspoon vanilla

CREAM butter and sugars, and add beaten egg yolks. Sift flour and soda together three times. Add half the dry ingredients to the creamed mixture, alternately with the milk. Then add chocolate, part of the egg whites, beaten stiff, more flour, more milk, and finally the rest of the egg whites. Add vanilla. Pour the batter into cake tins. Cut through the batter with a knife and pound the tins several times on a flat surface to remove any bubbles. Bake 23 to 25 minutes at 350 to 375 degrees.

Icing:

¼ pound butter
2½ cups powdered sugar
2 squares unsweetened chocolate, melted

Cream
½ teaspoon vanilla
A pinch of salt

MIX butter with powdered sugar and melted chocolate. Thin with cream to a consistency for spreading. Add vanilla and salt.

Onion Salad Dressing

Makes almost a pint—enough for several salads

½ cup sugar
1 teaspoon salt
1 teaspoon dry English mustard
1 teaspoon poppy seed

1 teaspoon celery seed
2 tablespoons onion juice
1 cup salad oil
4 tablespoons lemon juice

MIX together sugar, salt, mustard, poppy seed, celery seed, and onion juice. Add salad oil slowly, 1 tablespoon at a time, beating well after each addition. Add lemon juice. Serve the dressing on a fruit salad.

Canada

Marjorie Elwood

THE TORONTO STAR
TORONTO, ONTARIO

Every spring and early summer there occurs one of nature's miracles —the salmon run. On both the east and west coasts of Canada, thousands upon thousands of the "king of fish" journey up from the ocean to the spawning grounds. It is said that instinct sends the vast majority of these silvery fish to the very same river down which they traveled as small fish, and to the same spawning ground where they themselves were born. It is at this time of year that the salmon fishermen have a very busy time.

Salmon from our Pacific Coast province, British Columbia, is canned in tremendous quantities and has an unequaled reputation for quality and flavor. On the other hand, the salmon from the East, caught in the Restigouche and Matapedia rivers of the Maritime provinces, though not as good as the British Columbia variety when canned, is marvelous cooked fresh. In fact, in the month of May it vies with spring lamb and young broilers in its appeal to jaded winter appetites.

Simmered Salmon

Serves 10 to 12

4- to 5-pound piece of Cana-   2 tablespoons vinegar or
   dian Restigouche salmon   lemon juice
Water to cover fish   1 teaspoon salt
3 bay leaves

MAKE a court bouillon of water, bay leaves, vinegar, and salt, and bring to the boiling point in a large kettle.

Set the salmon on a heatproof plate and then on a large piece of cheesecloth, bringing the corners together to be tied like a bag. Or wrap the fish in cheesecloth and put it in a wire basket such as that used for deep-fat frying. After wrapping the fish, lower it into the court bouillon; reduce the heat to simmering. If the water is allowed to boil the salmon loses much of its delicate flavor.

Allow about 12 minutes to the pound. When cooked, drain the salmon and remove it to a hot platter; reserve the stock for making sauce. Garnish with lemon wedges and sprigs of parsley, or lemon slices dipped in chopped parsley. Serve with melted butter or a fish sauce such as cucumber, maître d'hôtel, or mustard sauce.

Glazed Cold Salmon

Glazed cold salmon is very decorative and appetizing for a buffet supper or luncheon.

TO prepare it, follow the recipe for simmered salmon. When the fish is cooked, remove it from the liquid, drain, but allow it to cool in the cheesecloth. Then remove the cloth, skin the fish, and glaze it with aspic made from the stock in which the fish was cooked. In making the aspic, first be sure the stock is well seasoned with vinegar or lemon juice, salt, and pepper. Strain. Make aspic using the proportion of 1 tablespoon unflavored gelatin to 2 cups stock. Mix the gelatin first with a little cooled liquid, then dissolve in the hot stock. As the gelatin mixture starts to set, brush it over the cold salmon as a glaze. Sprinkle lightly with paprika.

Arrange the glazed salmon on a bed of water cress and garnish with cucumbers, hard-cooked eggs, or stuffed olives. Mayonnaise is usually served with the cold salmon.

If desired, the gelatin mixture may be allowed to jell in a bowl, then it can be turned out on a board, chopped fine, and placed around the fish as a decorative border.

Wild Rice

In the marshes of Rice Lake in Ontario, Lake Winnipeg in Manitoba, and other northern lakes, wild rice grows and is harvested in the autumn by the Indians. The kernels of rice are long and thin and of an almost black color. (It is often called black rice.)

Wild rice may be used much like white rice in a pudding. For this purpose, it is best steamed for a long period of time in a double boiler. We like it better cooked and served with mushrooms, as a vegetable, as in the following recipe.

Serves 4

1 cup wild rice	4 cups boiling water
1 teaspoon salt	¼ teaspoon thyme
1 small onion	1 teaspoon chopped parsley
2 tablespoons butter or margarine	1 cup mushrooms, sautéed

COMBINE rice, salt, onion, and boiling water in the top part of a double boiler. Cook the rice over boiling water until tender—about 45 minutes. Stir with a fork occasionally. Add the remaining ingredients and place in a well-buttered, 7-inch ring mold or casserole.

Set in a pan of warm water and bake in a moderate oven (350 degrees) for 20 minutes. This is delicious with poultry or game.

Pickled Corncobs

In Canada we do not grow enough corn for all our needs, but we do have, starting about August, some mighty good varieties for eating on the cob. The Golden Bantam develops first. As the name implies, it is yellow in color and small in size. In September the Wintergreen variety starts appearing on the market. It is a delicious juicy corn, sweeter than the Golden Bantam, and is the one eaten with such gusto by the fire at corn roasts.

This recipe is one of those family traditions handed down from one generation to the next but never put on paper. It is an old German recipe, and since the district around Kitchener, Ontario, is full of people of German descent, that is where we finally located it. Actually, tiny immature corncobs are used for this pickle, and the only place they are sold is in the farmers' markets.

2 pounds tiny, premature corncobs, 1½ to 2 inches long	1 cup white wine vinegar
	1 pound granulated sugar
½ ounce alum	1 bay leaf
	2 sticks whole cinnamon

TRIM cobs of all corn silk and husks.

Boil alum in ½ gallon water. Pour over cobs and let stand in a warm place for 1 hour. Drain; chill in cold water.

Make a syrup of vinegar, sugar, and the spices tied in a cheese-cloth bag. Bring to the boiling point and add corncobs. Cook 5 minutes. Remove the spice bag. Fill sterilized jars with cobs and liquid. Seal and store in a cool, dark place.

Yorkshire Pudding

This is an Old Country dish which at one time was cooked along with the roast of beef or under it, allowing the beef drippings to fall upon it. However, since it is now customary to roast beef in a slow oven, and Yorkshire Pudding requires a hot oven to make it puff, the two cannot be cooked together satisfactorily. Yorkshire Pudding is popular in Canada—and in most other countries—as an accompaniment for roast beef.

Serves 6

1 cup sifted pastry flour	2 eggs, separated
½ teaspoon salt	½ cup water
½ cup milk	Beef drippings

SIFT flour and salt into a bowl and stir in milk. Beat the mixture until foamy. Beat egg yolks until thick and lemon colored. Beat whites until stiff, and fold into yolks. Beat eggs into the flour-and-milk batter. Then add water and beat until large bubbles rise to the surface. Allow the batter to stand 1 hour (optional).

Beat lightly again before using. Preheat the oven to 400 degrees. Have ready a hot baking dish (about 10 by 6 by 2 inches), with about ¼ inch hot beef drippings in it. Pour the batter into the prepared baking dish to a depth of ⅝ inch. Bake in a hot oven (450 degrees) for 20 minutes, then reduce the temperature to 350 degrees, and bake 10 to 15 minutes longer. Cut in squares and serve very hot.

Peach Pudding

There are no finer peaches than those grown in the Niagara district of Ontario. British Columbia peaches are also favorites in all parts of Canada, but because of the long distances they have to be shipped, they are picked before full maturity and are not as juicy and luscious as those from the Niagara fruit belt.

This Peach Pudding is rather unusual in preparation, and so good to eat!

Serves 6

1 cup sifted pastry flour	½ cup milk
2 teaspoons baking powder	1 cup brown sugar
2 teaspoons sugar	2 cups boiling water
Few grains salt	2 tablespoons butter
1 cup fresh, sliced peaches	

MIX and sift together flour, baking powder, sugar, and salt. Add peaches and milk. Pour into a deep buttered baking dish. Mix brown sugar, boiling water, and butter. Pour this over the pudding. Bake in a moderate oven (350 degrees) for 25 to 30 minutes. Serve hot.

Margaret Henderson

THE VANCOUVER DAILY PROVINCE

VANCOUVER, BRITISH COLUMBIA

Baked Peaches and Sausage

Serves 3 or 4

1 pound bulk pork sausage	4 tablespoons brown sugar,
6 cooked or canned peach	syrup, or honey
halves, drained	¼ teaspoon cloves
½ teaspoon cinnamon	¼ cup peach juice

FLATTEN sausage into six thin patties. Fry in a hot frying pan over medium heat until well browned, about 15 minutes, turning once. Place peach halves in a single layer in a well-greased baking dish or casserole. Sprinkle with mixed brown sugar and spices. Add peach juice. Bake in a hot oven (450 degrees) for 15 minutes. Place the browned sausage patties on the peach halves and bake 15 minutes longer.

Note: 4 tablespoons maple-flavored syrup, corn syrup, or honey may be substituted for the brown sugar.

Steamed Marmalade Pudding

Serves 6

1 tablespoon butter or margarine, or ¼ cup finely chopped suet	1 cup sifted flour
	2 teaspoons baking powder
	½ teaspoon salt
½ cup sugar	½ cup milk
1 egg	3 tablespoons marmalade

CREAM butter and sugar together thoroughly; add unbeaten egg and beat well. Sift flour with baking powder and salt. Add the sifted dry ingredients to the creamed mixture alternately with the milk. Add marmalade and mix well. Turn into a well-buttered pudding mold, tie securely, steam 1 hour. Serve with lemon sauce.

Edith Adams

THE VANCOUVER SUN
VANCOUVER, BRITISH COLUMBIA

Johnny Canuck Game Dinner

Serves 2 or 3

1 rabbit or game bird	1 small onion, grated
3 tablespoons bacon fat	⅓ cup seedless raisins
2 cups apple juice	1 clove garlic
1 cup maple syrup	¼ teaspoon dry mustard
½ can condensed tomato soup	Salt and pepper

CLEAN and cut into serving portions a rabbit or game bird, setting aside the rib and neck sections. Use these to prepare a meat stock. Have an iron skillet sizzling hot. Grease with bacon fat, sear the game, then fry it to a golden brown in the remaining fat. Add the other ingredients. Cover and simmer slowly until the liquid is nearly evaporated and the sauce begins to thicken and brown in the pan. Then add 1 cup of stock from the neck and rib pieces, and again simmer the contents of the skillet until thick. Repeat adding a cup of stock and simmering it away until the meat is tender and beginning to leave the bones. Remove to a hot platter and serve with applesauce to which has been added grated horseradish in the ratio of 2 level tablespoons horseradish to 2 cups cold applesauce.

Owoyoos Tomato Fritters

Serves 4

2 cups canned tomatoes, drained
2 tablespoons melted butter
1 cup sifted flour

1 teaspoon baking powder
½ teaspoon sugar
1 teaspoon salt
¼ teaspoon pepper

MIX thoroughly. Drop into hot deep fat by small spoonfuls and brown on both sides.

Rose-Hip Jam

This is not only delicious but has a high vitamin C content.

2 cups fully ripe rose hips (best after frost has touched them)
4 cups boiling water

2 pounds sugar
¾ pound cooking apples, pared

WASH hips and put into boiling water. Boil gently until soft. Mash with a wooden spoon. Strain through a jelly bag, letting it drip overnight. Measure juice; make up to 3 cups with water, if necessary. Cook apples to a pulp in a little water; rub through a sieve.

Mix hip juice and apple pulp and bring to a boil. Stir in sugar and boil rapidly until the jelly stage is reached. Pour into sterilized jars, and seal.

Hawthorn haws can be used for a similar jam.

Sheila Craig

THE WINNIPEG TRIBUNE
WINNIPEG, MANITOBA

Blueberry Crisp

Wild blueberries are plentiful in this part of the country from the latter part of July to the first of September. They are delicious in pies, muffins, desserts, and jam. But Blueberry Crisp is everyone's favorite.

Serves 6

4 cups fresh blueberries
¼ cup granulated sugar
4 tablespoons butter or margarine
2 teaspoons lemon juice
¾ cup brown sugar
½ cup sifted flour

PLACE blueberries in a 1½-quart buttered baking dish. Sprinkle with granulated sugar and lemon juice.

Cream butter; gradually add brown sugar. Add flour and rub to a crumbly mixture. Spread this over the top of the fruit and bake in a moderate oven (350 degrees) for about 40 minutes.

Hawaii

Harriett Thomas

HONOLULU STAR-BULLETIN

HONOLULU, HAWAII

Hawaii is a melting pot of recipes reflecting both Occidental and Oriental influences. Each race represented in Hawaii has delicious dishes, and here are a few universal favorites: Hawaiian Curry, Teriyaki Steak, Beef and Tomatoes, and Pineapple, Luau style. (A "luau" is the name of a true Hawaiian feast.)

Hawaiian Curry

Serves 6 to 8

2 cups grated fresh coconut
3 cups milk
3 cloves garlic, chopped
1 tablespoon chopped, fresh ginger root
2 apples, cored and diced
2 medium onions, chopped

2 tablespoons curry powder
½ cup softened butter
½ cup enriched flour
½ teaspoon salt
½ cup light cream or top milk
2 to 3 cups cooked chicken, shrimp, or other meat

ADD milk to grated coconut and bring the mixture to a simmering temperature. Add garlic, ginger, apples, and onions. Blend curry powder with 2 tablespoons of the butter; add to the coconut mixture and cook slowly for 3 hours, stirring occasionally. Remove from the stove and place in a cool spot for several hours or until the next day. Then strain, using a poi cloth or jelly bag. Cook very slowly until thoroughly heated. Blend flour with the remaining butter and add to the warm, strained mixture. Cook, stirring constantly, until thickened. Add salt and cream. Add meat or fish and continue to simmer slowly for 30 minutes. If chicken is used in the curry, 1 cup of finely diced fresh pineapple may be added. Serve with rice and the following accompaniments:

Crisp chopped bacon	Chopped nuts
Chutney	Raisins
Sweet pickles	Grated cheese
Shredded coconut	Hard-cooked eggs, chopped or
Sliced lemon	sliced

CURRY is attractively served from a hollowed-out pineapple shell, with the rice molded in individual servings and garnished with chopped parsley.

Teriyaki Steak

This is a Hawaiian variant of a Japanese dish.

Serves 6

3 pounds beefsteak	1 small piece ginger root,
½ cup soy sauce	crushed, or 1 tablespoon
2 tablespoons sugar	ground ginger
1 clove garlic	

SLICE meat thin, across the grain if possible. Combine the remaining ingredients and soak meat in this sauce for 20 minutes or longer. Drain. Place on a rack and broil on each side for 5 to 10 minutes, or until brown. Serve immediately with rice and vegetables.

Beef and Tomatoes

This is a local adaptation of a Chinese dish.

Serves 4

1 pound beef	4 tablespoons peanut oil
2 medium onions	1 teaspoon soy sauce
1 green pepper	2 teaspoons enriched flour
3 medium tomatoes	1 clove garlic

CUT meat in thin slices, the onions and pepper in large pieces, and the tomatoes in wedges. Place meat in a bowl and pour over it a sauce made from 1 tablespoon peanut oil, soy sauce, and flour. Let stand 10 to 15 minutes. Heat 2 tablespoons peanut oil in a frying pan and add garlic. Press garlic against the sides of the pan; when browned and dry, remove garlic and add the meat and sauce. Cook 5 to 10 minutes, stirring frequently. Remove the meat and the gravy that has formed, and set aside. Heat remaining peanut oil in a pan and add to it the onions and green pepper. Cook slightly; add meat, gravy, and tomatoes. Blend well; when the gravy bubbles, remove and serve at once.

Note: Overcooking toughens the meat and causes the tomatoes to be mushy.

Fresh Pineapple, Luau Style

USING a long, thin-bladed knife, cut a thick slice from the top and bottom of the pineapple, reserving them for later use. Remove the fruit portion of the pineapple in one solid cylinder. Cut it in half lengthwise and remove the core. Cut in lengthwise spears and replace these spears in the pineapple shell. Replace the pineapple top and bottom, to resemble a whole pineapple. Hold the bottom in place with toothpicks. Place on the luau table and allow guests to eat the pineapple spears with their fingers.

Notes on Regional Terms and Unusual Ingredients

A head or bulb of garlic is one of Nature's neatest packages, with tidy sections separately sealed that may be used one at a time; but this piece may be called, among other things, a pod, a button, a bud, or a bean. Regional terms can be that confusing. And some combinations of foods or seasonings can seem equally peculiar and even unlikely. Some terms are listed here that might mystify, say, someone in Alabama who wants to make a dish from Minnesota or a woman brought up in Texas who is trying to duplicate the dishes of her husband's Vermont childhood.

Almost daily some new delicacy comes into national distribution that once could be found only in the esoteric food shops in large cities. Now almost all cities and many small towns have stores with large assortments of unusual herbs, seasonings, vinegars, and such that used to available and known only to those with recent contact with foreign countries. There are also many Italian, Chinese, Scandinavian, and Mexican stores catering to first- or second-generation familes and other addicts of that kind of food. If you are really stymied for a strange seasoning, write to the Atlas Importing Company, 1109 Second Avenue, New York, N. Y., which will fill mail orders for almost any known spice, herb, condiment, or dried legume (which means any kind of pea, bean, or lentil).

BEANS. This universal food is grown in countless varieties all over the world, with each region having its favorite sizes, types, and names for fresh beans served as a vegetable in the summer and the dried beans used in regional dishes such as chili con carne or Boston baked beans. Pea or navy are the smallest of the dried beans. These or the marrowfat beans, next larger in size, are most used in New England. Yellow-eye, pinto, black-eyed pea, or kidney beans are larger; they are more often used in soup or in Southern dishes. The garbanzo or Spanish bean, also called the chick-pea and *ceci,* is much used in Mexican, Spanish, or Italian cooking. The *fava,* horse, or broad bean, sometimes called the butter bean, is a robust relative of the lima bean and, like it, may be eaten fresh or dried.

Of the beans that are generally served straight from the garden, fresh-picked, frozen, or canned, the yellow wax bean is called a butter bean in New England and so are limas elsewhere; the green string beans are called snap beans in some regions, bush beans in others.

BLADE MEAT.   A very thin cut of beef, with short, flat bones. Also called short ribs. Corresponds to spare ribs of pork.

BURGOO.   Kentucky stew traditionally made in large quantities outdoors in huge iron kettles for special occasions.

CHORIZAS or Spanish sausage, are dark and highly spiced. Salami is probably the best substitute to be found easily, though hot Italian, Portugese, or Polish sausage would also serve.

COMINO SEED.   Cumin seed, available in most stores offering a good assortment of seasonings.

CREOLE MUSTARD.   A prepared mustard, mild in flavor but more distinctive in taste than the run-of-the-mill commercial mustards. If it is unobtainable, use a regular prepared mustard but increase the spices very slightly.

COURT BOUILLON.   Water, with fish bones and skin, boiled with salt, pepper, onions, garlic (for some dishes), lemon slices, and a bay leaf, used for poaching steaks or filets of fish, and used strained as the liquid in sauces served with fish.

FAT BACK.   Salt pork, not smoked, with no lean streak at all.

FETA CHEESE.   Greek white cheese preserved in a brine.

FILÉ POWDER.   A seasoning and a thickener made from leaves or roots of sassafras. Food should never be cooked after filé has been added.

GARLIC.   With the garlic, even more than with beans, regional nomenclature leads to confusion. It grows in heads or bulbs, each of which divides easily into small sections called variously pods, buttons, buds, cloves, or beans. It may be sold by the bulb, and almost always is in large vegetable markets and in stores with a foreign flavor, but it appears in many American markets and chain stores in little cellophane envelopes, each containing several cloves.

HUSH PUPPY.   A small, deep-fried corn cake.

KOLACKY.   Bohemian dumplings, usually with prune, poppy-seed, or other fruit filling.

METTWURST.   A rich, spicy beef sausage. The best readily available substitute would be teawurst or liverwurst.

PAN CREAM.   Thick cream skimmed from the top of fresh milk. Much thicker than city "heavy cream."

PASTIES.   Cornish meat turnovers that the miners take to work instead of our sandwiches.

PEPPERS.   The bell or sweet pepper, whether red or green, is not to be confused with the hot or chili (cayenne) pepper, which is to be treated with the greatest caution, especially by cooks unfamiliar with Mexican or Spanish dishes. Pimientos are smooth, sweet red peppers.

ROSE HIPS.   The fruit of the rose, often brightly colored. It is the calyx, and remains on the stem after the petals have fallen.

ROUX.   A mixture of equal amounts of melted fat and flour, cooked slowly together over direct heat with constant stirring until the flour has ceased to smell raw. It is the basis for cream sauces and gravies.

SAGO.   The dried, powdered pith of a palm tree, used as a thickening agent and in puddings.

SQUASH. The varieties of summer squash are picked early and used at once or preserved by freezing or canning. They include the yellow crookneck or straightneck soft-skinned types, white bush or patty pan, green, cucumberlike-looking *zucchini*, and the *cocozelle* or Italian vegetable marrow squash. Fall and winter squashes, hard-shelled vegetables which keep well for winter use, include the Hubbard, acorn, butternut, and buttercup squash. These bake well, and are commonly used for "pumpkin" pie, though some diehards continue to use the true pumpkin.

SOUR CREAM. Smooth, mild, artificially soured cream, called butter cream in the Midwest.

STOCK. Beef, veal, or chicken bones simmered with onion, carrot, leek, and seasonings, then skimmed and strained.

SWELLFISH. Small, tender seafish from the bones and skin of which it is easy to separate the chunks of flesh, yielding lots of delicate meat not particularly fishy tasting and with practically no bones. Also known as sea squab in some restaurants and fish markets.

SUGAR. Two varieties have different names in different parts of the country. Confectioner's sugar is an especially finely powdered sugar; loaf sugar is lump sugar.

TORTE PAN. A special kind of cake pan common in European households. If you want to make many fancy cakes of the torte variety, get one in a big housewares department, or order one from a big city specialty store like Lewis and Conger in New York, or Macy's; for occasional use, try a spring-form cake pan with straight sides.

WRIGHT'S LIQUID SMOKE. A barbecue accompaniment in general use in the Far West. There is no substitute.

WILD ONION. Not readily available to most city people—try substituting chives or scallions.

Index

Contributors and Papers

A CATALOGUE OF SELECTED DOVER BOOKS
IN ALL FIELDS OF INTEREST

A CATALOGUE OF SELECTED DOVER BOOKS
IN ALL FIELDS OF INTEREST

LEATHER TOOLING AND CARVING, Chris H. Groneman. One of few books concentrating on tooling and carving, with complete instructions and grid designs for 39 projects ranging from bookmarks to bags. 148 illustrations. 111pp. 7⅞ x 10.
23061-9 Pa. $2.50

THE CODEX NUTTALL, A PICTURE MANUSCRIPT FROM ANCIENT MEXICO, as first edited by Zelia Nuttall. Only inexpensive edition, in full color, of a pre-Columbian Mexican (Mixtec) book. 88 color plates show kings, gods, heroes, temples, sacrifices. New explanatory, historical introduction by Arthur G. Miller. 96pp. 11⅜ x 8½.
23168-2 Pa. $7.50

AMERICAN PRIMITIVE PAINTING, Jean Lipman. Classic collection of an enduring American tradition. 109 plates, 8 in full color—portraits, landscapes, Biblical and historical scenes, etc., showing family groups, farm life, and so on. 80pp. of lucid text. 8⅜ x 11¼.
22815-0 Pa. $4.00

WILL BRADLEY: HIS GRAPHIC ART, edited by Clarence P. Hornung. Striking collection of work by foremost practitioner of Art Nouveau in America: posters, cover designs, sample pages, advertisements, other illustrations. 97 plates, including 8 in full color and 19 in two colors. 97pp. 9⅜ x 12¼.
20701-3 Pa. $4.00
22120-2 Clothbd. $10.00

THE UNDERGROUND SKETCHBOOK OF JAN FAUST, Jan Faust. 101 bitter, horrifying, black-humorous, penetrating sketches on sex, war, greed, various liberations, etc. Sometimes sexual, but not pornographic. Not for prudish. 101pp. 6½ x 9¼.
22740-5 Pa. $1.50

THE GIBSON GIRL AND HER AMERICA, Charles Dana Gibson. 155 finest drawings of effervescent world of 1900-1910: the Gibson Girl and her loves, amusements, adventures, Mr. Pipp, etc. Selected by E. Gillon; introduction by Henry Pitz. 144pp. 8¼ x 11⅜.
21986-0 Pa. $3.50

STAINED GLASS CRAFT, J.A.F. Divine, G. Blachford. One of the very few books that tell the beginner exactly what he needs to know: planning cuts, making shapes, avoiding design weaknesses, fitting glass, etc. 93 illustrations. 115pp.
22812-6 Pa. $1.50

CREATIVE LITHOGRAPHY AND HOW TO DO IT, Grant Arnold. Lithography as art form: working directly on stone, transfer of drawings, lithotint, mezzotint, color printing; also metal plates. Detailed, thorough. 27 illustrations. 214pp.
21208-4 Pa. $3.00

DESIGN MOTIFS OF ANCIENT MEXICO, Jorge Enciso. Vigorous, powerful ceramic stamp impressions — Maya, Aztec, Toltec, Olmec. Serpents, gods, priests, dancers, etc. 153pp. 6⅛ x 9¼.
20084-1 Pa. $2.50

AMERICAN INDIAN DESIGN AND DECORATION, Leroy Appleton. Full text, plus more than 700 precise drawings of Inca, Maya, Aztec, Pueblo, Plains, NW Coast basketry, sculpture, painting, pottery, sand paintings, metal, etc. 4 plates in color. 279pp. 8⅜ x 11¼.
22704-9 Pa. $4.50

CHINESE LATTICE DESIGNS, Daniel S. Dye. Incredibly beautiful geometric designs: circles, voluted, simple dissections, etc. Inexhaustible source of ideas, motifs. 1239 illustrations. 469pp. 6⅛ x 9¼.
23096-1 Pa. $5.00

JAPANESE DESIGN MOTIFS, Matsuya Co. Mon, or heraldic designs. Over 4000 typical, beautiful designs: birds, animals, flowers, swords, fans, geometric; all beautifully stylized. 213pp. 11⅜ x 8¼.
22874-6 Pa. $5.00

PERSPECTIVE, Jan Vredeman de Vries. 73 perspective plates from 1604 edition; buildings, townscapes, stairways, fantastic scenes. Remarkable for beauty, surrealistic atmosphere; real eye-catchers. Introduction by Adolf Placzek. 74pp. 11⅜ x 8¼.
20186-4 Pa. $2.75

EARLY AMERICAN DESIGN MOTIFS, Suzanne E. Chapman. 497 motifs, designs, from painting on wood, ceramics, appliqué, glassware, samplers, metal work, etc. Florals, landscapes, birds and animals, geometrics, letters, etc. Inexhaustible. Enlarged edition. 138pp. 8⅜ x 11¼.
22985-8 Pa. $3.50
23084-8 Clothbd. $7.95

VICTORIAN STENCILS FOR DESIGN AND DECORATION, edited by E.V. Gillon, Jr. 113 wonderful ornate Victorian pieces from German sources; florals, geometrics; borders, corner pieces; bird motifs, etc. 64pp. 9⅜ x 12¼.
21995-X Pa. $2.75

ART NOUVEAU: AN ANTHOLOGY OF DESIGN AND ILLUSTRATION FROM THE STUDIO, edited by E.V. Gillon, Jr. Graphic arts: book jackets, posters, engravings, illustrations, decorations; Crane, Beardsley, Bradley and many others. Inexhaustible. 92pp. 8⅛ x 11.
22388-4 Pa. $2.50

ORIGINAL ART DECO DESIGNS, William Rowe. First-rate, highly imaginative modern Art Deco frames, borders, compositions, alphabets, florals, insectals, Wurlitzer-types, etc. Much finest modern Art Deco. 80 plates, 8 in color. 8⅜ x 11¼.
22567-4 Pa. $3.00

HANDBOOK OF DESIGNS AND DEVICES, Clarence P. Hornung. Over 1800 basic geometric designs based on circle, triangle, square, scroll, cross, etc. Largest such collection in existence. 261pp.
20125-2 Pa. $2.50

150 MASTERPIECES OF DRAWING, edited by Anthony Toney. 150 plates, early 15th century to end of 18th century; Rembrandt, Michelangelo, Dürer, Fragonard, Watteau, Wouwerman, many others. 150pp. 8⅜ x 11¼.   21032-4 Pa. $3.50

THE GOLDEN AGE OF THE POSTER, Hayward and Blanche Cirker. 70 extraordinary posters in full colors, from Maîtres de l'Affiche, Mucha, Lautrec, Bradley, Cheret, Beardsley, many others. 9⅜ x 12¼.   22753-7 Pa. $4.95
21718-3 Clothbd. $7.95

SIMPLICISSIMUS, selection, translations and text by Stanley Appelbaum. 180 satirical drawings, 16 in full color, from the famous German weekly magazine in the years 1896 to 1926. 24 artists included: Grosz, Kley, Pascin, Kubin, Kollwitz, plus Heine, Thöny, Bruno Paul, others. 172pp. 8½ x 12¼.   23098-8 Pa. $5.00
23099-6 Clothbd. $10.00

THE EARLY WORK OF AUBREY BEARDSLEY, Aubrey Beardsley. 157 plates, 2 in color: Manon Lescaut, Madame Bovary, Morte d'Arthur, Salome, other. Introduction by H. Marillier. 175pp. 8½ x 11.   21816-3 Pa. $3.50

THE LATER WORK OF AUBREY BEARDSLEY, Aubrey Beardsley. Exotic masterpieces of full maturity: Venus and Tannhäuser, Lysistrata, Rape of the Lock, Volpone, Savoy material, etc. 174 plates, 2 in color. 176pp. 8½ x 11.   21817-1 Pa. $4.00

DRAWINGS OF WILLIAM BLAKE, William Blake. 92 plates from Book of Job, Divine Comedy, Paradise Lost, visionary heads, mythological figures, Laocoön, etc. Selection, introduction, commentary by Sir Geoffrey Keynes. 178pp. 8½ x 11.
22303-5 Pa. $3.50

LONDON: A PILGRIMAGE, Gustave Doré, Blanchard Jerrold. Squalor, riches, misery, beauty of mid-Victorian metropolis; 55 wonderful plates, 125 other illustrations, full social, cultural text by Jerrold. 191pp. of text. 8⅛ x 11.
22306-X Pa. $5.00

THE COMPLETE WOODCUTS OF ALBRECHT DÜRER, edited by Dr. W. Kurth. 346 in all: Old Testament, St. Jerome, Passion, Life of Virgin, Apocalypse, many others. Introduction by Campbell Dodgson. 285pp. 8½ x 12¼.   21097-9 Pa. $6.00

THE DISASTERS OF WAR, Francisco Goya. 83 etchings record horrors of Napoleonic wars in Spain and war in general. Reprint of 1st edition, plus 3 additional plates. Introduction by Philip Hofer. 97pp. 9⅜ x 8¼.   21872-4 Pa. $3.00

ENGRAVINGS OF HOGARTH, William Hogarth. 101 of Hogarth's greatest works: Rake's Progress, Harlot's Progress, Illustrations for Hudibras, Midnight Modern Conversation, Before and After, Beer Street and Gin Lane, many more. Full commentary. 256pp. 11 x 14.   22479-1 Pa. $7.00
23023-6 Clothbd. $13.50

PRIMITIVE ART, Franz Boas. Great anthropologist on ceramics, textiles, wood, stone, metal, etc.; patterns, technology, symbols, styles. All areas, but fullest on Northwest Coast Indians. 350 illustrations. 378pp.   20025-6 Pa. $3.50

MOTHER GOOSE'S MELODIES. Facsimile of fabulously rare Munroe and Francis "copyright 1833" Boston edition. Familiar and unusual rhymes, wonderful old woodcut illustrations. Edited by E.F. Bleiler. 128pp. 4½ x 6⅜. 22577-1 Pa. $1.00

MOTHER GOOSE IN HIEROGLYPHICS. Favorite nursery rhymes presented in rebus form for children. Fascinating 1849 edition reproduced in toto, with key. Introduction by E.F. Bleiler. About 400 woodcuts. 64pp. 6⅞ x 5¼. 20745-5 Pa. $1.00

PETER PIPER'S PRACTICAL PRINCIPLES OF PLAIN & PERFECT PRONUNCIATION. Alliterative jingles and tongue-twisters. Reproduction in full of 1830 first American edition. 25 spirited woodcuts. 32pp. 4½ x 6⅜. 22560-7 Pa. $1.00

MARMADUKE MULTIPLY'S MERRY METHOD OF MAKING MINOR MATHEMATICIANS. Fellow to Peter Piper, it teaches multiplication table by catchy rhymes and woodcuts. 1841 Munroe & Francis edition. Edited by E.F. Bleiler. 103pp. 4⅝ x 6.
22773-1 Pa. $1.25
20171-6 Clothbd. $3.00

THE NIGHT BEFORE CHRISTMAS, Clement Moore. Full text, and woodcuts from original 1848 book. Also critical, historical material. 19 illustrations. 40pp. 4⅝ x 6. 22797-9 Pa. $1.00

THE KING OF THE GOLDEN RIVER, John Ruskin. Victorian children's classic of three brothers, their attempts to reach the Golden River, what becomes of them. Facsimile of original 1889 edition. 22 illustrations. 56pp. 4⅝ x 6⅜.
20066-3 Pa. $1.25

DREAMS OF THE RAREBIT FIEND, Winsor McCay. Pioneer cartoon strip, unexcelled for beauty, imagination, in 60 full sequences. Incredible technical virtuosity, wonderful visual wit. Historical introduction. 62pp. 8⅜ x 11¼. 21347-1 Pa. $2.50

THE KATZENJAMMER KIDS, Rudolf Dirks. In full color, 14 strips from 1906-7; full of imagination, characteristic humor. Classic of great historical importance. Introduction by August Derleth. 32pp. 9¼ x 12¼. 23005-8 Pa. $2.00

LITTLE ORPHAN ANNIE AND LITTLE ORPHAN ANNIE IN COSMIC CITY, Harold Gray. Two great sequences from the early strips: our curly-haired heroine defends the Warbucks' financial empire and, then, takes on meanie Phineas P. Pinchpenny. Leapin' lizards! 178pp. 6⅛ x 8⅜. 23107-0 Pa. $2.00

WHEN A FELLER NEEDS A FRIEND, Clare Briggs. 122 cartoons by one of the greatest newspaper cartoonists of the early 20th century — about growing up, making a living, family life, daily frustrations and occasional triumphs. 121pp. 8½ x 9½.
23148-8 Pa. $2.50

THE BEST OF GLUYAS WILLIAMS. 100 drawings by one of America's finest cartoonists: The Day a Cake of Ivory Soap Sank at Proctor & Gamble's, At the Life Insurance Agents' Banquet, and many other gems from the 20's and 30's. 118pp. 8⅜ x 11¼. 22737-5 Pa. $2.50

THE BEST DR. THORNDYKE DETECTIVE STORIES, R. Austin Freeman. The Case of Oscar Brodski, The Moabite Cipher, and 5 other favorites featuring the great scientific detective, plus his long-believed-lost first adventure — 31 New Inn — reprinted here for the first time. Edited by E.F. Bleiler. USO 20388-3 Pa. $3.00

BEST "THINKING MACHINE" DETECTIVE STORIES, Jacques Futrelle. The Problem of Cell 13 and 11 other stories about Prof. Augustus S.F.X. Van Dusen, including two "lost" stories. First reprinting of several. Edited by E.F. Bleiler. 241pp.
20537-1 Pa. $3.00

UNCLE SILAS, J. Sheridan LeFanu. Victorian Gothic mystery novel, considered by many best of period, even better than Collins or Dickens. Wonderful psychological terror. Introduction by Frederick Shroyer. 436pp.   21715-9 Pa. $4.00

BEST DR. POGGIOLI DETECTIVE STORIES, T.S. Stribling. 15 best stories from EQMM and The Saint offer new adventures in Mexico, Florida, Tennessee hills as Poggioli unravels mysteries and combats Count Jalacki. 217pp.   23227-1 Pa. $3.00

EIGHT DIME NOVELS, selected with an introduction by E.F. Bleiler. Adventures of Old King Brady, Frank James, Nick Carter, Deadwood Dick, Buffalo Bill, The Steam Man, Frank Merriwell, and Horatio Alger — 1877 to 1905. Important, entertaining popular literature in facsimile reprint, with original covers. 190pp. 9 x 12.   22975-0 Pa. $3.50

ALICE'S ADVENTURES UNDER GROUND, Lewis Carroll. Facsimile of ms. Carroll gave Alice Liddell in 1864. Different in many ways from final Alice. Handlettered, illustrated by Carroll. Introduction by Martin Gardner. 128pp. 21482-6 Pa. $1.50

ALICE IN WONDERLAND COLORING BOOK, Lewis Carroll. Pictures by John Tenniel. Large-size versions of the famous illustrations of Alice, Cheshire Cat, Mad Hatter and all the others, waiting for your crayons. Abridged text. 36 illustrations. 64pp. 8¼ x 11.   22853-3 Pa. $1.50

AVENTURES D'ALICE AU PAYS DES MERVEILLES, Lewis Carroll. Bué's translation of "Alice" into French, supervised by Carroll himself. Novel way to learn language. (No English text.) 42 Tenniel illustrations. 196pp.   22836-3 Pa. $2.50

MYTHS AND FOLK TALES OF IRELAND, Jeremiah Curtin. 11 stories that are Irish versions of European fairy tales and 9 stories from the Fenian cycle — 20 tales of legend and magic that comprise an essential work in the history of folklore. 256pp.   22430-9 Pa. $3.00

EAST O' THE SUN AND WEST O' THE MOON, George W. Dasent. Only full edition of favorite, wonderful Norwegian fairytales — Why the Sea is Salt, Boots and the Troll, etc. — with 77 illustrations by Kittelsen & Werenskiöld. 418pp.
22521-6 Pa. $4.00

PERRAULT'S FAIRY TALES, Charles Perrault and Gustave Doré. Original versions of Cinderella, Sleeping Beauty, Little Red Riding Hood, etc. in best translation, with 34 wonderful illustrations by Gustave Doré. 117pp. 8⅛ x 11.   22311-6 Pa. $2.50

EARLY NEW ENGLAND GRAVESTONE RUBBINGS, Edmund V. Gillon, Jr. 43 photographs, 226 rubbings show heavily symbolic, macabre, sometimes humorous primitive American art. Up to early 19th century. 207pp. 8⅜ x 11¼.
21380-3 Pa. $4.00

L.J.M. DAGUERRE: THE HISTORY OF THE DIORAMA AND THE DAGUERREOTYPE, Helmut and Alison Gernsheim. Definitive account. Early history, life and work of Daguerre; discovery of daguerreotype process; diffusion abroad; other early photography. 124 illustrations. 226pp. 6⅙ x 9¼.
22290-X Pa. $4.00

PHOTOGRAPHY AND THE AMERICAN SCENE, Robert Taft. The basic book on American photography as art, recording form, 1839-1889. Development, influence on society, great photographers, types (portraits, war, frontier, etc.), whatever else needed. Inexhaustible. Illustrated with 322 early photos, daguerreotypes, tintypes, stereo slides, etc. 546pp. 6⅛ x 9¼.
21201-7 Pa. $5.95

PHOTOGRAPHIC SKETCHBOOK OF THE CIVIL WAR, Alexander Gardner. Reproduction of 1866 volume with 100 on-the-field photographs: Manassas, Lincoln on battlefield, slave pens, etc. Introduction by E.F. Bleiler. 224pp. 10¾ x 9.
22731-6 Pa. $5.00

THE MOVIES: A PICTURE QUIZ BOOK, Stanley Appelbaum & Hayward Cirker. Match stars with their movies, name actors and actresses, test your movie skill with 241 stills from 236 great movies, 1902-1959. Indexes of performers and films. 128pp. 8⅜ x 9¼.
20222-4 Pa. $2.50

THE TALKIES, Richard Griffith. Anthology of features, articles from Photoplay, 1928-1940, reproduced complete. Stars, famous movies, technical features, fabulous ads, etc.; Garbo, Chaplin, King Kong, Lubitsch, etc. 4 color plates, scores of illustrations. 327pp. 8⅜ x 11¼.
22762-6 Pa. $6.95

THE MOVIE MUSICAL FROM VITAPHONE TO "42ND STREET," edited by Miles Kreuger. Relive the rise of the movie musical as reported in the pages of Photoplay magazine (1926-1933): every movie review, cast list, ad, and record review; every significant feature article, production still, biography, forecast, and gossip story. Profusely illustrated. 367pp. 8⅜ x 11¼.
23154-2 Pa. $6.95

JOHANN SEBASTIAN BACH, Philipp Spitta. Great classic of biography, musical commentary, with hundreds of pieces analyzed. Also good for Bach's contemporaries. 450 musical examples. Total of 1799pp.
EUK 22278-0, 22279-9 Clothbd., Two vol. set $25.00

BEETHOVEN AND HIS NINE SYMPHONIES, Sir George Grove. Thorough history, analysis, commentary on symphonies and some related pieces. For either beginner or advanced student. 436 musical passages. 407pp.
20334-4 Pa. $4.00

MOZART AND HIS PIANO CONCERTOS, Cuthbert Girdlestone. The only full-length study. Detailed analyses of all 21 concertos, sources; 417 musical examples. 509pp.
21271-8 Pa. $4.50

THE FITZWILLIAM VIRGINAL BOOK, edited by J. Fuller Maitland, W.B. Squire. Famous early 17th century collection of keyboard music, 300 works by Morley, Byrd, Bull, Gibbons, etc. Modern notation. Total of 938pp. 8³/₈ x 11.
ECE 21068-5, 21069-3 Pa., Two vol. set $14.00

COMPLETE STRING QUARTETS, Wolfgang A. Mozart. Breitkopf and Härtel edition. All 23 string quartets plus alternate slow movement to K156. Study score. 277pp. 9³/₈ x 12¼. 22372-8 Pa. $6.00

COMPLETE SONG CYCLES, Franz Schubert. Complete piano, vocal music of Die Schöne Müllerin, Die Winterreise, Schwanengesang. Also Drinker English singing translations. Breitkopf and Härtel edition. 217pp. 9³/₈ x 12¼.
22649-2 Pa. $4.50

THE COMPLETE PRELUDES AND ETUDES FOR PIANOFORTE SOLO, Alexander Scriabin. All the preludes and etudes including many perfectly spun miniatures. Edited by K.N. Igumnov and Y.I. Mil'shteyn. 250pp. 9 x 12. 22919-X Pa. $5.00

TRISTAN UND ISOLDE, Richard Wagner. Full orchestral score with complete instrumentation. Do not confuse with piano reduction. Commentary by Felix Mottl, great Wagnerian conductor and scholar. Study score. 655pp. 8¹/₈ x 11.
22915-7 Pa. $10.00

FAVORITE SONGS OF THE NINETIES, ed. Robert Fremont. Full reproduction, including covers, of 88 favorites: Ta-Ra-Ra-Boom-De-Aye, The Band Played On, Bird in a Gilded Cage, Under the Bamboo Tree, After the Ball, etc. 401pp. 9 x 12.
EBE 21536-9 Pa. $6.95

SOUSA'S GREAT MARCHES IN PIANO TRANSCRIPTION: ORIGINAL SHEET MUSIC OF 23 WORKS, John Philip Sousa. Selected by Lester S. Levy. Playing edition includes: The Stars and Stripes Forever, The Thunderer, The Gladiator, King Cotton, Washington Post, much more. 24 illustrations. 111pp. 9 x 12.
USO 23132-1 Pa. $3.50

CLASSIC PIANO RAGS, selected with an introduction by Rudi Blesh. Best ragtime music (1897-1922) by Scott Joplin, James Scott, Joseph F. Lamb, Tom Turpin, 9 others. Printed from best original sheet music, plus covers. 364pp. 9 x 12.
EBE 20469-3 Pa. $6.95

ANALYSIS OF CHINESE CHARACTERS, C.D. Wilder, J.H. Ingram. 1000 most important characters analyzed according to primitives, phonetics, historical development. Traditional method offers mnemonic aid to beginner, intermediate student of Chinese, Japanese. 365pp. 23045-7 Pa. $4.00

MODERN CHINESE: A BASIC COURSE, Faculty of Peking University. Self study, classroom course in modern Mandarin. Records contain phonetics, vocabulary, sentences, lessons. 249 page book contains all recorded text, translations, grammar, vocabulary, exercises. Best course on market. 3 12" 33¹/₃ monaural records, book, album. 98832-5 Set $12.50

MANUAL OF THE TREES OF NORTH AMERICA, Charles S. Sargent. The basic survey of every native tree and tree-like shrub, 717 species in all. Extremely full descriptions, information on habitat, growth, locales, economics, etc. Necessary to every serious tree lover. Over 100 finding keys. 783 illustrations. Total of 986pp.
20277-1, 20278-X Pa., Two vol. set $8.00

BIRDS OF THE NEW YORK AREA, John Bull. Indispensable guide to more than 400 species within a hundred-mile radius of Manhattan. Information on range, status, breeding, migration, distribution trends, etc. Foreword by Roger Tory Peterson. 17 drawings; maps. 540pp.
23222-0 Pa. $6.00

THE SEA-BEACH AT EBB-TIDE, Augusta Foote Arnold. Identify hundreds of marine plants and animals: algae, seaweeds, squids, crabs, corals, etc. Descriptions cover food, life cycle, size, shape, habitat. Over 600 drawings. 490pp.
21949-6 Pa. $5.00

THE MOTH BOOK, William J. Holland. Identify more than 2,000 moths of North America. General information, precise species descriptions. 623 illustrations plus 48 color plates show almost all species, full size. 1968 edition. Still the basic book. Total of 551pp. 6½ x 9¼.
21948-8 Pa. $6.00

AN INTRODUCTION TO THE REPTILES AND AMPHIBIANS OF THE UNITED STATES, Percy A. Morris. All lizards, crocodiles, turtles, snakes, toads, frogs; life history, identification, habits, suitability as pets, etc. Non-technical, but sound and broad. 130 photos. 253pp.
22982-3 Pa. $3.00

OLD NEW YORK IN EARLY PHOTOGRAPHS, edited by Mary Black. Your only chance to see New York City as it was 1853-1906, through 196 wonderful photographs from N.Y. Historical Society. Great Blizzard, Lincoln's funeral procession, great buildings. 228pp. 9 x 12.
22907-6 Pa. $6.00

THE AMERICAN REVOLUTION, A PICTURE SOURCEBOOK, John Grafton. Wonderful Bicentennial picture source, with 411 illustrations (contemporary and 19th century) showing battles, personalities, maps, events, flags, posters, soldier's life, ships, etc. all captioned and explained. A wonderful browsing book, supplement to other historical reading. 160pp. 9 x 12.
23226-3 Pa. $4.00

PERSONAL NARRATIVE OF A PILGRIMAGE TO AL-MADINAH AND MECCAH, Richard Burton. Great travel classic by remarkably colorful personality. Burton, disguised as a Moroccan, visited sacred shrines of Islam, narrowly escaping death. Wonderful observations of Islamic life, customs, personalities. 47 illustrations. Total of 959pp.
21217-3, 21218-1 Pa., Two vol. set $10.00

INCIDENTS OF TRAVEL IN CENTRAL AMERICA, CHIAPAS, AND YUCATAN, John L. Stephens. Almost single-handed discovery of Maya culture; exploration of ruined cities, monuments, temples; customs of Indians. 115 drawings. 892pp.
22404-X, 22405-8 Pa., Two vol. set $8.00

CONSTRUCTION OF AMERICAN FURNITURE TREASURES, Lester Margon. 344 detail drawings, complete text on constructing exact reproductions of 38 early American masterpieces: Hepplewhite sideboard, Duncan Phyfe drop-leaf table, mantel clock, gate-leg dining table, Pa. German cupboard, more. 38 plates. 54 photographs. 168pp. 8⅜ x 11¼. 23056-2 Pa. $4.00

JEWELRY MAKING AND DESIGN, Augustus F. Rose, Antonio Cirino. Professional secrets revealed in thorough, practical guide: tools, materials, processes; rings, brooches, chains, cast pieces, enamelling, setting stones, etc. Do not confuse with skimpy introductions: beginner can use, professional can learn from it. Over 200 illustrations. 306pp. 21750-7 Pa. $3.00

METALWORK AND ENAMELLING, Herbert Maryon. Generally conceded best all-around book. Countless trade secrets: materials, tools, soldering, filigree, setting, inlay, niello, repoussé, casting, polishing, etc. For beginner or expert. Author was foremost British expert. 330 illustrations. 335pp. 22702-2 Pa. $3.50

WEAVING WITH FOOT-POWER LOOMS, Edward F. Worst. Setting up a loom, beginning to weave, constructing equipment, using dyes, more, plus over 285 drafts of traditional patterns including Colonial and Swedish weaves. More than 200 other figures. For beginning and advanced. 275pp. 8¾ x 6⅜. 23064-3 Pa. $4.00

WEAVING A NAVAJO BLANKET, Gladys A. Reichard. Foremost anthropologist studied under Navajo women, reveals every step in process from wool, dyeing, spinning, setting up loom, designing, weaving. Much history, symbolism. With this book you could make one yourself. 97 illustrations. 222pp. 22992-0 Pa. $3.00

NATURAL DYES AND HOME DYEING, Rita J. Adrosko. Use natural ingredients: bark, flowers, leaves, lichens, insects etc. Over 135 specific recipes from historical sources for cotton, wool, other fabrics. Genuine premodern handicrafts. 12 illustrations. 160pp. 22688-3 Pa. $2.00

THE HAND DECORATION OF FABRICS, Francis J. Kafka. Outstanding, profusely illustrated guide to stenciling, batik, block printing, tie dyeing, freehand painting, silk screen printing, and novelty decoration. 356 illustrations. 198pp. 6 x 9.
21401-X Pa. $3.00

THOMAS NAST: CARTOONS AND ILLUSTRATIONS, with text by Thomas Nast St. Hill. Father of American political cartooning. Cartoons that destroyed Tweed Ring; inflation, free love, church and state; original Republican elephant and Democratic donkey; Santa Claus; more. 117 illustrations. 146pp. 9 x 12.
22983-1 Pa. $4.00
23067-8 Clothbd. $8.50

FREDERIC REMINGTON: 173 DRAWINGS AND ILLUSTRATIONS. Most famous of the Western artists, most responsible for our myths about the American West in its untamed days. Complete reprinting of *Drawings of Frederic Remington* (1897), plus other selections. 4 additional drawings in color on covers. 140pp. 9 x 12.
20714-5 Pa. $3.95

How to Solve Chess Problems, Kenneth S. Howard. Practical suggestions on problem solving for very beginners. 58 two-move problems, 46 3-movers, 8 4-movers for practice, plus hints. 171pp. 20748-X Pa. $2.00

A Guide to Fairy Chess, Anthony Dickins. 3-D chess, 4-D chess, chess on a cylindrical board, reflecting pieces that bounce off edges, cooperative chess, retrograde chess, maximummers, much more. Most based on work of great Dawson. Full handbook, 100 problems. 66pp. 7⅞ x 10¾. 22687-5 Pa. $2.00

Win at Backgammon, Millard Hopper. Best opening moves, running game, blocking game, back game, tables of odds, etc. Hopper makes the game clear enough for anyone to play, and win. 43 diagrams. 111pp. 22894-0 Pa. $1.50

Bidding a Bridge Hand, Terence Reese. Master player "thinks out loud" the binding of 75 hands that defy point count systems. Organized by bidding problem—no-fit situations, overbidding, underbidding, cueing your defense, etc. 254pp. EBE 22830-4 Pa. $2.50

The Precision Bidding System in Bridge, C.C. Wei, edited by Alan Truscott. Inventor of precision bidding presents average hands and hands from actual play, including games from 1969 Bermuda Bowl where system emerged. 114 exercises. 116pp. 21171-1 Pa. $1.75

Learn Magic, Henry Hay. 20 simple, easy-to-follow lessons on magic for the new magician: illusions, card tricks, silks, sleights of hand, coin manipulations, escapes, and more —all with a minimum amount of equipment. Final chapter explains the great stage illusions. 92 illustrations. 285pp. 21238-6 Pa. $2.95

The New Magician's Manual, Walter B. Gibson. Step-by-step instructions and clear illustrations guide the novice in mastering 36 tricks; much equipment supplied on 16 pages of cut-out materials. 36 additional tricks. 64 illustrations. 159pp. 6⅝ x 10. 23113-5 Pa. $3.00

Professional Magic for Amateurs, Walter B. Gibson. 50 easy, effective tricks used by professionals —cards, string, tumblers, handkerchiefs, mental magic, etc. 63 illustrations. 223pp. 23012-0 Pa. $2.50

Card Manipulations, Jean Hugard. Very rich collection of manipulations; has taught thousands of fine magicians tricks that are really workable, eye-catching. Easily followed, serious work. Over 200 illustrations. 163pp. 20539-8 Pa. $2.00

Abbott's Encyclopedia of Rope Tricks for Magicians, Stewart James. Complete reference book for amateur and professional magicians containing more than 150 tricks involving knots, penetrations, cut and restored rope, etc. 510 illustrations. Reprint of 3rd edition. 400pp. 23206-9 Pa. $3.50

The Secrets of Houdini, J.C. Cannell. Classic study of Houdini's incredible magic, exposing closely-kept professional secrets and revealing, in general terms, the whole art of stage magic. 67 illustrations. 279pp. 22913-0 Pa. $2.50

THE MAGIC MOVING PICTURE BOOK, Bliss, Sands & Co. The pictures in this book move! Volcanoes erupt, a house burns, a serpentine dancer wiggles her way through a number. By using a specially ruled acetate screen provided, you can obtain these and 15 other startling effects. Originally "The Motograph Moving Picture Book." 32pp. 8¼ x 11.   23224-7 Pa. $1.75

STRING FIGURES AND HOW TO MAKE THEM, Caroline F. Jayne. Fullest, clearest instructions on string figures from around world: Eskimo, Navajo, Lapp, Europe, more. Cats cradle, moving spear, lightning, stars. Introduction by A.C. Haddon. 950 illustrations. 407pp.   20152-X Pa. $3.00

PAPER FOLDING FOR BEGINNERS, William D. Murray and Francis J. Rigney. Clearest book on market for making origami sail boats, roosters, frogs that move legs, cups, bonbon boxes. 40 projects. More than 275 illustrations. Photographs. 94pp.
                                                                           20713-7 Pa. $1.25

INDIAN SIGN LANGUAGE, William Tomkins. Over 525 signs developed by Sioux, Blackfoot, Cheyenne, Arapahoe and other tribes. Written instructions and diagrams: how to make words, construct sentences. Also 290 pictographs of Sioux and Ojibway tribes. 111pp. 6⅛ x 9¼.   22029-X Pa. $1.50

BOOMERANGS: HOW TO MAKE AND THROW THEM, Bernard S. Mason. Easy to make and throw, dozens of designs: cross-stick, pinwheel, boomabird, tumblestick, Australian curved stick boomerang. Complete throwing instructions. All safe. 99pp.   23028-7 Pa. $1.50

25 KITES THAT FLY, Leslie Hunt. Full, easy to follow instructions for kites made from inexpensive materials. Many novelties. Reeling, raising, designing your own. 70 illustrations. 110pp.   22550-X Pa. $1.25

TRICKS AND GAMES ON THE POOL TABLE, Fred Herrmann. 79 tricks and games, some solitaires, some for 2 or more players, some competitive; mystifying shots and throws, unusual carom, tricks involving cork, coins, a hat, more. 77 figures. 95pp.   21814-7 Pa. $1.25

WOODCRAFT AND CAMPING, Bernard S. Mason. How to make a quick emergency shelter, select woods that will burn immediately, make do with limited supplies, etc. Also making many things out of wood, rawhide, bark, at camp. Formerly titled Woodcraft. 295 illustrations. 580pp.   21951-8 Pa. $4.00

AN INTRODUCTION TO CHESS MOVES AND TACTICS SIMPLY EXPLAINED, Leonard Barden. Informal intermediate introduction: reasons for moves, tactics, openings, traps, positional play, endgame. Isolates patterns. 102pp. USO 21210-6 Pa. $1.35

LASKER'S MANUAL OF CHESS, Dr. Emanuel Lasker. Great world champion offers very thorough coverage of all aspects of chess. Combinations, position play, openings, endgame, aesthetics of chess, philosophy of struggle, much more. Filled with analyzed games. 390pp.   20640-8 Pa. $3.50

SLEEPING BEAUTY, illustrated by Arthur Rackham. Perhaps the fullest, most delightful version ever, told by C.S. Evans. Rackham's best work. 49 illustrations. 110pp. 7⅞ x 10¾. 22756-1 Pa. $2.00

THE WONDERFUL WIZARD OF OZ, L. Frank Baum. Facsimile in full color of America's finest children's classic. Introduction by Martin Gardner. 143 illustrations by W.W. Denslow. 267pp. 20691-2 Pa. $2.50

GOOPS AND HOW TO BE THEM, Gelett Burgess. Classic tongue-in-cheek masquerading as etiquette book. 87 verses, 170 cartoons as Goops demonstrate virtues of table manners, neatness, courtesy, more. 88pp. 6½ x 9¼. 22233-0 Pa. $1.50

THE BROWNIES, THEIR BOOK, Palmer Cox. Small as mice, cunning as foxes, exuberant, mischievous, Brownies go to zoo, toy shop, seashore, circus, more. 24 verse adventures. 266 illustrations. 144pp. 6⅝ x 9¼. 21265-3 Pa. $1.75

BILLY WHISKERS: THE AUTOBIOGRAPHY OF A GOAT, Frances Trego Montgomery. Escapades of that rambunctious goat. Favorite from turn of the century America. 24 illustrations. 259pp. 22345-0 Pa. $2.75

THE ROCKET BOOK, Peter Newell. Fritz, janitor's kid, sets off rocket in basement of apartment house; an ingenious hole punched through every page traces course of rocket. 22 duotone drawings, verses. 48pp. 6⅞ x 8⅜. 22044-3 Pa. $1.50

PECK'S BAD BOY AND HIS PA, George W. Peck. Complete double-volume of great American childhood classic. Hennery's ingenious pranks against outraged pomposity of pa and the grocery man. 97 illustrations. Introduction by E.F. Bleiler. 347pp. 20497-9 Pa. $2.50

THE TALE OF PETER RABBIT, Beatrix Potter. The inimitable Peter's terrifying adventure in Mr. McGregor's garden, with all 27 wonderful, full-color Potter illustrations. 55pp. 4¼ x 5½. USO 22827-4 Pa. $1.00

THE TALE OF MRS. TIGGY-WINKLE, Beatrix Potter. Your child will love this story about a very special hedgehog and all 27 wonderful, full-color Potter illustrations. 57pp. 4¼ x 5½. USO 20546-0 Pa. $1.00

THE TALE OF BENJAMIN BUNNY, Beatrix Potter. Peter Rabbit's cousin coaxes him back into Mr. McGregor's garden for a whole new set of ·dventures. A favorite with children. All 27 full-color illustrations. 59pp. 4¼ x 5½. USO 21102-9 Pa. $1.00

THE MERRY ADVENTURES OF ROBIN HOOD, Howard Pyle. Facsimile of original (1883) edition, finest modern version of English outlaw's adventures. 23 illustrations by Pyle. 296pp. 6½ x 9¼. 22043-5 Pa. $2.75

TWO LITTLE SAVAGES, Ernest Thompson Seton. Adventures of two boys who lived as Indians; explaining Indian ways, woodlore, pioneer methods. 293 illustrations. 286pp. 20985-7 Pa. $3.00

HOUDINI ON MAGIC, Harold Houdini. Edited by Walter Gibson, Morris N. Young. How he escaped; exposés of fake spiritualists; instructions for eye-catching tricks; other fascinating material by and about greatest magician. 155 illustrations. 280pp. 20384-0 Pa. $2.50

HANDBOOK OF THE NUTRITIONAL CONTENTS OF FOOD, U.S. Dept. of Agriculture. Largest, most detailed source of food nutrition information ever prepared. Two mammoth tables: one measuring nutrients in 100 grams of edible portion; the other, in edible portion of 1 pound as purchased. Originally titled Composition of Foods. 190pp. 9 x 12. 21342-0 Pa. $4.00

COMPLETE GUIDE TO HOME CANNING, PRESERVING AND FREEZING, U.S. Dept. of Agriculture. Seven basic manuals with full instructions for jams and jellies; pickles and relishes; canning fruits, vegetables, meat; freezing anything. Really good recipes, exact instructions for optimal results. Save a fortune in food. 156 illustrations. 214pp. 6⅛ x 9¼. 22911-4 Pa. $2.50

THE BREAD TRAY, Louis P. De Gouy. Nearly every bread the cook could buy or make: bread sticks of Italy, fruit breads of Greece, glazed rolls of Vienna, everything from corn pone to croissants. Over 500 recipes altogether. including buns, rolls, muffins, scones, and more. 463pp. 23000-7 Pa. $3.50

CREATIVE HAMBURGER COOKERY, Louis P. De Gouy. 182 unusual recipes for casseroles, meat loaves and hamburgers that turn inexpensive ground meat into memorable main dishes: Arizona chili burgers, burger tamale pie, burger stew, burger corn loaf, burger wine loaf, and more. 120pp. 23001-5 Pa. $1.75

LONG ISLAND SEAFOOD COOKBOOK, J. George Frederick and Jean Joyce. Probably the best American seafood cookbook. Hundreds of recipes. 40 gourmet sauces, 123 recipes using oysters alone! All varieties of fish and seafood amply represented. 324pp. 22677-8 Pa. $3.00

THE EPICUREAN: A COMPLETE TREATISE OF ANALYTICAL AND PRACTICAL STUDIES IN THE CULINARY ART, Charles Ranhofer. Great modern classic. 3,500 recipes from master chef of Delmonico's, turn-of-the-century America's best restaurant. Also explained, many techniques known only to professional chefs. 775 illustrations. 1183pp. 6⅝ x 10. 22680-8 Clothbd. $17.50

THE AMERICAN WINE COOK BOOK, Ted Hatch. Over 700 recipes: old favorites livened up with wine plus many more: Czech fish soup, quince soup, sauce Perigueux, shrimp shortcake, filets Stroganoff, cordon bleu goulash, jambonneau, wine fruit cake, more. 314pp. 22796-0 Pa. $2.50

DELICIOUS VEGETARIAN COOKING, Ivan Baker. Close to 500 delicious and varied recipes: soups, main course dishes (pea, bean, lentil, cheese, vegetable, pasta, and egg dishes), savories, stews, whole-wheat breads and cakes, more. 168pp. USO 22834-7 Pa. $1.75

COOKIES FROM MANY LANDS, Josephine Perry. Crullers, oatmeal cookies, chaux au chocolate, English tea cakes, mandel kuchen, Sacher torte, Danish puff pastry, Swedish cookies — a mouth-watering collection of 223 recipes. 157pp.
22832-0 Pa. $2.00

ROSE RECIPES, Eleanour S. Rohde. How to make sauces, jellies, tarts, salads, pot-pourris, sweet bags, pomanders, perfumes from garden roses; all exact recipes. Century old favorites. 95pp.
22957-2 Pa. $1.25

"OSCAR" OF THE WALDORF'S COOKBOOK, Oscar Tschirky. Famous American chef reveals 3455 recipes that made Waldorf great; cream of French, German, American cooking, in all categories. Full instructions, easy home use. 1896 edition. 907pp. 6⅝ x 9⅜.
20790-0 Clothbd. $15.00

JAMS AND JELLIES, May Byron. Over 500 old-time recipes for delicious jams, jellies, marmalades, preserves, and many other items. Probably the largest jam and jelly book in print. Originally titled May Byron's Jam Book. 276pp.
USO 23130-5 Pa. $3.00

MUSHROOM RECIPES, André L. Simon. 110 recipes for everyday and special cooking. Champignons à la grecque, sole bonne femme, chicken liver croustades, more; 9 basic sauces, 13 ways of cooking mushrooms. 54pp.
USO 20913-X Pa. $1.25

FAVORITE SWEDISH RECIPES, edited by Sam Widenfelt. Prepared in Sweden, offers wonderful, clearly explained Swedish dishes: appetizers, meats, pastry and cookies, other categories. Suitable for American kitchen. 90 photos. 157pp.
23156-9 Pa. $2.00

THE BUCKEYE COOKBOOK, Buckeye Publishing Company. Over 1,000 easy-to-follow, traditional recipes from the American Midwest: bread (100 recipes alone), meat, game, jam, candy, cake, ice cream, and many other categories of cooking. 64 illustrations. From 1883 enlarged edition. 416pp.
23218-2 Pa. $4.00

TWENTY-TWO AUTHENTIC BANQUETS FROM INDIA, Robert H. Christie. Complete, easy-to-do recipes for almost 200 authentic Indian dishes assembled in 22 banquets. Arranged by region. Selected from Banquets of the Nations. 192pp.
23200-X Pa. $2.50

Prices subject to change without notice.
Available at your book dealer or write for free catalogue to Dept. GI, Dover Publications, Inc., 180 Varick St., N.Y., N.Y. 10014. Dover publishes more than 150 books each year on science, elementary and advanced mathematics, biology, music, art, literary history, social sciences and other areas.